Demons

Phantoms

and Me

"A Love Affair with Flying"

ISBN: 1-4140-1706-5 (e-book)
ISBN: 1-4140-1704-9 (Paperback)
ISBN: 1-4140-1705-7 (Dust Jacket)

Library of Congress Control Number: 2003097749

This book is printed on acid free paper.

Printed in the United States of America
Bloomington, IN

1stBooks – rev. 10/30/03

As is true of the restless sea, the huge Aircraft Carrier never ceases to be in motion. Even when securely attached to the harbor pier or anchored two miles off the shore, the Carrier faithfully obeys the commands of the sea. During flight operations its flight deck is an organized chaos of activity, day and night. Aircraft appear and disappear on huge elevators that transport them between decks. A myriad of color-coded people cluster around and weave their way among the endless parade of aircraft, tractors, ammunition dollies, and other assorted equipment required to make the ship a mighty weapon of war. At night the chaos continues but is recognizable only by the motion of dim yellow wands and red flashlights used by the flight crews and deck hands to ensure the aircraft are ready and capable of projecting the awesome power of the ship. Night Carrier flight operations qualify as the most dangerous of all flying activities. Prior to a night launch, the normally lively pilot's Ready Room takes on a quiet "deadly serious" hush as the crews prepare to man their aircraft. The tiny butterflies that precede a day launch suddenly become monster moths. Every flight crewman recognizes that the information required to thread their aircraft through the tiny margins of safety to an often pitching and rolling flight deck are drastically reduced. The night Carrier landing accident rate exceeds the day rate by a factor of ten. The time between the manning of the aircraft and the engine start is a period of intense introspection. *Why would anyone ever volunteer to do this?*

Acknowledgements

I'd like to thank all the characters that appear in this book for they are the ones that created the stories and events that occur within. My wife Linda deserves special thanks for her encouragement, editing, and putting up with my considerable absences during the writing. I thank Barrett Tillman for his review of an early manuscript and for passing it on to the Tail Hook Association for review and comment. Mr. Doug Siefield of the Tail Hook Association who made the phone call that resulted in a final sprint to complete the book. I thank Linda Hereth of the State University of New York at Buffalo who was kind enough to edit the first attempt at putting the words on paper. George Shirley and George Patton provided numerous photographs greatly enhancing the book. Guy Jones of the Experimental Aircraft Association is recognized for his excellent review and ability to take my engineering writing style and making it readable. I appreciate the efforts of Lynn Albaugh and Bill Rieke for their review, encouragement and endorsement of the book. I am indebted to James Donald of Boomerang Design Group for his masterful editing and the layout of the final version.

Demons, Phantoms and Me
"A love affair with flying"

Demons, Phantoms and Me is a love story. More precisely, it is a story of a love affair. The characters and events are real, modified only by the lapses in memory between their occurrence and their transference to the written word. Most would agree that love is our strongest emotion and the keynote to life. A love affair is often thought of as a deeply intense relationship that defies rational thought and behavior. Normally short-lived, a love affair consumes one's soul with passion, creates its own mystery, has its own intrigue, and is not without its dangerous and potentially destructive elements.

Demons, Phantoms and Me is two chapters from a lifetime love affair with flying. More than anything else, it is about the feelings and emotions of one pilot's experience as he falls in love with, pursues, and even thrives on the dangers of Naval Carrier Aviation. It is a story that could not have been written while it was happening. My youthful macho image would not have allowed an honest outpouring of the real feelings I experienced at that time. Only in my later years have I felt sufficiently comfortable and secure with my flying accomplishments to admit what was really going on in my mind and heart during that exciting period in my aviation career. While this is a story about flying, and a story about feelings and emotions, it is mostly a story about love.

Any adventure is determined largely by the route traveled, the people we meet, and the events that occur along the way. In my case, the love affair started at an early age and was influenced by many circumstances, people and considerable luck.

The Yellow Navy Trainer

It was a mild October afternoon in 1946. The dim yellow sun was not quite capable of penetrating the high, gray, thickening overcast. Four young boys, two sets of brothers actually, were busy at play in a broom straw hued field in a northern suburb of Richmond, Virginia. Residue from the soot and cinders deposited over the years by the numerous steam-powered locomotives traveling the main artery of the Richmond, Fredericksburg, and Potomac (R.F.&P.) Railway between Richmond and Washington, D.C. camouflaged the clothes and skin of each youngster.

From the south a barely audible staccato sound, more like a rhythmic Ca-puck-a-da, slowly increased in intensity until it commanded the attention of the four boys. The sound emanated from a small, yellow, blunt-nosed, stub-winged Navy trainer. As if on cue, abeam the field, the Navy SNJ began a series of acrobatics. The yellow airplane, with the whine of its engine alternating between sharp crescendo and near silence, held the attention of three of the young boys for only a few moments. The next to the youngest boy, however, was totally captivated, mesmerized. His large dark-brown eyes traced every turn, every loop, every roll, and every

The yellow Navy trainer

pitching motion. "Warren, come and play," his playmates prodded; but to no avail. It seemed important that every movement of the trainer be committed to memory. The plane turned and slowly disappeared in the direction from whence it came. Turning to rejoin my playmates, I knew at that moment I wanted to become the "Superman" who must have been piloting the yellow Navy trainer. Thus began a love affair with flying that would last a lifetime.

The Young Years

Following the encounter with the yellow Navy trainer, "The Hardy Boys" gave way to the "Yankee Flyer." Airplane books, aviation magazines, and model airplanes became an obsession. Not being noted for keeping a particularly neat room in the first place, model airplane building turned mine into a certifiable disaster area. Many a new bedspread quickly accumulated globs of glue and multi-colored speckles of model airplane paint. The area over my bed was filled with models not so carefully suspended from the ceiling.

Mom used to get thoroughly irritated with me when I would bolt from the dinner table and crash out the door whenever the sound of an aircraft engine or jet was nearby, "Gene Warren, get back in here this minute and finish your dinner!" When bored in class, my mind wandered to airplanes and my fingers doodled aircraft. Scrapbooks of aircraft photographs filled my bookshelves, and a fair share of my weekly allowance was invested in airplane models and aviation paraphernalia.

In the summertime, it was fun to lie on my back in the yard and envy the buzzards soaring high in the sky, lazily circling the billowing cumulus clouds. Oh how I wanted to touch and play with the clouds. Clouds were fascinating. They could float along effortlessly, as if they had no place in particular to go, or rush past at a racer's pace, as if their very existence depended on getting to wherever clouds went. Clouds could appear dark and angry or light and fluffy. The dark and angry ones often raced across the countryside like big bullies, indiscriminately tossing bolts of lightning in all directions and creating scary thunder. The light and puffy ones seemed soft, playful and fun, like giant marshmallows. The thin icy ones looked like huge paintbrush strokes splashed across the sky. Clouds could fashion themselves into any number of shapes, limited only by the imagination of a young aspiring aviator. Clouds had mystery, magic, and majesty. But most important, clouds could fly.

The White Wooden Roller Coaster

One of the highlights of summer was the annual train trip to Buckroe Beach, Virginia sponsored by our own Bethlehem Baptist Church. Everyone went. One of the prime attractions at Buckroe Beach was a gigantic white wooden roller coaster. Most of us kids couldn't wait to get there. The beach was fun, with waves to dive through and sand castles to build. The beach, however, stood in the shadow of that foreboding

White wooden roller coaster

roller coaster. The ominous clatter of rattling wheels and the screech of metal against metal rose above the roar of the dashing waves. As the little cars rounded sharp corners and climbed and dived, fighting against, or giving into the force of gravity, fear was evident in the screams that accentuated every acceleration and centrifugal turn. As I listened to the excitement of my friends, all of whom had ridden it before, and took every opportunity to boast of that fact, deep inside I was afraid to ride that roller coaster.

The vivid memory of the small yellow Navy trainer, with "Superman" at the controls; twisting, diving, climbing and turning in the sky kept saying: "Warren, flying has got to be like riding that roller coaster. If you ever expect to fly, you must go on that ride." Reluctantly, I gave in. The first ride was a blur and every bit as frightening as I imagined. Walking down the whitewashed platform at the end of the ride, avowing, "Never again," the yellow Navy trainer reminded me there was no choice. Three rides later, with my allowance nearly spent, and absolutely certain I did *NOT* like it, but no longer afraid of it, I boasted to my friends what great rides they had been and secretly filed away the experience as a victory for the yellow Navy trainer.

My First Airplane Ride

My family shared a summer cottage on the Rappahanock River with Horace and Alice Jones and their three daughters. The cottage was about an hour and a half drive from Richmond. Horace had recently qualified for his private pilot's license when one Saturday afternoon he invited his nephew, Donnie Holmes, and me to go flying. At the old Central Airport, east of Richmond, Horace strapped both of us into the back seat of an Aeronca Champion. His plan was to overfly the river cottage and land on the unattended airstrip at Tappaha-nock, Virginia. We fash- ioned a parachute from

Aeronca 7AC Champion

a handkerchief and attached it to a glass bottle with a note crammed inside inviting the families to go for a flight and to give me a ride to the cottage.

The delightful transition from the noisy bouncing and bumping of the takeoff roll to the smooth exhilaration of being airborne remains an indelible memory. Like two buoys riding the same wave, Donnie and I swayed in unison, as we leaned away from every turn, trying desperately to keep our world right side up. Flying was pure magic. How could air possibly hold us up? I watched the world shrink below us. Details disappeared, as the surrounding landscape became amorphous. Individual trees blended into forests, cars converted to toys, houses became Monopoly pieces, roadways and railroad tracks etched lines in the predominately green carpet below and the world extended further in all directions than I ever imagined possible.

From the air, the Rappahanock River was narrower than expected. Horace quickly located the cabin and started a steep descending left turn from over the river toward the shoreline. One low pass brought people out of every cottage. Adults were waving and kids were set into various combinations of vertical and circular motions with as many permutations as there were children. The seat tugged at my body as Horace pulled up sharply, and slowly released me

The Early Years   5

as the speed decreased and the loud swoosh of rushing air faded to a whisper. He made a steep turn back for a second pass. Again I was pressed against the seat. Of course! It was the white wooden roller coaster with another dimension. On the third pass, he slowed, opened the sliding Plexiglas window, and dropped the homemade parachute. The chute streamed and the bottle shattered as it crashed into the river. The paper note, marked by the soaked handkerchief, floated long enough to be retrieved, getting the message across, but not in the elegant manner we had envisioned.

About a half-mile south of the cottage was Mark Haven Beach, which at that time was a segregated Negro beach. It was a beautiful Saturday. The beach and its wooden pier were covered with people. Horace made one low altitude, high-speed (for an Aeronca Champ) pass at the pier. The water churned white as bodies vacated the wooden structure en masse. We later discovered that, while we had cleared the pier of people, we had barely missed an electrical wire running the length of the structure. We had been lucky.

We were on the ground at Tappahanock only a few minutes when two carloads of river folk arrived with kids stacked one on top of the other, all excited over the opportunity to experience the miracle of flight. As promised, Horace took the kids for a trip around the field, sometimes two at a time and the smaller ones, three at a time. I no longer wanted to stay at the river through Sunday. I desperately wanted to fly back to Richmond.

Bobby

Bobby, not Robert, Brown was much taller than I, had unruly reddish brown hair and more than a smattering of

Bobby Brown, 1955

freckles. We were best friends and shared the same intense interest in aviation. Bobby had an attic "heaven" with a large wooden worktable that filled half the room. We spent many wonderful, tedious hours there; gluing, covering, and painting carefully crafted strips of balsa and fabric, creating model airplanes, which we flew from the schoolyard. We flew U-control models off the baseball diamond and chased free-flight models for miles on our bikes. We also did our share of aeronautical experimentation, some of which worked and some that didn't.

Bobby's friendship provided my first opportunity to pursue the "Superman" in the yellow trainer.

Feeling Poorly

The Boy Scouts provided my second flying experience. Seventeen scouts from our troop were invited to Langley Air Force Base to take a flight in a C-47. As we caravanned from Richmond to Hampton, all were in great spirits and looking forward to flying, some for the first time, and old hands like me looking forward to flying in a large transport. I eagerly shared my wealth of aeronautical knowledge gained from my one flight in the Aeronca Champ.

Air sickness epidemic

It was incredibly hot when we boarded the venerable C-47, climbed the steep incline and were strapped into the canvas troop seats extending the length of the fuselage. Several of the boys were apprehensive and it showed. The taxi and takeoff went fine but as soon as we were airborne, convective currents started to batter the transport. It pitched and rolled, bucked and bounced, all at the same time. The motion was continuous. The combination of anxiety, heat, and excessive turbulence took its toll. Within minutes young stomachs began to empty. Motion sickness became epidemic. No one was spared. That flight goes down as the most miserable flight experience I ever had and represents one half of the number of flights on which I actually tossed my cookies. As far as I was concerned, we couldn't get back on the ground fast enough.

F-86 Sabres at Langley Air Force Base, circa 1951

We had relatives in Newport News, Virginia, not too far from Buckroe Beach and near Langley Air Force Base. Whenever we went to visit, I was a real pest, persistently pleading to be taken to Langley to look at the shiny new jets that populated the field. Republic F-84 "Thunderjets" and North American F-86 "Sabres" and B-45 "Tornadoes" roared overhead. Awestruck is the best description of a young lad watching these fast, sleek machines racing through the sky propelled only by black smoke.

Northfield Airport

During our junior year of high school, Bobby turned his paper route over to me and went to work for Arnette's Ice Cream Shoppe. The job lasted only a few months then the break of a young lifetime occurred: Bobby took a job at Northfield Airport as a line boy. In a matter of weeks, we *both* were pumping gas, washing windshields, propping engines, and absolutely getting rich. We earned a whole dollar an hour, which included fifty cents in real money and fifty cents in flying time.

Northfield Airport, circa 1951

Northfield Airport was a small grass field located on Route 301 twelve miles north of Richmond and eight miles from our homes. The airport had one long and one short grass runway, a maintenance hangar, a long strip of metal nose-to-tail aircraft hangars along the long runway, and an open area for tying down aircraft. The heart of the operation was a small, white, rectangular, one-story building where the Airport Manager had his office, a small flight planning

Northfield Operations Building

room, a briefing room, and a glass enclosed area that overlooked the long runway. One of our many duties was to service a canned soup and pre-packaged sandwich bar located in the main building. Another was to hawk rides to the many visitors who arrived in the parking lot to watch the airplanes. Adjacent to the parking lot, a large, orange, corrugated metal tetrahedron stood sentinel duty amidst a circle of white-painted cement blocks. It creaked and groaned, especially at night, as it turned to face the changing wind or stood at silent rigid attention when we locked it in place to indicate the active runway. Additional white cement blocks communicated to airborne pilots the proper traffic pattern direction.

Northfield lounge and snack bar

Northfield's entrance added to the mystique of the airport. A short but steep, winding, poorly graveled road climbed from the highway to the airport. A green broadleafed vine covered the

Northfield entrance

hillside and all the trees in the surrounding area. Because of its rapid spreading and climbing ability, we called the vine "mile-a-minute weed." The area was eerie and deserved the name "Spooks Hollow." Northfield was, however, an aspiring young aviator's idea of heaven.

We worked for Mr. Elmer Durand "Dee" Bailey, Airport Manager and flight instructor. Mr. Bailey had a narrow angular face, a large, parrot-beak nose, and could have claimed the Guinness record for being the thinnest man alive. Bobby always said,

Mr. Bailey and Bobby

"If Mr. Bailey were to put on a herring-bone suit and stick out his tongue, he would look like a zipper." Mr. Bailey was soft-spoken and usually very calm. On numerous occasions, however, Bobby and I demonstrated an ability to ruffle his calm exterior. Despite his serious manner, we enjoyed working for Mr. Bailey. He was an excellent flight instructor. Mr. Bailey was affectionately known to us as "The Spook," because he possessed an uncanny ability to appear out of nowhere, especially when Bobby and I were "Hangar Flying" or doing something else we weren't supposed to be doing. He always called Bobby, "Bop."

One day the two of us were playing in the maintenance hangar rather than working. Mr. Tanner's "Tri-pacer" provided the perfect simulator for practicing loops and rolls with all the attendant sound effects and running commentary that went along with it. Bobby, not quite tall enough to see out of the small windows, was periodically leaping in the air, on the lookout for Mr. Bailey. Our precautions proved in vain. Mr. Bailey mysteriously materialized and calmly asked, "What you doing, Bop?" Bobby was hard pressed to explain that he was looking for him and I dumbly continued my simulated acrobatics oblivious to it all. It was my turn next, "Warren, isn't there someplace else you're supposed to be?"

"Uh, oh, YES SIR, Mr. Bailey."

Runway Maintenance

Of our many chores, the two that created the most frustration had to do with runway maintenance. Mr. Bailey had acquired a diesel-powered "steamroller" to roll the runway. After a minimal checkout by Bobby, i.e., how to start it, gear it, steer it, and stop it, I headed for the runway for my first experience as a road, uh, runway grader. The steering mechanism was a horizontal hand crank arrangement that guided the front roller. The gear ratio was at least a hundred-to-one, which meant it took a hundred turns of the crank to turn the front roller one degree.

Runway roller

Getting to the runway was easy since only a minor turn was required and it was slightly downhill. Making the ninety degree left turn onto the runway, however, was a totally different matter.

While cranking as fast as my arm would allow, I nearly ran off the right edge. Bobby's laughter could be heard over the loud popping of the diesel engine even though he was way back at the gas pump.

It only took a few yards of travel down the runway to figure out that the steamroller didn't like soft spots, high grassy spots, wet spots, or uphill grades. It would simply come to a halt while the rear wheels continued to slowly spin. The only solution (provided you didn't spin the wheels too long) was to negotiate the complicated sequence of levers and clutches to select reverse, back up, and get a running start toward the offending spot on the runway. It worked most of the time. The ninety degree turn onto the runway was minor, compared to my first one hundred eighty degree turn back down the runway. Crank, crank, crank, clutch, gear, clutch, back up, crank, crank, crank, clutch, gear, clutch, slowly forward, then back, then forward. It seemed to take forever to get turned around. My tiring arm began to ache. What had looked like fun turned out to be nothing but pure hard work. It took the better part of a day to do the long runway. We never tried rolling the short runway. Ironically because it was much too uneven.

The second contraption we drove was the grass cutter, an open, converted jeep-chassis with a rotating circular metal disk mounted underneath. The disk had four dull, but functional, triangular blades attached to the outer edge. The disk turned any time the jeep was in motion. Had the equivalent of the Office of Safety and Health Administration (OSHA) existed at that time, the grass cutter would surely have been condemned as hazardous to our health. It went a lot faster than the steamroller; too fast, according to Mr. Bailey, who was always admonishing us to slow down. We delighted in drag racing the grass cutter up and down the runway with grass flying in all directions. It was a "fun job" that actually turned out to be "fun."

One day while charging down the left edge of the runway at my usual high rate of speed, the steering wheel suddenly ceased to have any effect on the direction the grass cutter had decided it wanted to go. Actuating the one remaining control, the brakes, only exacerbated my already considerable left turn. The cutter careened off the side of the runway and bounced over a drainage ditch in a dusty trail of grass, weeds, dirt, and rocks. The only thing keeping me attached to the wildly bucking machine was the freely rotating, nonfunctioning steering wheel. The cutter and I finally came to an abrupt halt in a billowing cloud of powdery white dust in a plowed field about twenty-five feet off the runway. Covered with dirt and debris from head to toe, I could easily have passed for an Aboriginal ceremonial dancer. Only when it was over did I realize how lucky I had been not to be thrown off and hit by the menacing blades.

As was most often the case, my immediate concern was less for my own safety than, "What was Mr. Bailey going to say?" The problem with the grass cutter was minor. The linkage between the base of the steering wheel and its attachment to the steering mechanism had popped off the ball-socket. It was easily replaced. At least there was a recognizable mechanical malfunction. The cutter was OK, but as it careened off the runway, it made a clean cut in the electrical wire to the runway lights. Mr. Bailey was not pleased. I don't think he even said he was glad I wasn't hurt, but he also didn't chide me for driving too fast, as I'm sure he knew I was.

Aeronca Champs

The majority of our attention was devoted to servicing the four Aeronca 7AC "Champion" airplanes, the primary trainers, tied down outside the main building by the gas pump. The Aeronca Champ was about the size of the venerable Piper J-3 "Cub." It was powered by a sixty-five horsepower Continental engine and distinguished by a mild dihedral in its wings and a slightly "pregnant guppy" shape to its tandem-seating fuselage. Unlike the Piper Cub, the Champ was soloed from the front seat, which was especially nice, because you could see where you were taxiing.

Aeronca 7AC Champion

Learning to Fly

Bobby and I loved the airplanes and loved to fly. We couldn't earn flying time fast enough. Mr. Bailey was an excellent instructor. He always wore a dark-blue base-

Aeronca instrument panel

ball cap with a bill that seemed too large for the hat. He communicated with his student through a battery-powered microphone connected to a set of large, round, World War II earphones. "Switch off." The line boy turns the prop. "Contact." Another turn of the prop and the engine sputters to life. The fire in its cylinders is mild compared to the fire of excitement ignited in a young boy's heart as he begins to live his fantasy of learning to fly.

The Champs cost $8 an hour solo, and $12 with Mr. Bailey as the instructor. With an earning power of only fifty cents an hour, it seemed it would take forever to learn to fly. Mr. Bailey could not have had two more dedicated and enthusiastic students. Though he never showed much emotion, I believe he actually enjoyed watching "his" two boys, as much as they enjoyed working for him.

Lessons were only a half-hour long. Every flight started with a proper pre-flight. Mr. Bailey was meticulous about pre-flighting the airplane. It was important that every cotter pin in every control surface be checked and don't forget the pitot tube to ensure no insects had taken up residence there. Checking the fuel in the tanks and oil in the engine was critical.

Mr. Bailey demonstrated the patience of Job while teaching me how to fly. He must have told me a thousand times, "a little more rudder, nose up some, add some power, don't forget the carburetor heat, start your flare, easy now, stick back." When I first started the learning process it all seemed so complicated. A simple turn not only required the right blend of stick and rudder, but up elevator as well; and if you expected to keep the same airspeed, some throttle. While convinced I would never learn to fly, it was the thrill of my life and I loved every minute we spent in the air.

We started out with basic air work. Incapable of analyzing it all, I simply mimicked Mr. Bailey's inputs until I began to get the picture and the feel of what to do. Mr. Bailey demonstrated how to trim the airplane in straight-and-level flight and how to make turns. He was a stickler for keeping the airplane trimmed; a good lesson to learn. Actually the basic air work came fairly easy. With Mr. Bailey's excellent coaching, and after he reminded me for the umpteenth time as I rolled into a turn, "more rudder, nose up some," it wasn't long before I developed the feel for how much rudder was required as I banked the airplane. Soon I recognized how much elevator was needed to keep from losing altitude in a turn; and lastly, how much throttle movement was necessary to keep the airspeed reasonably constant.

Once the basic air work became reasonably natural, we concentrated on takeoffs and landings. Understanding the mechanics of making a takeoff or landing was relatively easy compared to actually achieving the necessary judgment to accomplish them. I never seemed to use enough rudder as I added power for takeoff and my directional control suffered as I concentrated on getting the tail off the ground or fixated on the airspeed indicator to determine the takeoff speed. It was landings, however, that required the most judgment. When do you start the turn to base and final? How much rate of descent is required? How high should you be when you arrive over the runway? When do you start the flare? How much elevator do you hold? What do you do if you're too high? What do you do if you're too low and bounce back into the air? How do you decide if you need more or less power? What about crosswinds? I learned very early that landings were important and needed lots of practice. Mr. Bailey taught with patience and understanding and had the enviable ability to critique my flying without making me feel like the clumsy oaf I must have seemed. Many times in my later years of flying, Mr. Bailey's calm matter-of-fact voice would remind me, "Nose up some, nose up some."

Every pilot must have his own concept of what it means to become an integral part of the airplane. For me, I'm not exactly sure when it happened, or how it happened. It just happened. In my early training, I "drove" the airplane more or less mechanically, reacting to Mr. Bailey's calm mono-tone voice. I simply converted Mr. Bailey's instructions into control inputs to force the airplane to go where I thought Mr. Bailey wanted it to go, perceiving what I was doing as some-thing I did to the airplane, as if external to it. I envisioned the airplane as it banked, turned, and pitched above the planar surface of the stationary earth. The motion of the airplane simply confounded and confused me more than it helped.

Gradually I was drawn into a set of axes located near the airplane's center. My reference changed perceptively from one of being outside the airplane looking in, to one of being inside looking out. No longer did I do things to the airplane as it flew over the earth. It was the world that tilted and turned. It was the world that climbed and dived. Ultimately, I could make the world spin in almost any direction I wanted it to go. The power I commanded in flight was enormous. If I didn't like the world where it was, I simply moved it to someplace else. The motions, the feelings, the sights, and the sounds of the airplane, added to my ability to control the attitude and location of the world. What an ego trip! Certainly the closest I would ever come to having the power of "Superman." I reveled in my command over the orientation of the earth, forever in love with flying.

The First Solo

The nominal flight time leading up to solo was around eight hours. I was getting close. As you approach that ever-important first solo flight, you're hopeful, but you never really know when the instructor will feel he can turn you loose on your own. It is an awesome responsibility. For me it happened one calm cool April afternoon after school. Mr. Bailey and I spent a half-hour in the landing pattern. Knowing I was close to soloing, made me anxious and amplified every mistake. The flying period passed quickly and Mr. Bailey instructed me to taxi back to the tie down area. How disappointing, I would not solo today. To my surprise, rather than instructing me to shut down, he simply said, "Warren, take her around the pattern, two touch-and-goes and a full stop," and climbed out of the back seat leaving me with the headphones on.

Without a second thought, I taxied to the far end of the

You always remember your first solo

field, looked both ways, turned onto the runway, took a deep breath, added power and started down the grassy strip. The tail lifted off the ground almost as soon as the stick moved forward. The Aeronca flew off smoothly at forty-five miles per hour. The takeoff was easy. My next thought came with a little more apprehension, "Well, I've got it up here; now all I have to do is get it down safely." I was acutely aware of the loudness of the silence from the headphones. Having watched Mr. Bailey solo a number of students, I knew exactly where to look for him. Sure enough, he was standing beside the tetrahedron adjacent to the parking lot. It was somehow comforting to know he was there.

As I started my left gliding turn toward the runway, pulling out the carburetor heat knob was a natural reaction. On the landing, I leveled off high and got too slow. The forgiving Champ settled ingloriously onto the grass and bounced a couple of times. It is an understatement to say it was an exhilarating experience, although I knew Mr. Bailey had surely observed every wrong input. As I added power, the engine coughed, reminding me to push in the carburetor heat knob. Quickly airborne, I could not have been more elated. I turned and looked behind me to make sure Mr. Bailey really wasn't there and let out the biggest YAHOO-O-O I could muster and shouted, "I'm doing it, I'm really flying all by myself. YAHOO-O-O!" I rocked the wings to let the Champ know who was in control but mostly to make sure this wasn't just a dream.

I don't remember the second touch-and-go, and my recollection of the final landing was only that it must have been perfect. Mr. Bailey met me at the gas pump and in his usual non-emotional way, shook my hand and said, "Nice job." I was pleased he was the first to congratulate me, but couldn't wait to tell Bobby I had soloed. The tail of my undershirt was unceremoniously scissored off, suitably stenciled with a black marking pen and thumb tacked on the wall of the Operations Building for all to see. It was April 5, 1955.

After the wonderful solo experience, instructional flights continued. Emphasis was placed on slow flight, straight and turning stalls, constant turns around a point, sideslips to a landing, wheel landings, and the ever-important emergency landing. Solo flights were interspersed with instructional flights to allow me to practice the maneuvers introduced during the dual flights. During the first solo flight on which I was allowed to leave the field, I wanted to do two things; one was to fly over my house; the other was to touch a cloud. It was important to emulate the buzzards and find out for myself what a cloud was really like. I accomplished both. I didn't actually fly through the cloud; I just gently nudged it with my wing tip.

Stalls were a little scary at first because they never seemed to be totally predictable and I didn't like the feeling of not being in control. I practiced them a lot. Wheel landings were fun because they required a high degree of judgment and weren't very forgiving of error. Turns about a point were confusing until I began to understand how to compensate for the wind by varying bank angle to hold a constant radius turn. Constantly being ready for the inevitable simulated emergency landing created a high degree of situational awareness and required the most planning and judgment. Mr. Bailey made it abundantly clear that I must be able to demonstrate that I could actually get the airplane safely on the ground should the engine quit. I loved the solo flying and freely admit I didn't use every minute of my solo time practicing maneuvers, as I should have. The miracle of flying needed to be enjoyed for the amazing wonder it was.

Flying Cross-country

The next major milestone toward earning my private pilot's license was to get clearance to fly cross-country. Since lessons were typically a half-hour long, we never strayed very far from the field. As an introduction, Mr. Bailey patiently and carefully taught map reading, ground speed calculations, wind effects and cross-country flight planning.

My first solo cross-country was not exactly a difficult one. I flew from Northfield Airport to the Fredericksburg Airport, a distance of about fifty miles. The two airports are bracketed by the two major north-south highways in Virginia and, to make navigation even easier, the R.F.&P. Railroad tracks the Navy trainer had used, also pass by the Fredericksburg Airport. In other words, it is virtually impossible to get lost.

It was a pleasant Sunday afternoon when I lifted off and turned north toward Fredericksburg. A gentle breeze nudged puffy summertime cumulus clouds across the field well above my intended flight altitude. The flight up was uneventful and the Fredericksburg Airport easily located. In my inexperience, I had failed to consider what the airport would look like and was confused by its layout. Northfield was the only airport at which I had ever landed and I had a difficult time determining which runway was in use. I started to circle the field a second time anxiously looking for a stiffened windsock or tetrahedron in a white cement circle to give me a clue. Ah good, a tetrahedron not unlike the one at home, but h-m-m-m, not so good; it's pointed between the two runways. About halfway around my second orbit, a yellow Piper Cub turned

Piper Cub shows the way

left out of the parking area toward Runway 23. I didn't have to make a choice; the yellow Cub made it for me, "Thanks." I landed, had my logbook signed, and was soon airborne for the return trip.

On the way back, the wind picked up noticeably, the puffy clouds weren't as white as when I started, and it got quite turbulent. I was becoming concerned. As Northfield appeared in the distance, the airplane was being buffeted about considerably. Over the airport, my attention was drawn to a small crowd gathered around a yellow and orange Champion that lay at a crazy angle off the right side of the long runway. My already shaken confidence level dropped to near zero. My only thought was, "Look out folks, because here comes another one." On final, the turbulence decreased slightly but there was still considerable crosswind. "Now what did I remember about crosswind landings?" I should never have asked myself the question, I should have only continued to fly the airplane. "If the cross-wind is from the left, does that mean left wing down or does it mean left rudder?" At the field boundary a big gust upset the airplane totally captivating my attention. Before I knew it, I was safely on the ground obviously having done the right thing without fully analyzing it in my mind. It made me appreciate how good Mr. Bailey's instruction was. The student pilot in the yellow and orange Champ had ground-looped and run off the runway. The Aeronca was fine and the only damage was to the student's ego. I had successfully completed my first cross-county flight.

A Muddy Airplane

The worst chewing out Bobby or I ever got happened to Bobby when he came back from a cross-country with enough mud on the airplane to advertise that it had been someplace it should not have been. Bobby got sufficiently lost that he decided to land in a farmer's field and ask his location and get directions. It sounded like a good plan to me. Mr. Bailey, obviously, did not share this opinion and proceeded to let Bobby know it in no uncertain terms. I concluded one should be especially careful on cross-country flights.

My Turn

One of the requirements for a private pilot's license was to successfully fly a solo cross-country of at least three hundred miles. Out of Northfield, the standard flight was to Rocky Mount, North Carolina. At the time it seemed so far away and presented a huge financial burden to save up enough flying hours to pay for it. After plotting and studying the route, the only navigation problem seemed to be the requirement to pick the proper railway line out of Petersburg, Virginia. By this time I was sophisticated enough to calculate ground speeds and times over check points.

Finally I accumulated enough flight time to make the trip. Weather checked, flight plan filed, I lifted off and headed south. Although the visibility was not the greatest, the route was free of clouds. The little sixty-five horsepower Continental purred nicely, driving the tiny wooden prop at 2150 rpm, pulling the Aeronca through the air at ninety miles per hour. I arrived at my first major checkpoint, Petersburg, earlier than expected and noted that it was rather smoky down low. Now, let's see, match the ground to map, or is it the other way around? The railroad tracks are not as distinct as they should be according to the map. Check the magnetic compass, don't forget the variation, h-m-m-m, fourteen degrees east, do I add or subtract? What did Mr. Bailey say?

East is least … Dummy, check your flight card, OK, 182 degrees. According to my time estimate, it should be about eight minutes to Bugg's Island Lake but that sure looks like it up ahead. Match the ground to the map. I

That looks like Bugg's Island Lake

can't possibly be here this early. The lake looks about right but that tower doesn't seem to be on the map. Enter images of Bobby's muddy airplane. Enter stronger images of Mr. Bailey's ire.

While not as easy as Fredericksburg, the little town of Rocky Mount should not be difficult to find. It lies at the intersection of a double north-south railroad and a single track to the west. The westward track runs right by the airport. I hope I didn't take the wrong set of railroad tracks out of Petersburg. My flight plan calls for a heading of 187 degrees but the compass is bouncing around so much it is practically useless. If only I could go faster to see if I'm going to end up with a muddy airplane or if the Rocky Mount Airport is actually going to be there. Please God let it be there.

The world turned mostly green and I didn't see a recognizable landmark anywhere. I should have paid more attention when I had good landmarks rather than simply enjoying the scenery. A little late, but if I had only done a ground speed check I'd have a much better idea of where I am. According to my flight plan, I should have almost ten minutes to go and the map shows a reasonably large roadway angling off to the left. But I don't see one. The fuel is okay because I seem to be getting everywhere ahead of schedule. Mr. Bailey is not going to like this. I began to wonder if I hadn't already passed Rocky Mount. I made a conscious decision not to panic until the time ran out. I'll muddy up the airplane at that time and not before.

After an eternity of twelve minutes a small town on the double railway comes into view, but alas, no single track heading west. Maybe there's another town further down the tracks. Most likely it's going to be a muddy airplane. A little closer, Eureka! A westerly single railway track, but where's the airport? All I see are green fields. Turn right just a little, look straight down, green fields. Turn left, more green fields, sigh, wait, what's that? A tetrahedron, a windsock, a green grassy runway. I continued the left turn, no traffic in sight, nice landing. "Thank you Lord. Happiness is not having a muddy airplane." This cross-country stuff isn't so bad after all.

When I looked for my logbook to get it signed, I discovered I had left it at Northfield. Does this mean I'll have to do it again? I can't afford it! The nice lady at the counter reminds me to close my flight plan. She obviously has encountered students before who had left their logbooks at home. She signed my flight plan and told me to show it to Mr. Bailey when I got home. That flight plan is still stapled in my

Refueling Northfield Aeronca Champion

logbook today. It was a luxury having another "line boy" refuel my Champ. He looked like a cross between Bobby and me. I wondered how far along he was toward learning to fly.

The trip home was a lot easier but slower. The sun was in a better position and the visibility considerably improved. Safely on the ground at Northfield, I was tired, never having flown that long before, but elated not to have a muddy airplane. Mr. Bailey mildly chided me for not taking my logbook with me as he reminded me to close my flight plan. Another major hurdle in my quest for my Private Pilot's license was completed.

I was excited and had to tell someone. I'll stop by my girlfriend's house on the way home. My mind was obviously someplace else because I never saw the car as it crossed from my left and didn't quite make it out the right side. I turned the wheel hard left but chipped the right taillight and bumper with a glass-tinkling thud. Reality has a way of rudely reappearing at the most inopportune times. The driver of the other car was not pleased, angry is more accurate. All I could think of was, call Dad; he could fix anything. Fortunately, Dad knew the people in the other car. He really could fix anything, including my car.

The Big Boys

Quite often, the airport mechanic needed a part on short notice that could only be obtained from a supplier located on Byrd Field, Richmond's municipal airport. Bobby or I occasionally got the opportunity to fly over and pick it up. Since none of our Champions were equipped with radios, we had to call ahead and make arrangements with the Byrd Field Control Tower to give us a light signal for landing. The thrill of flying in the same airspace as the "Big Boys" was as exciting as the prospect of "free" flight time.

I carefully studied the list of Control Tower light signals, not really sure what I was going do if the Tower flashed any light other than the steady green, cleared to land, signal. The idea was to fly close to the Tower and watch for the light. Fortunately I always got a green light. On the final approach, I was amazed how long and how wide the runway looked. I had never imagined there might be so much concrete in the entire world. What a thrill to cross the threshold and see a DC- 6 or DC-7 waiting to take the runway for takeoff. Imagine, the "Big Boys" waiting for me to land. How embarrassing if they were to see me bounce on touchdown. On the ground, surrounded by the huge expanse of concrete, the little Champ seemed mighty small.

A phone call from the parts vendor alerted the Tower to give me a light signal for taxi. The airport world was certainly a lot simpler then. Even though the Aeronca could easily takeoff in the last one thousand feet, I liked to use the full runway. It was fun to see the end of the runway disappear well beneath the airplane on climb out. Oh, how I wanted to be one of the "Big Boys" some day.

The aircraft maintenance hangar reminded me of working at my Dad's automobile repair shop and I enjoyed lending a hand when I could. It also gave me an appreciation of the structural and mechanical aspects of aircraft, albeit simple ones. Applying fabric to the various surfaces is an art very few people are able to do these days, yet it was the essence of aircraft overhaul at that time. I especially liked the smell of newly applied dope to the cloth surfaces.

Linda

Linda entered my life during my senior year in high school. She had transferred to Hermitage in her sophomore year from a big city school, Thomas Jefferson High. We were assigned to the same fifth-period study hall. Linda was a tall, thin blonde with a small waist and ample hips. She had the clearest, creamiest white skin I had ever seen. Her oval face was framed by exceptionally fine, shiny, blonde hair, cut relatively short. Her sparkling blue eyes and slightly pouty lower lip made her irresistibly sexy. While Linda seemed quiet and a bit shy, she was not beyond responding to my obvious interest and flirtation. She would become my wife.

Fledgling Test Pilots

Mr. Bailey acquired an early model Ercoupe airplane for the airport. The Ercoupe is a low-wing, side by side, two-seater, with tricycle landing gear. The uniqueness of the airplane was that it did not have rudder pedals, but used an aileron-rudder interconnect for flight coordination with the control wheel. It was advertised as making flying "as easy as driving your car." It also had limited elevator authority, which theoretically meant you couldn't stall the airplane and thus could not spin it. There were two problems. The first involved takeoffs and landings in crosswinds and the

Budding test pilots

second was, never tell two seventeen-year-old budding test pilots you couldn't do something in an airplane, for they will most certainly try to prove you wrong.

By this time Bobby had his Private Pilot's license, which meant we could fly together. We carefully tufted the wings of the Ercoupe with short strips of black yarn and took off to play test pilot. We found, indeed, that we could not stall the Ercoupe by flying straight-and-level and pulling slowly back on the wheel, it simply mushed along. We further discovered that if we got it going fast and zoomed upward, we could get it to stall. We experimented only enough to convince ourselves it could be done. The tufts fascinated me as they reacted to the changing airflow over the wing and the long yarn string we had attached to the wing tip rotated continuously in the hurricane vortex generated at the tip. My interest in aerodynamics was strong and would never diminish.

Formation Flying?

One day Bobby and I tried our hand at flying formation. I think the only briefing we did was to make sure we were far enough away from Northfield that Mr. Bailey wouldn't see us. We completely ignored such important items as who was going to be the leader and who was going to be the wing man. Since the Champs didn't have radios, all communications had to be done by hand signals, which only worked if we were able to join up. We met overhead Hermitage High School and engaged in what looked more like a World War I dog fight than two airplanes trying to join up with one another. There were as many head-on passes as there were side by side ones. Eventually Bobby got joined up on me but, as we both attempted to compensate for the movement of the other aircraft, we ended up looking more like we were on separate roller coasters than we did like two aircraft in formation. We were lucky we didn't run into each other.

After I got my Private license, Bobby and I flew a very ragged formation from Northfield to Park Hall, Maryland to attend an air show at the Naval Air Test Center. Linda flew with me and Bobby's future wife, Judy, flew with him. The motion was too much for Judy who bolted from Bobby's airplane to the nearest rest room with a bad case of air sickness as soon as we stopped. It was at this air show I would see my first F3B "Demon" without knowing the role it would ultimately play in my life. We decided not to fly formation on the return trip.

Acrobatics 101

Another dimension of flying was introduced by a young flight instructor who enjoyed flying more for the females his pilot image allowed him to attract, than for his love of flying. One day Harvey Bloodworth invited me to go flying when, unbeknownst to me, he planned to practice acrobatics, which, in the Aeronca Champ, meant steep turns, wingovers, and loops. His goal was likely twofold: one to impress me with his aeronautical prowess and the other, to see if he could make me sick. The wingovers were fun and I was impressed with his precision; but by far the most exhilarating was turning the world upside down in a loop. He made it look so easy; I couldn't wait until my next solo flight.

Within a couple of days I set out to impress myself with my own newly acquired aeronautical knowledge, hopefully without making myself sick. I was sure I had carefully memorized all the airspeeds and "g" forces. I did wingovers with nowhere near Harvey's skill. They were certainly not impressive. That's okay. I would recover my tarnished image by executing the perfect loop. Highway 1 provided the appropriate ground reference. Nose down, throttle forward, 80-85-90 miles per hour, stick back, back some more, up, up, stick further back, all I can see is sky, straight up, h-m-m-m, seems a little slow? Something doesn't feel quite right, the horizon finally came into view in the top of the windshield, come on, almost upside down, keep going, keep going, whew! Inverted at last. Speed much, much too slow. Suddenly the world came to a complete standstill. I was suspended, dangling upside down in the sky. My mind forever being imprinted with the sickening feeling of the fabric covered wings as they rocked

Not as it's supposed to be!!!

back-and-forth. Once. Twice. In my mind I visualized the struts that normally suspend the fuselage in tension begin to collapse in the unfamiliar compression of the wings as they now lifted toward the sky in the inverted position. This was not the way it was supposed to be. The wings did two more sickening teeters before the horizon slowly dropped upward in the windscreen toward the nose of the airplane. I throttled back and had absolutely no trouble whatsoever keeping the airspeed below 90 miles per hour. I recovered the Champ somewhere near the original heading and experienced the worst case of spatial disorientation I would ever know.

It was a wise decision to terminate my acrobatics and return to Northfield. The airport was visible in the distance, but my vestibular system was sending such strong and erroneous information to my brain that I literally had to force myself to turn in the proper direction toward the field. The whole world had somehow rotated and couldn't possibly exist in the direction my eyes perceived it to be. It was several minutes before I was able to orient the Champ in the direction of home. That poorly executed loop taught me an important lesson I would carry with me forever: the world is indeed not always "WHAT" it appears to be, and especially in flying, it is not always "WHERE" it appears to be.

In my Navy Flight Training, I discovered my vestibular system was almost perfect, almost perfectly wrong that is. While under the hood or in the clouds, I could enter a fifteen degree banked turn, hold it for a while, roll the wings level, only to discover I was precisely in a fifteen degree banked turn in the opposite direction. Vertigo, to some degree continued to haunt me my entire flying career. It was a conscious decision to tuck the memory of that loop into an easily accessible part of my mind. I didn't even tell Bobby about it. I had discovered real flying could easily exceed the thresholds established on the white wooden roller coaster at Buckroe Beach.

Beware the Night

If anyone ever had the slightest doubt that Northfield deserved the label "Spooks Hollow," they obviously had never been there after dark. Bobby was checked out to fly at night and we decided to combine some of our hard-earned flying time for a night flight. We purposefully picked a night with a partial moon. This was when we discovered that Harvey used the airport for activities other than just flight instruction. As we made the last twist in the vine-covered entrance to the field, our headlights rested squarely on the rear window of Harvey's distinctive 1954 Ford. We laughed, craned our necks, and took our own sweet time making the turn. There was a tremendous flurry of hands, skin, eyes, cloth, elbows, and other less often exposed anatomy as the cover up commenced. Harvey was relieved we were not the cops, or an irate husband, but was quick to let us know we had ruined the best part of his evening.

For night flying, the Aeronca Champ is equipped with a small cylindrical receptacle under the left wing into which you insert the stem of what looks like a streamlined automobile headlight. There is a control switch in the cockpit to turn it on and off.

After takeoff, we circled over the city, which was absolutely gorgeous. Richmond was an oasis of sparkling lights in an otherwise dark expanse of black. We made a pylon turn around the blinking lights atop the huge WLEE radio tower and headed back to Northfield. Bobby shot a touch-and-go landing on the long runway and it went so well he decided to try one on the short runway.

Besides being only half the length of the main runway, the short runway lacked runway lights and had tall trees at the north end. The approach was purposely steep to avoid the trees, which we did, but near the ground it was almost impossible to judge the altitude for landing. We hit the ground with a loud whoomp and bounced back into the air. Bobby added power but we hit the ground hard again, and in a considerable skid. The rough runway amplified the resulting pilot/airplane/ground oscillation. Bobby got the airplane stopped but we were both noticeably shaken. We decided we had had enough night flying that evening and taxied back to the fuel pump.

I concluded that night flying, while absolutely beautiful, needed to be approached with caution. I also began to realize how quickly airplanes and ground proximity could join forces to exceed the limits designed into the machine and that the machine almost always loses in a contest with the ground.

My Private Pilot's License

Having accrued the required forty hours of flight time and passed my FAA written exams, I was ready for my Private Pilot's flight check which, at that time, could and was, given to me by Mr. Bailey. The flight check was done in two parts, the basic air work maneuvers and the cross-country part. Both went very well and I was awarded my Private Pilot's license on September 14, 1957. My first passenger seat was reserved for my Mom. We essentially reconstructed my first solo flight where I was allowed to leave the

My first passenger; my Mom

field but without touching the cloud. Mom was very proud of me. Unfortunately my Dad never got to fly with me. To have a son who loved to fly, my Dad was deathly afraid of flying. For the half-dozen commercial flights he made, he turned ashen white three days prior to and remained so for three days after every flight.

College

There was never any doubt that I wanted to study Aeronautical Engineering when I went to college. My first choice was Virginia Polytechnic Institute (VPI) and my second choice was the University of Virginia. VPI clearly had the better reputation as an engineering school but I ended up getting a partial scholarship to the University of Virginia, so there was really no choice since Mom and Dad had very little money to pay for my college education. In the fall of 1956, I entered the Aeronautical Engineering curriculum at the University of Virginia.

My college roommate was from Roanoke, Virginia. We were both taking potluck on roommates letting the University assign them. Don Henderson and I were exactly the same size even down to shoe size. Don was an Aeronautical Engineering major, his father was a diesel mechanic, we were both Baptist, non-smokers, and non-

Captain Don Henderson, USAF

drinkers. The major difference was that Don was a fair-skinned blonde with blue eyes and I had dark hair and skin and brown eyes. Our taste in females was just the opposite, Don liked brunettes and I liked fair-skinned blondes. We were exceptionally compatible and complemented each other in many ways. Don went on to become a Major General in the Air Force Space Command and I went into the Navy and ultimately became a NASA Test Pilot.

As are most college students, I was broke and could only fly when someone else came up with the money. I did get checked out in a Piper PA-11 "Super Cub" at the Charlottesville-Albemarle Airport and we pooled our money on a couple of occasions to fly around the University and ultimately to check out some of the aeronautical theory we were studying. Shades of Bobby and me playing test pilots in the Ercoupe. At Northfield I checked out in the Cessna 172 and flew friends when they, or their parents, paid the cost of the airplane. I learned never to turn down anyone who wanted to pay for me to fly an airplane. It was infinitely better to have someone pay me to fly than it was for me to pay them to let me fly. That axiom has served me well through the years. I also used this as my definition of a "good job." That is: a job where I get paid to do something, I would pay someone to let me do.

Bobby attended Virginia Polytechnic Institute (VPI); however; his influence over my love affair with flying did not end when we graduated from high school. Bobby entered a Co-op program sponsored by VPI and worked as a student engineer at the Naval Air Test Center, NATC, at Patuxent River, Maryland. Once again he shared this experience with me. At his suggestion, Don and I applied for summer jobs at the Test Center and worked there two summers. We lived in the BOQ with up to thirty other student engineers.

I was assigned to the Aeromedical Branch of the Service Test Division and worked directly for a Civil Service engineer, Roger Seltz, and indirectly for a Navy Flight Surgeon, LT "Doctor" Herb Kelly. The Head of the Branch was another Flight Surgeon, LCDR Frank Austin who was also a pilot. My Civil Service boss was Mr. Hank Dobson. The job was fun but not particularly challenging. Most of our effort was devoted to perfecting a full-pressure suit for high altitude

Smile for the camera

flying. I spent many hours in pressure suits in the low-pressure chamber and became very familiar with oxygen equipment. We also mapped the noise fields under helicopters. I had the "pleasure" of walking around beneath hovering helicopters with a hand held microphone while Roger Seltz recorded acoustic data in a nearby van. It is amazing how much oil a piston-powered helicopter can eject as it hovers over your head. It never occurred to me that it could fall on my head.

Dr. Austin pro-
vided the real high-
light of the Naval Air
Test Center experience.
Frank gave me my first
jet ride in a Lockheed
T2V trainer and I was
immediately hooked
on becoming a Naval
Aviator. Words cannot

First jet ride with LCDR Austin

begin to describe the
excitement a young lad feels as he is strapped in for his
first jet ride. Once the canopy was closed, I was surprised
how quiet it was. The outwardly noisy jet engine seemed
no louder than a washing machine motor. On takeoff the
ground whizzed by at rate of speed I never dreamed was
possible. The climb out was steep and rapid. Once at altitude
Frank put the trainer through its paces but was considerate
enough to keep checking to see if I was all right. The high "g"
forces took some getting used too but I assured him I was OK
and was in fact having the time of my life, as I was. Frank
asked if I wanted to fly the airplane. Timidly I grabbed the
stick and made a small input, the rapid and solid response
of the controls was fantastic. Frank said, "Pull back on the
stick and push it to the left." The world did a series of rapid
rolls to the right. It was incredible how fast things happened.
Much too soon it was time to head back to the field. Frank
did a series of touch-and-go landings with steep pull-ups
to the downwind leg. In typical Navy fashion all patterns
were made with the gear down. As I climbed down from the
cockpit I was beaming from ear to ear. If there ever had been,

there was no longer any doubt what I wanted to do after graduating from the University.

The Flight Test Center was an exciting place to work. All the latest Navy aircraft were there. Dr. Austin participated in the transcontinental speed record flight set by then Marine Major John Glenn in the F8U-1P "Crusader" from Los Alamos, CA to Floyd Bennett Field, NY on July 16, 1957. We were treated to all the exciting stories that went along with the record flight.

The Navy was testing the Temco TT-1 "Pinto" trainer and I had the opportunity to fly in it a couple of times. The

Temco TT-1 Pinto Trainer

TT-1 was the Navy's attempt to replace the T-34 and provide an all-jet training syllabus for its aviators. It was about the same size as the T-34 and had a 920-pound thrust Continental J-69-T-9 turbojet engine. The two crew members sat in tandem in front of the mid-mounted straight, but slightly tapered wing. The horizontal and vertical tails were attached to a tapered tubular structure that extended aft of the wing. The large single clamshell canopy was hinged behind the instructor's seat. Shortly after I had my first flight in the TT-1, the canopy fell and broke the arm of the pilot with whom I had flown. It was a very simple aircraft and participated for a short time in the flight-training syllabus at the Naval Auxiliary Air Station, Saufley Field in Pensacola, Florida before the Navy discontinued its usage.

In my humble and unqualified opinion, the TT-1 was fun to fly but seriously under-powered. We shot a touch-and-go landing at Webster Field and just barely got airborne before running off the end of the runway. It had a serious problem whenever it taxied or attempted to takeoff through standing water. The water tended to be sucked into the low intakes and drown out the engine.

The Navy's latest trainer, the T2J "Buckeye," had just arrived on the Center for testing. Unfortunately I did not get to fly in it because of a restriction on the ejection seat system. Little did I know at the time that I would end up doing my Navy flight training in the T2J.

NATC T2J Trainer

The Naval Air Test Center taught me that aviation could be a dangerous undertaking. I witnessed two aircraft accidents on the Center, the first was a wheels-up landing by an F11F "Tiger" and the other was a takeoff accident of an A4D "Skyhawk." The F11F was experiencing an engine problem

NATC Grumman F11F Tiger

and the pilot had advised the tower that he needed to land as soon as possible and could not accept a wave-off. The tower dutifully notified the "wheels watch" personnel at the end of the runway. The F11F made a normal approach for landing with one exception, no gear. Apparently the pilot was distracted by the engine problem and simply landed wheels up. Huge balls of fire trailed behind the airplane as it slid along the runway on its belly. When the airplane stopped, the canopy popped open and a streak of orange raced from the cockpit to the side of the runway. It was the unhurt but very embarrassed pilot.

The A4D "Skyhawk" was conducting heavy-weight takeoffs on Runway 14. When the pilot attempted to raise the nose for takeoff he over rotated and the aircraft stopped accel- erating. He lowered

Beware of "Ground Effect," or the lack thereof

the nose, attained sufficient flying speed to get airborne, but only enough to remain airborne in the ground effect of the runway. When the Skyhawk crossed the end of the runway, which is about thirty feet above the bay, the ground effect cushion was lost and the airplane settled into the water just off the end of the runway. The airplane was a loss but the pilot was fine.

Back at the University, Don and I made extra money working as laboratory assistants in the wind tunnel. We set up experiments and graded the lab reports once the experiments were written up. The wind tunnel experience further cemented my interest in aerodynamics. It also gave me a feel for how many variables can, and do, affect the outcome of an engineering experiment, and thus how careful you have to be to gather meaningful test data.

Aviation Officer Candidate Hall, SIR!

During my senior year at the University of Virginia, I applied to the Navy's Aviation Officer Candidate (AOC) program. The program took qualified college graduates for Naval Aviator and Naval Flight Officer positions. In the early Spring I passed the qualifying exams and a stringent flight physical. On August 6, 1960 Commander F. O. Ralston officially swore me into the Naval Air Reserves at the

Swearing in by CDR Rolston

Norfolk Naval Air Station. My reporting date for Pre-Flight Training was one week later. A major step toward making a dream come true. The opportunity to directly pursue the "Superman" in the yellow Navy trainer was becoming a reality.

After graduation, I spent the summer working for Dad at the garage. We enjoyed the time together and as usual he worked my tail off. Those times were very special. I was overjoyed when he offered to drive to Pensacola with me and take the bus back. We had never done anything like that together before. I really appreciated his attention and it seemed somehow appropriate that my father should deliver me into "manhood." Also that summer, Linda and I announced our engagement.

NAS Pensacola Main Gate, 1960

It took a day and a half to reach Pensacola with an overnight stop in a nondescript motel somewhere in central Georgia. Following lunch at a drug store counter in downtown Pensacola, I delivered Dad to the Greyhound bus station, and drove straight to the Pensacola Naval Air Station (NAS). Everyone seemed cordial and helpful as I presented my "official" brown U.S. Navy envelope to the NAS OOD (Officer of the Day). I was told where to park my car since, "You won't need it for a while." In turn he directed me to a large brick building that housed the Indoctrination Battalion. A number of my classmates were already there when I arrived. We were escorted to the evening meal by several of the Senior Class Officers and in general enjoyed the evening relaxing and making new acquaintances. At the time I had no idea what all this was about to mean to me. At six o'clock the following morning, the cordiality of the previous evening changed dramatically.

"Reveille! Reveille! Reveille! All right you Civilians, up and at um, I want everyone outside standing tall in *twenty minutes*, I repeat *twenty minutes*, not *twenty-one*, Do you understand? Move it, MOVE IT!" A few of my new classmates did not meet the twenty minute deadline and endured the wrath of the Cadet Officers in charge.

Once outside, we were formed into two sections and introduced to our Drill Instructor, Marine Gunnery Sergeant Hustler. Sergeant Hustler appeared to be in his late thirties, wasn't any taller than my five foot eight inches, but must have weighed close to one hundred eighty pounds, not an ounce of which was fat. His arms

Marine Gunnery Sergeant Hustler

were as thick as my thighs and hung down at his side like the bowlegs of a cowboy. His barrel chest angled into a flat stomach, thin waist and slight hips. His "Smokey the Bear" hat was pulled down close to his small dark eyes and there was no hint of sideburns beneath the brim. His ears stuck out as if standing at attention. His head and neck were the same size, making it difficult to tell where one ended and the other began. His immaculately pressed uniform fit him like a glove, giving him the appearance of an inverted oblique trapezoid.

Sergeant Hustler's introduction and welcome was more of a tirade than a speech. "Gentlemen," he barked, "It's my job to turn 'you boys' into men and I only have sixteen weeks in which to do it. Many of 'you boys' won't make it, because you don't have what it takes to be a man." He paused for effect. "It's important that you know, you will do WHAT I say, WHEN I say it, and HOW I say it will be done,

Do you understand?" He stared expectantly at the group. "I can't hear you! When I ask a question I expect an answer, is that clear?"

We responded with a weak combination of yeses, yeahs and some yes sirs.

He turned in anger. "The answer is: YES SIR! Is that understood?"

"YES SIR!" We shouted, not totally in unison.

"Now that's better." He walked slowly up and down every line, stopping and looking each of us over very carefully. There were a few nervous snickers as we watched the drama unfold. When he returned to the front, he said, "Who dressed 'you boys' this morning, YOUR MAMAS?"

"NO SIR!" Was the reply. We were getting better already.

"I think the first thing we've got to do is get 'you boys' properly dressed, is that correct?"

"YES SIR!" We replied loudly and more in unison.

"I see that some of 'you boys' are pretty boys and like to wear your hair long like the girls do. I think we'd better fix that and right now, isn't that true?"

"YES SIR!"

Sergeant Hustler turned to the Cadet Officer and instructed him to take "these boys" to breakfast, to the barber and then to supply to get some "proper clothes." The Cadet Officer responded with a loud, "YES SIR" and saluted smartly.

After breakfast we returned to the Indoctrination Barracks in a clumsy formation and lined up for our first military haircut. The young barber delighted in asking each of us how we wanted our hair trimmed before taking the clippers and completely shaving our heads. To add further indignity to the hair cut, he charged seventy-five cents for the experience.

At Supply we were issued "proper clothing," most of which was too large. Many of us spent our first meager paycheck having the garments tailored to fit. In its great wisdom, the Navy had carefully calculated my monthly pay as a Seaman Apprentice to precisely match my monthly laundry bill. There was precious little money leftover for anything else. Not that I had any time or place to spend it.

AOC Hall official photo

Entry Math Exam

On Tuesday we took the mandatory entry math exam the passing of which was required to continue in the program. Failing the exam required a two-week math refresher course and reassignment to the next class. The test was easy, but a number of my classmates were sweating the results, which would be posted on Thursday.

The week in the Indoctrination Barracks was primarily used to teach us the basics of military etiquette, military discipline, and how to speak and understand "Navyese." For all practical purposes it was boot camp. One of our many requirements, whenever a Cadet Officer was nearby, was to "brace the bulkhead," i.e., come smartly to attention against the nearest bulkhead (wall). One day three of us were in the "passageway" (hallway), when a Cadet Officer appeared.

"Ah-ten-shun," was called and two of us "braced the bulk-head" amidst a tremendous clatter of metal on metal. Our third classmate had braced the slightly ajar door to the "swab" (mop) closet and disappeared through the now open doorway. The Officer tried his best to keep a stern expression as he chewed out the two of us for not maintaining a serious composure.

Indoctrination training maintained a grueling pace with near constant harassment. Good was never good enough. My Boy Scout experience paid off as many of the basic skills required by the military had already been learned in the Scouts. A number of my classmates were not faring as well. It was obvious that surviving the next fifteen weeks was going to require a major individual and group effort. While not fully appreciated at the time, a complex set of group dynamics was developing. As we were being care-fully molded into a disciplined organization, individually we competed fiercely with each other in everything we did. Our leadership skills were being scrupulously observed, tested, and evaluated. Each of us responded in our own way and contributed to the unity of the whole.

As promised, the results of the math exam were posted on Thursday. Seven of our classmates would have to take the two weeks of remedial math and therefore would not be joining the rest of us. What? I couldn't believe my eyes. I was one of the seven who had failed the exam. Surely there must be some mistake? It was an easy exam. How could anyone fresh out of engineering school possibly fail such an elemen-tary math test? I would never live this one down. My ego was destroyed. I pleaded my case to see if there could have been some grading error or if it were possible to retake the exam. I was told neither option was likely. I was extremely disappointed in myself and totally distraught over the prospect of spending two more harassing weeks in the Indoctrination Battalion.

On Friday I was ordered to report to the Cadet Officer of the Day, who in turn escorted me to the Academics Officer. "Aviation Officer Candidate, Hall, reporting as ordered Sir," I recited to the Navy Lieutenant seated behind the steel gray desk.

"Stand easy, Mr. Hall. We have reviewed your math exam answer sheet and have found an answer sheet that matches 'your' answers. While this is highly irregular, We do not believe you need the two weeks of remedial math."

"Thank you Lord," I said to myself.

The Lieutenant continued, "We feel, however, that you have demonstrated a serious inability to follow instructions and a complete lack of attention to detail; neither of these characteristics can be tolerated in a Naval Aviator." My heart sank. I was about to be terminated from the program without even getting the opportunity to try. The Lieutenant paused long enough to let the full impact of his statement sink in. I waited for the inevitable dismissal. As if reading my mind, he continued, "Mr. Hall, you will be allowed to continue with your Class, but you are being awarded five demerits for the 'improper filling out of official papers,' you are dismissed."

I came to attention with a snappy, "YES SIR, Thank you Sir," did an about face and exited his office. I didn't like the idea of the demerits but at least I was still in the program, and best of all, wouldn't have to spend two more weeks in the Indoctrination Battalion. Possessing an uncanny ability to misinterpret on which line and/or in which block to enter the required information, I continued to have trouble with the "improper filling out of official papers" throughout my entire military career and still do. Unfortunately, the five demerits would present a problem for me sooner than expected.

Class 30-60, Charlie Section

The weeks of indoctrination passed by excruciatingly slow but they did come to an end. We were officially designated Class 30-60 and assigned to Marine Captain Black, the commissioned officer responsible for overseeing our Class in Battalion II. The Class was divided into two Sections, Alpha and Charlie. Alpha Section consisted of those AOCs destined to become Naval Flight Officers and Charlie Section comprised the Pilot candidates. We were alphabetically assigned four to a room. My roommates were Henry "Hank" Harder, Charles "Chuck" Hottle and Robert "Bob"

Harder   Hottle   Kelly

Kelly. I lost contact with Hank and Chuck shortly after graduation. Bob was killed in an A4 Skyhawk accident attributed to high altitude hypoxia. While I did not miss the open bay barracks of the Indoctrination Battalion, I did miss its red brick polished newness. Batt II, as it was called, was housed in a classic World War II, white, wooden barracks with well-worn paint and rough wooden flooring. The two sections of Class 30-60 were housed at either end of the building with offices and a recreation room between.

Two days after moving into Batt II, I was summoned to Captain Black's office. He informed me that I was the only person in the Class who had come from the Indoctrination Battalion with demerits and was therefore labeled a trouble-maker. He wanted to personally let me know I would be closely watched and that he would not tolerate any unof-ficer-like conduct. Obviously I had not made a good first impression and was off to a lousy start. I did wonder if he had bothered to look at the reason for the demerits. Never-theless I took the message to heart.

Sergeant Hustler delighted in drilling us by the hour on a large macadam area behind Batt II affec-tionately known as the "grinder." We marched there, rain or shine. The hot Florida sun turned the grinder into a humongous

The "Infamous" Grinder

steam bath. Heavy M-1 rifles cut deeply into our shoulders and burned our fingers. Blisters were more common than not, as new combat boots reluctantly yielded to the contours of our feet or vice versa.

During the first couple of weeks in Batt II, several class-mates were afforded the opportunity to lead the Section. Some were noticeably better than others; but apparently we were not doing as well as we should have been. More by happenstance than skill, my chance came about the time we began to get in sync with each other. I became the leader of Class 30-60 "Charlie" Section and remained so until we graduated in December.

Good Morning Cadets

Morning formation was held on the grinder everyday, rain or shine. Some type of inspection followed the morning report.

Salute. "Class Thirty Sixty, Charlie Section, All present and accounted for SIR!"

"Prepare for inspection." Salute.

"Class Thirty Sixty, Charlie Section, Open ranks, Harch! (You never said March)."

"Charlie Section, At close interval, dress right, dress."

"Red-ee front."

AOC Class 30-60, November 1960

Salute. "Class Thirty Sixty, Charlie Section ready for inspection, SIR!"

Sergeant Hustler scrutinized each of us at close quarters front and back. No wrinkle, no overdue haircut, no shoe shine that didn't live up to his lofty expectations and no crooked or unpolished insignia went unnoticed.

Several classmates were singled out to answer important questions like: "What is your rifle number Cadet?"

"My rifle number is 5-2-6-0-9-9-7, SIR!" Returned in a loud sing song manner.

"What is your service number, Cadet?"

"My service number is 6-4-4-4-6-8, SIR!"

It was all part of getting us to think on our feet and developing the required discipline to meet the Navy's needs.

In a surprisingly few weeks, a number of my classmates decided that military life was not their forte and DORed (Dropped on Request). One day they simply disappeared. We all worried about it. I know I did. I couldn't imagine myself serving a two year tour as a Seaman Apprentice on a ship somewhere. It made us work all the harder. We formed support groups to help each other with academics, military, physical fitness or whatever might be creating a problem. With my aeronautical engineering background, the technical academics were easy and I enjoyed the military subjects. Many an evening was spent coaching some of my less technically minded classmates.

A fierce competition developed between the two Sections within the Class. It was particularly exacerbated by the fact that half of the class was destined to become pilots and the other half Naval Flight Officers. A pilot's ego is not something that is developed during Pre-Flight Training; it is already larger than life and only further refined during the training process.

Military courtesies were taken seriously. For fear of not saluting someone who deserved one, we saluted almost anything that moved. It was not unusual to cross the street to avoid chance meetings and, heaven forbid, if you were behind an officer and wanted to pass. We marched everywhere: to class, to movies, to meals, to athletic events, to swimming, to church, everywhere that is, except to the obstacle course.

Marching to church

The Obstacle Course

With the ubiquitous Sergeant Hustler prodding us on and our M-1 rifles held at arms length in front of us or over our heads, we ran the nearly two miles to and from the obstacle course. As we made our way back from the course in full stride, it was not unusual for a classmate or two to fall out beside the sun-drenched road.

The obstacle course included sufficient torture devices to guarantee every muscle in our bodies was taxed. To make matters worse, the entire course meandered through uneven, deeply sanded, scrub pine. Over the years the sand had become more and more refined by the thousands of Naval Cadets who had pounded the course. Just plain running was laborious and slow. Every time we negotiated the course our completion times were

The obstacle course...   It goes on forever...

carefully recorded. In other words, you competed with yourself as well as everyone else. As always, there was the ever-present competition between the two Sections.

When I reported for training, I thought I was in pretty good physical shape but my body was not up to the physical punishment it was asked to endure so early in the program. Each of us found our nemesis in at least one or more of the obstacles. Mine was a twelve-foot vertical wooden wall (although it looked more like fifty to me) with several large ropes hanging from the top. The theory was simple. You ran full speed at the wall, grabbed one of the ropes and half walked and half pulled your way up and over the top. As is often the case, putting theory into practice is not so easy. I was consistently inconsistent. My feet either

My Nemesis

got ahead of my hands and I found myself hanging inverted halfway up the wall or, conversely, my hands outran my feet at which time I found myself dangling by my hands with my feet bumping uselessly against the well-worn polished surface of the wall. The result was the same no matter what. The only recourse was to let go of the rope, crumple into a heap in the sandy pit below, retreat and make yet another running attempt as precious competitive seconds ticked away.

In the end, we all made it through the course. It was a test of strength and endurance for sure, but mostly a test of will. The course was designed to show us how much further we could push ourselves, or be pushed, when we were absolutely certain we had reached our limit weeks ago. It was rewarding to see classmates who had completed the course only moments before, back track to provide encouragement and moral support to the remainder of the Class as each took their turn.

Life Gets Easier

We were finally allowed to have some Saturday afternoons free from the military grind. Most Saturday nights

Aviation Cadet Recreation Center

were spent at the ACRAC (pronounced ack-rack). The Aviation Cadet's Recreation and Activities Center was a small brick building located next to the grinder.

Girls from the surrounding area poured in for the evening, most looking for a husband. While many of the Cadets were interested, alcohol seemed to be the first priority. The girls knew these most eligible bachelors would soon become Naval Officers and were in general a well-screened batch of virile males. More Naval Aviators are married to females from the Pensacola area than any other single location in the United States.

The primary night attraction in downtown Pensacola was Trader Jon's, a single, large, dark, and smoke-filled room with bizarre memorabilia on the walls and hanging from the ceiling. A small dance floor, a live band, and lots and lots of beer provided the entertainment. It was a rowdy place, ideal for Cadets to let off steam and indulge in pleasures not available inside the confines of NAS Pensacola.

NAVCAD Haven

Midway through Pre-Flight Training, I invited Linda to fly down for the weekend. The primary event was a formal dance held at the NAS Pensacola Officer's Club. The rules for her were as strict as were mine. She was required to stay in the Wave's quarters located across the street and three buildings down from Batt II. We had the same curfew.

Linda looked especially lovely in her long white evening gown. It was my first time in a Navy dress uniform and I felt handsome in the stiffly starched, high collar, dress whites. The brief excursion into the Officer's Club was a tantalizing peek into the future. It *was* a very impressive place to say the least. Linda and I enjoyed the dance but were careful to sneak away early enough to have some time alone before our mutual curfews expired. As the big hand on my watch ticked steadily toward the eleven o'clock curfew, we were not the only couple enjoying passionate good night kisses at the entry to the Wave's barracks.

I left Linda with barely three minutes to get the car parked and myself inside Batt II. While racing madly to the car, I stepped in a hole and crashed with a thud on a mound of red Pensacola clay, ruining the blouse and trousers of my dress whites after only one wearing. For having been in the Navy only a short time, I did a respectable job of expounding sufficient expletives to adequately express my displeasure.

Swimming Requirements

The obstacle course was only one part of the physical fitness program. We did progressively more strenuous tasks as we moved through the program. We were taught self-defense, gymnastics, wrestling and swimming. All were graded as competitive events. It was impera- tive to be at or near the top of the class. The swimming require- ments were manda- tory and tough. Three of my classmates were unable to complete them satisfactorily.

Swimming requirements, mandatory and tough

There were distance requirements on and under the water, endurance swims, and demonstrations of the mastery of several swimming techniques. We were dropped from the ceiling in parachute harnesses and towed the length of the pool by a cable to simulate a parachute dragging us through the water. We were taught how to use our clothing as a life preserver and required to swim several laps of the pool in full flight gear.

Dilbert Dunker

The last swimming test was accomplished in the infamous Dilbert Dunker, a clever red contraption resembling an open cockpit section of a single seat airplane mounted on two railings about twenty feet above the water. The two railings extended at a forty-five degree angle into the water. One student at a time was strapped into the cockpit which, when released, slid down the rails, crashed into the water, flipped upside down and sank inverted into the deep end of the pool.

Dilbert Dunker halfway...

...crash with a splash, sink upside down

The crash into the water was considerably more violent than I had anticipated. The shock took away most of the huge breath so carefully inhaled too early in the descent down the rails. The turn-turtle flip fully induced the desired vertigo and the millions of bubbles obscured the immediate surroundings. The escape from the cockpit was accomplished solely by feel. As I undid the lap belt, my lungs were already beginning to burn as the elevated carbon dioxide level triggered the response to breathe. In an effort to achieve some sort of reference, I fumbled for the canopy bow supposedly somewhere in front of me, knowing that up was in fact opposite to the way the canopy bow was pointing. For a moment I tried to determine the direction the bubbles were going but my brain was more interested in telling my lungs to breathe than figuring out which way was up. I pushed off the canopy bow and kicked frantically toward what I believed to be the surface. Within microseconds of taking a huge gulp of green water, I popped out of the water gasping and sputtering for air, having successfully passed yet another milestone in my pursuit of the "Superman" in the yellow Navy trainer. Ironically it was from an inverted red cockpit very similar to the yellow one in which he flew.

Survival Training

One of the last sessions in Pre-Flight was survival training, which included three days and two nights in a survival situation in the woods on Eglin Air Force Base. We patiently sat through the survival lectures on everything; from don't eat Polar Bear hearts or fish that have poisonous spines near their tails, to how to prepare beetles and prickly pear roots for eating. For the three-day Eglin survival "ordeal" we were split into groups of four and given a ration of water but not enough food to last us for three days. Eglin is mostly sand, scrub pine, mesquite bushes and a few prickly pears. Not exactly an Eden.

Survival Training Center

The four of us made a halfhearted attempt to cook prickly pear roots but unanimously found them unpalatable. What the Pre-Flight instructors didn't know was how much we actually enjoyed our three-day "ordeal." It was the first time any of us had the opportunity to relax "on company time" since we started Pre-Flight in August. We enjoyed the leisurely pace as we lounged around a gently flowing stream in the shadow of the scrawny pine woods. On the second day, a couple of us fashioned fishing hooks from pins and feigned fishing in the stream. Mostly, I think, because we felt guilty if we weren't doing something. Our disinterested attempt wasn't about to catch a fish, even if there was one to catch. Lo and behold, we saw a large (by Eglin standards) dead fish come floating by upside down in the stream. As it went by, I jabbed at it with my fishing pole and it wiggled. "It's alive," I shouted. For a moment nothing happened and then four hungry cadets simultaneously jumped into the water trying to grab the half-dead fish. After several splashing grabs we finally batted it up on the shore, not unlike a Grizzly bear might do to a tired salmon. We eagerly roasted the fish and enjoyed a delicious dinner that evening. As best we could figure, the fish had been damaged by the tons of explosive ordnance being tested by the Air Force on the bombing ranges at Eglin. Thanks Air Force, the Navy owes you a meal someday.

Swords

Toward the end of Pre-Flight training we started drilling with our official Officer's swords. Many a "Zorro" incident accompanied our early attempts at drawing and sheathing the swords. We should have started collecting hazardous duty pay at that time. While no one was seriously injured, clothing was occasionally torn and many a close call occurred. It was not unusual to see a cadet cover (hat) go flying in the air when a sword salute was required.

Graduation

Our standing in the class was determined by a combination of our grades in academics, physical fitness and military. The head of Alpha section, Andre Marechal, led the class in physical fitness and I led the class in academics. The final standing hinged on the military grade, a largely subjective evaluation by Captain Black and Sergeant Hustler. The well-deserved honor went to Andre: I would be second. The Class enjoyed its week of running the Indoctrination Battalion as much as the Class Officers had done when we first reported to Pensacola. It seemed so long ago but we knew we had earned, even deserved, the respect; no, make that the "forced attention" afforded us by the new Class.

Graduation day parade and graduation

Mother and Linda drove to Pensacola for graduation and stayed at the old San Carlos Hotel. A reception followed the graduation parade and commissioning ceremony. It was December 2, 1960.

Sergeant Hustler strategically positioned himself to ensure he presented us our first salute as newly commissioned Ensigns. We proudly returned his salute, handed him a shiny Silver dollar and reveled in his "Congratulations Sir," response. I would not have wanted that important dollar to go to anyone else. Sergeant Hustler had my utmost respect and I hoped I had earned his.

Ensign Hall

Saufley Field

Sporting shiny new gold Ensign bars, I packed, drove the nine short miles to Naval Auxiliary Air Station (NAAS) Saufley Field and checked into the Bachelor Officer's Quarters (BOQ). Boy that sounded good! It had been an arduous but  highly rewarding four months. At last flight training was about to begin.

At the time, the Saufley Field flight line was populated with acres of dirty-yellow and shiny-red and white T-34s. Students and instructors with parachutes draped across their shoulders or backs, singularly and in pairs, strode purposefully among the orderly trainers. In a more disorganized manner, whirling propellers accelerated blue-white smoke along fuselages as engines burst into life. Overhead the traffic pattern buzzed in organized chaos. Saufley Field was vibrantly alive. I couldn't wait to fly.

Flight, however, was still several study filled weeks away. Ensign Stan Primmer and I presented our orders to the clerk at Flight Gear Issue, signed the official forms (properly this time), and received two orange flight suits, a pair of brown flight boots, yellow leather gloves, a gold helmet with a boom mike, knee board, a blue log book and most important of all, the official brown Naval Aviator leather flight jacket with the soft fur collar.

Back at the BOQ, and acting at least ten years younger than our chronological ages indicated, we stripped off our khaki uniforms and inserted ourselves into the surprisingly stiff orange flight suits. We paraded about as in new Easter finery, shamelessly admiring ourselves in any reflective medium we encountered. We briefly discussed the possibility of

Anxious to fly

walking to the flight line and taking each other's pictures beside one of the newer looking trainers. We prudently decided to wait until the weekend for fear there was some written or unwritten rule that said only pilots, not mere perspective pilots, were permitted to cross the painted yellow line that guarded the perimeter of the flight line. Instead, we took pictures in the room and stuck them in the Exchange to get them developed as soon as possible.

The Navy's Primary Trainer was the Beechcraft T-34B, "Mentor," which meant it would not be possible to directly emulate the "Superman" in his yellow Navy SNJ trainer. The yellow SNJs could not wait the twelve years it had taken the young boy in the broom straw field to reach the gateway to his planet Krypton.

Ground school took on an entirely new meaning, it was definitely procedurally oriented, more "hands on", and deadly serious. From the start, it was clear there was

A new T-34B trainer at NAAS Saufley Field

only one way to fly the T-34 and that was the "NAVY" way. Departures and arrivals at the airfield followed seemingly complex routes known as course rules. We committed these procedures to memory as if our lives depended on them, for indeed they did. Emergency procedures were likewise committed to memory and recited aloud in precise staccato language. We drilled and critiqued each other on demand. Normal flight procedures developed into singsong sentences

that helped guide us through the proper sequence of events. For example, once in the landing pattern, you open the canopy, retard the throttle, push the propeller lever full forward, and at 110 knots lower the

T-34B Procedural Trainers

landing gear. This procedure became: pop, chop, prop, one ten drop. We all used it. We practiced these procedures in the rows of cockpit trainers located in the Ground Training Building under the watchful eye of knowledgeable enlisted instructors. The final exam was to perform a blindfold cockpit check. In retrospect, it's hard to believe an airplane as simple as the T-34B could have seemed so complicated.

As time marched on, it was increasingly obvious we were not going to start flight training before the Christmas break occurred. I hated the idea that we wouldn't fly until next year and even more that when I was home, after having been in Navy "Flight" Training for five months, I would have to admit I had not yet flown an airplane. Next year seemed like an eternity. The Navy had evidently faced this situation before and much to our delight decided, "weather permitting," each of us would get one flight before we scattered to all parts of the country for the Christmas holidays.

Early in the last week of ground school, we eagerly crowded around the bulletin board to determine which "Flight" we were assigned, but more important to see whom our Primary Flight instructor would be. My Flight was Fourteen and my flight instructor was LTJG Ramsey. The next few days were spent ferreting out as much information as possible about LTJG Ramsey. Most of what I heard, I didn't like. The one trait we least wanted to hear, was the one constant everyone mentioned who had flown with LTJG Ramsey. His unquestioned reputation was one of being a "screamer." A training command "plow back" (a pilot who did not receive a fleet squadron assignment out of flight training but returned to the training command as an instructor pilot), he was considered a perfectionist with little tolerance for student error and was noted for his loud diatribes berating hapless students for any and all lapses of memory or improper technique. The perfectionist label was not a problem but I was definitely not looking forward to having my, sure to be numerous, mistakes criticized in what I was certain to take as personal attacks on my manhood. I was hoping for the Navy's equivalent of Mr. Bailey, not the ogre I created in my mind of LTJG Ramsey.

Several of my friends flew first and came back with enthusiastic reports of how much fun it had been and how they would rather stay in Pensacola and fly than go home for Christmas. While certain I was going to feel the same way, the nagging agony of my idea of one LTJG "Screamer" Ramsey hovered like a menacing black cloud over a holiday picnic. It hadn't rained yet but it seemed likely.

On the morning of my "Dollar Ride" flight, I met LTJG Ramsey next to the scheduling board at precisely 0730. We were scheduled for a 0900 takeoff. LTJG Ramsey did not look like the ogre his reputation had engendered. He was no more than three years older than me, about my height, dark hair, medium build, and actually a nice looking guy. His body language, however, was more consistent with his reputation. He wore a stern, almost pained expression, alternately accented by a slight pulse of his lower jaw muscles. His posture was best described as one of controlled impatience. Without even knowing his reputation, you sensed he was the kind of person you approached with caution.

I took a deep breath, let it out slowly and approached him with my hand extended. Before I could speak, he turned his head, looked squarely at me and asked, "Are you Ensign Hall?"

"Yes Sir," I replied.

"Lieutenant Ramsey," he said, and grasped my hand in a firm but otherwise expressionless handshake. Glancing at my leather name tag, he queried, "Why are you called Warren? In your flight folder you are listed as Gene, you'd better get used to that name."

"Yes Sir."

He gestured toward one of the precisely arranged tables, "Come with me." As we sat down, he opened my flight folder and studied it for a few moments. "I see you already have a Private Pilot's license. That may not be in your best interest, you know?" I looked inquisitive but made no reply. He continued, "Now, before I can teach you how to fly, I've got to teach you how NOT to fly. That makes my job twice as hard." I started to apologize for something I was especially proud of, but decided against it. We had been together for almost ten minutes now and I had said exactly four words, two of which were the same.

"Have you studied the profile for Flight One?"

"Yes Sir, I have."

"Do you have any questions?"

"No Sir, but I'm sure I will as we go along."

"I'd rather have you ask them now, things go pretty fast once we get started."

I thought for a moment. I didn't know what to say. "No questions."

"Good, let's get on with it." I followed as LTJG Ramsey strode out of the flight briefing area at a steady pace. We picked up and inspected two parachutes without a word being spoken. Again I followed a couple of steps behind and to his left, the heavy parachute awkwardly bumping me first behind one knee and then the other. The next stop was the line shack to check the "yellow sheets" for T-34B Number 186. LTJG Ramsey provided a terse explanation of the "official forms" and reminded me how important it was to fill them out accurately and completely. Images of demerits for the "improper filling out of yellow sheets" flashed across my mind. I tried to pay careful attention but he went so fast, I honestly didn't understand them. I knew, however, I was going to be responsible for them on the next flight.

I trailed him to the airplane in silence. He was not exactly "Mister Sociability." For having the reputation as a "screamer" he sure didn't have much to say. At the airplane he pointed me toward the front cockpit. After placing our parachutes in their respective seats, he did an excellent job of walking me through the pre-flight inspection of the airplane. He was indeed a perfectionist. I recognized most of his explanations as being verbatim from the flight manual.

Once in the airplane, we made an inter phone check and he allowed I could, "Start the checklist anytime now because he didn't have all day." I did my best to be professional and complete each item on the checklist as we had been instructed and practiced in ground school. I wasn't exactly spooked but felt uneasy because of the tense atmosphere already existing between LTJG Ramsey and myself. As my luck would have it, the reluctant engine didn't fire once on my first start attempt. No comment from the rear seat. On my second try, the engine backfired once, came to life with a roar, and promptly oversped in response to my having the throttle too far forward. I quickly snatched the throttle back and the engine quit. The tirade started, "Didn't you attend ground school before this flight? Didn't they teach you how to start the engine? Here, let me start it for you. It's obvious you need a couple more ground periods before I let you ruin a perfectly good engine. Our lives depend on this engine and don't you forget it!" His next statement was the clincher, "I thought you already knew how to fly and you can't even get the damn engine started." Of course the engine started perfectly for him.

"Well what are we waiting for now? Call Ground Control for taxi clearance."

I made the call but was really expecting a little more coaching from him on my first flight. I signaled the Plane Captain to pull the chocks and started to taxi forward.

"Which way do you want me to turn, Sir?" I asked.

"What do you think?" Was the curt reply.

"It looks like I should go to the right, Sir."

"Well then do it!"

Already I felt in trouble and we were barely out of the chocks. Luckily, at the end of the row there were several other T-34s taxiing out so I simply followed them.

During the engine run up, he corrected me for not precisely setting 1800 rpm for the propeller check, remarked that I pulled the propeller rpm knob back too slowly and advanced it too rapidly. Naturally I got a soft backfire on the magneto "off" check and could not tell him the exact rpm drop during the individual magneto checks. Lastly, he wanted to know if this was the way I always flew. I was looking less and less forward to attempting to fly, for there was no way I could do it with the perfection he demanded. I was actually relieved when he allowed that I had demonstrated enough "unsafe" tendencies that he had better make the takeoff and departure to keep us from getting killed. I was, however, to talk him through the departure course rules to demonstrate that I knew them.

I successfully guided him through the departure and as long as he was flying it was relatively quiet. Having flown only once since arriving in Pensacola and that as a passenger in a T-28 with my Aerodynamics Instructor as a reward for having the highest grade in his class, it was indeed great to be back in the air.

LTJG Ramsey continued to fly and I relaxed a bit as we toured the extreme corners of the practice area. To the south the morning sun glinted off the glassy surface of the Gulf of Mexico and its warmth felt good through the Plexiglas canopy. The calm cool December air was turbulence free. We saw several other T-34s in the area but none were very close. I loved being in the pilot's world.

At last he either got up enough nerve or had flown sufficiently himself that he felt I should have a try at it. "You've got the airplane. Fly heading one two zero, maintain 140 knots and hold 4,000 feet," he instructed. I must have been

"Fly Navy"

paying more attention to what was going on outside than what was happening inside because it took me several minutes to find and integrate the heading, altitude and airspeed. The requested numbers were exactly what we were already flying. Although I jostled the airplane as I grabbed the stick and placed my feet on the rudder pedals, the airplane was perfectly trimmed and continued to fly on course and altitude with no inputs required and no comment from the rear seat. Inwardly I smiled.

LTJG Ramsey instructed, "Come right to one eight zero degrees." I rolled slowly into somewhere near a thirty degree bank and stared at the heading indicator. Almost immediately the nose dropped and we started to lose altitude and gain airspeed. Mr. Bailey's calm voice echoed in my mind, "nose up some, nose up...," when it was abruptly drowned out by a much louder and harsher voice through the earphones, "Where are you going? I said maintain 4,000 feet, and check your airspeed." I immediately fixated on the altitude and pulled the nose up too far. As I tried to get the altitude under control I overshot the one hundred eighty degree heading. When I rolled the wings level, I ended up high, slow, at least twenty degrees too far to the right and still climbing. "All right, see if you can get us back to 4,000 feet and headed south." I eased the nose down and gently banked about ten degrees to the left. Having second thoughts, I decided to try to solve one problem at a time and rolled the wings level. At 4,000 feet, I pulled the nose up to what I hoped would be the level flight attitude. The stick felt heavy as the nose tried to drop in response to its natural tendency to reacquire the trim airspeed. Continuing to hold the stick back, I turned left toward the south, and rolled out near the correct heading and only fifty feet low. "Look at your airspeed, I said one hundred forty knots." I focused all my attention on the airspeed indicator and lost more altitude in a slight descending left turn.

I had completely forgotten about the throttle. I added a little power, the airspeed increased slowly and I regained most of my altitude. I was trying to get the airplane better trimmed when he asked, "Where are we? Do you know where we are?" I looked around and tried to get my bearings. We were headed toward the gulf but other than that I wasn't exactly sure where we were. I couldn't decide which was worse, admit to being lost or make a WAG (Wild Ass Guess). To my left was a small town. The only name I even remembered was the town of Foley, Alabama. Why not? "We're west of Foley Sir."

"Good, at least you know where you are."

We flew around for a while longer. I got slightly better, but as expected it was impossible for me to fly with the perfection LTJG Ramsey demanded. Invariably I under corrected or overshot into yet another deviation. I was terribly behind the airplane and always seemed to be trying to catch up with my own mistakes, all of which were dramatically narrated by the "screamer" in the rear seat. It wasn't obvious whether it was more important to focus my attention inside the cockpit or outside; clearly I was more used to the latter. If only Mr. Bailey were here to help me. In a very short time both hands ached from holding the controls so tightly and my legs were cramped from being jammed against the rudder pedals. The sun that had felt so warm and comfortable at the beginning of the flight was suddenly uncomfortably hot. Small rivulets of perspiration escaped from beneath my helmet.

LTJG Ramsey instructed me to fly back to the field. As we approached the initial to Runway 23, T-34s seemed to be everywhere. I had never seen so many airplanes in the same sky at the same time. I overshot the initial and needed a fairly large correction to get aligned with the runway. With an abrupt shaking of the stick, and in what I interpreted as an irritated voice, LTJG Ramsey said, "I've got it!" He took the airplane and flew in silence to the final landing. As he taxied off the runway, he instructed, "Take it and taxi us back to the parking spot." My mind was blank. I had no idea what spot we came out of. I had simply followed him to the airplane. I remembered we made a right turn out of parking and thought we had been in the third row of airplanes but I wasn't even sure of that. "I'm sorry Sir, I don't remember which parking spot we came out of," I confessed.

"That does make it more difficult doesn't it?" He said. I waited expectantly for some help but none was forthcoming. He was obviously waiting to see what I would do. I continued taxiing, made a right turn into the parking area, stopped, and repeated my dilemma, "I'm sorry Sir but I don't know which parking spot we came out of."

"Sorry Sir, I don't remember our parking spot"

"Second row, spot Bravo nineteen, nine slots down to the left." I parked the airplane and shut it down in silence, apparently without commentable error.

According to military etiquette a junior enters first and leaves last. Once LTJG Ramsey got out of the rear cockpit, I lifted the heavy parachute and myself out of the seat. A chill spread through my body as the cool December air encompassed my perspiration soaked flight suit. LTJG Ramsey was halfway to the line shack when I stepped off the rear of the wing. My parachute and I lumbered to catch up. He was closing the yellow sheet book when I reached him. I followed him inside to the flight debriefing area without a word. The silent treatment was hard to take. What was worse, I had not enjoyed the flight like the rest of my contemporaries. I felt deflated and defeated. I should have done better. I wondered what Mr. Bailey would say? Maybe the Navy-way wasn't fun; maybe it was another "fun job" that would turn out to be all work.

LTJG Ramsey recounted the flight in excruciating detail. "On your first start attempt, you had the throttle too closed, which is why it didn't start. On the second, you moved it too far forward and oversped the engine. Aside from that, your pre-start procedures were OK. You need to study the ground patterns to improve your confidence on the field. It is always a good idea to write down your parking spot when you leave the line shack. Starting right now, I want you to perform all ground and flight procedures as accurately as possible. There is little margin for error in this business, so you need to get off on the right foot on the first step. By the way, I had always intended to make the first takeoff myself anyway."

"It is obvious you have flown before. Your air presence and orientation were good. I believe in pushing my students. It makes them good or breaks them early. I think I will enjoy flying with you. Are there any questions?" For the first time since the ten seconds before I met LTJG Ramsey I finally relaxed. "No questions, thank you Sir, have a nice holiday." What a relief, I had felt absolutely miserable about the entire flight until the debrief. "Thank you Lord, but I'm still not looking forward to flying with LTJG 'Screamer' Ramsey."

The Christmas Holidays went quickly. It was enjoyable being at home and with Linda but I was anxious to get back to Pensacola and mastering the T-34. The books so purposely taken home to study, were right where I set them down when I picked them up to leave.

Upon return to Saufley, I only had one more flight with LTJG Ramsey and, for reasons unknown, was reassigned to LT Charlie Noss, the antithesis of "Screamer" Ramsey. LT Noss had been a P5M pilot on active duty, was a devout Christian, led the youth group at the Warrington Baptist Church, which I attended, and planned to enter the ministry when his Navy tour was completed. LT Noss was indeed the NAVY equivalent of a much younger Elmer Durand Bailey. He was an excellent instructor and I responded positively to his

Getting serious about flying

calm instructional manner and technique. We became friends.

The T-34 was a pleasure to fly, and after the Aeronca Champ, felt like a fighter. It was honest, responsive and best of all, reasonably forgiving of mistakes. If all went well, you soloed on your thirteenth flight (an ominous number); assuming of course you got through the dreaded A-12 flight check. In retrospect, the only skills required were a good procedural knowledge of the airplane, course rules, prac-

tice area and a dem-
onstrated ability to
takeoff and land. I was
absolutely certain I was
going to draw LTJG
"Screamer" Ramsey as
the instructor for my
A-12 check ride, I just
knew it.

T-34B Trainer on final approach

Check rides are interesting tests. They are really a two-part test. While you can cram for the procedural knowledge, a la college days, the flying skills cannot be faked. You either have it or you don't. In college you either pass or fail. In the Navy, you are given an up, the direction of the sky, or a down, the direction of the ground.

Soloing the T-34 lacked the excitement I had experienced in the lowly Aeronca Champ. Not that it wasn't enjoyable because it was. I was more excited about the prospect of having this really marvelous airplane completely under my control than about simply soloing. I had already accomplished that important first and enjoyed every minute of it. Like a lot of things in life, there is only one first time. After

Soloing the T-34B

thirteen flights in the T-34, I felt quite comfortable and was anxious to get into serious acrobatics, something I had never had the opportunity to do, with the single exception of my nearly disastrous loop in the Champ. I hoped I was going to be better in the T-34.

Acrobatics were fun. Acrobatics combined the "inside out" of the pilot's world with a strong "inside in." You try to accurately maneuver the outside world while meeting precise airspeed, altitude, heading and "g" values registered on "inside" instruments. A loop and a barrel roll are two excellent examples. An ideal loop maneuvers the world through a full three hundred sixty degrees of overhead and ends up at the same altitude, airspeed and heading from which it started. A barrel roll maneuvers the world through a full three hundred sixty degree roll, with two ninety degree turns included in it, ending up at the same altitude, airspeed and heading from which it started.

Mayday, Mayday, Maybe?

My first in-flight emergency occurred on my third solo flight. As I leveled off at the specified course-rule altitude en route to the acrobatics practice area, it was obvious something was wrong. Nearly full power was barely holding 120 knots, when I should be indicating at least 140 knots with considerably less power. I studied the engine instruments intently for several seconds. Everything seemed to indicate the engine was functioning normally but unquestionably it wasn't putting out enough power to accelerate the airplane. The only reasonable conclusion was that I was experiencing a partial engine failure. Instinctively I began to look for a place to land should the engine decide to quit altogether. Mr. Bailey would have been proud of me.

Trying to sound calm and professional, I called, "Saufley Field Tower, this is Two Sierra One Three Nine; I'd like to declare an emergency, Over."

"Roger Two Sierra One Three Nine, this is Saufley Tower, state the nature of your emergency, Over."

"Saufley Tower, this is Two Sierra One Three Nine, I'm experiencing a partial engine failure and need to return to base, Over."

Another voice different to the tower calmly inquired, "Two Sierra One Three Nine, explain your problem, Over."

"Roger, this is Two Sierra One Three Nine; with full power I'm only able to get one hundred twenty knots, Over."

The same calm voice replied, "Roger Two Sierra One Three Nine, raise your gear."

Sure enough, the gear handle was down and the indicators confirmed what the calm voice knew they would. I raised the gear; the airplane accelerated and no further conversation ensued.

Something's wrong here!

The World Turns

I had never spun an airplane intentionally or otherwise until spins were introduced during our acrobatic phase of training. Spins are the most disorienting maneuver I ever encountered. Perfecting spins is unusual because it is really an attempt to perfect the art of "not flying." A spin requires two conditions be met; first the airplane must be fully stalled, i.e., not flying, and second, it must have some amount of yawing motion imparted to it.

Fortunately the T-34 is an honest spinning airplane. To enter a spin, you pull back on the stick until the airplane stalls and kick the rudder in the direction you want to spin. The nose falls through until it looks about sixty degrees nose down and the ground spins wildly around at an ever-increasing rate. When LT Noss demonstrated the first spin, I became completely disoriented. While he calmly counted off the number of turns, all I saw was a rotating green blur. My body, however, knew immediately it didn't like the feeling of being out of control. It was reminiscent of my first ride on the white wooden roller coaster. Following the recovery, he gave me the airplane and we climbed back to altitude. I made the required clearing turns to make sure no one was underneath us, reduced the power, eased the stick back until we stalled, and hesitantly added rudder. Evidently I didn't put in enough rudder because we didn't spin very fast. I felt LT Noss add more rudder and we really started to rotate. I had no idea how many turns we made as LT Noss instructed, "Start your recovery now!" I neutralized the controls and if the spinning showed any signs of slowing down, it wasn't obvious to me. Again the controls moved on their own as LT Noss added rudder in the direction to stop the rotation. I had never seen the world move so fast, nor had my head ever felt like it was still spinning when my eyes told me otherwise. I expect LT Noss made the full recovery, for unquestionably I was merely along for the ride. After only two spins, my body was ready to return to Saufley and talk about it for a while and let my stomach and head come to some agreement about this whole idea. That was not to be the case.

LT Noss instructed me to be more positive with my rudder input at the stall and to establish a ground reference to help count the number of turns in the spin. He also told me to locate the turn needle and use it as an aid in determining the direction of spin and thus which direction to apply the rudder to stop the rotation. Before I even started the clearing turns for my second spin, my head and stomach were already in their own tailspin. The message was loud and clear, neither body part wanted to do another spin. Following the old adage for student pilots, namely; when responding to an instructor's critique, it is better to overcompensate than under; at the stall I crammed in full left rudder. The left wing dropped rapidly and the right wing raced up and over,

I swore we went inverted. LT Noss didn't say anything and we did end up in an upright spin (Although at that time I didn't know there was any other kind). The T-34 wound up like a

Spins are fun?

top. I was so taken by surprise, that by the time I counted three turns, we must have done at least five, because LT Noss was calling for me to recover well before I counted to three. I stopped the rotation of the T-34, but not the rotation of my brain. I promptly stalled again as I tried to pull out of the ensuing dive. LT Noss must have recognized I wasn't going to last at this much longer and pulled the throttle back to simulate an engine failure. I was never happier to have a simulated emergency. The brain finally settled down and I was able to complete the checklist items for the engine failure. The stomach, however, continued on it's own schedule, sending out ominous warning signals, indicating it was on the verge of tossing its cookies. The gentle glide to a successful simulated emergency landing only renewed part of the confidence lost during the introduction to spins.

My heart was not in the rest of the flight. My stomach commanded center stage. I didn't feel well. More than anything else I wanted the world to stand still for a few moments. The return to Saufley Field was unusually quiet. I don't remember the debrief for I couldn't wait to get back to the BOQ room. I lay catatonic on the bunk and stared at the slowly revolving ceiling. Closing my eyes couldn't even make it stop. My stomach ultimately settled down but not enough to risk subjecting it to the evening meal. For the first time I went to sleep dreading tomorrow's flight.

As we made our way to the acrobatic area, my apprehension showed in the tentativeness with which I flew the airplane. I made the required clearing turns, stalled the T-34 and pressed the left rudder pedal. The airplane responded nicely and entered a gentle spin to the left. The world rotated as before but with less violence and with noticeably more predictability. I counted the first turn as the east-west highway through Foley, Alabama passed the center of the windscreen for the second time. On the third turn I neutralized the stick and pressed the right rudder pedal. The rotation stopped in less than half-a-turn. As I started the nose up to stop the descent, LT Noss complimented me on the recovery and instructed me to stop the rotation earlier to keep from exceeding the three-turn limit. My stomach didn't feel great but nothing like yesterday. At least I was not afraid to try the second spin. I stopped the second spin within twenty degrees of the reference and felt my confidence begin to return. I must have gotten overconfident for I jammed in too much rudder during the third spin entry. The T-34 responded accordingly and wound up rapidly. TOO rapid for me. The required three turns rushed by and I overshot the recovery by at least half-a-turn. I learned a good lesson: smooth application of the pro-spin rudder was the key. My stomach and my brain seemed to have reached an agreement; at least they weren't fighting each other. The fourth and fifth spins were actually fun but I wasn't totally disappointed when LT Noss suggested we go on to something else.

At the debrief, LT Noss cleared me to practice spins on my own. Unwittingly I had taken the same approach to spins as I had to the white wooden roller coaster. The difference was, I ended up liking spins. I ultimately got to the point where, if I wanted to lose a couple of thousand feet of altitude, a spin was an excellent way to do it. The T-34 was the only Navy airplane I flew that we were allowed to spin intentionally. In my later years of flying I continued to have similar experiences with spins. After a layoff, I usually didn't like the first few spins, but really enjoyed them once I had done several.

Upon completion of Primary Flight Training at Saufley Field, there were two choices, or pipelines, as the Navy called

them, for Basic Training. You were either assigned to props or jets. As always, the selection depended first on "the needs of the service" and second on your class standing, which was determined by your academic and flight grades. There was never any doubt I wanted to fly jets. I was egotistical enough to not even have considered the other alternative.

My grades were good enough to place me in the top three students. Contrary to what LTJG Ramsey

Primary complete, jets next

had said, the flight experience at Northfield and Mr. Bailey's excellent flight instruction had paid off. Fortunately "the needs of the service" did not interfere with my desires and jets were assured. The only question was whether I would stay at Pensacola (which I wanted) and train at Forrest Sherman Field or be sent to NAAS Kingsville, Texas? The location was solely dependent on which week you graduated. Every two weeks students were assigned to one or the other Basic Training fields. Just when it was looking like I would get Pensacola, the Great God in the sky adjusted the weather such that I was assigned to Kingsville. The last thing I wanted was to go to the end of the world by myself. I called Linda and asked if she thought she could plan a wedding in a week's time. She assured me she could, and did. I'm sure we raised more than just a few eyebrows with the hurry up wedding.

I flew home commercial and Linda and I were married the next day, March 9, 1961. After the wedding we headed for Kingsville, Texas via Pensacola. We made it all the way from Richmond to Petersburg, a mere 25 miles. Linda looked over my shoulder as a nervous Warren signed the motel register as Ens. Gene Hall. Inquisitively Linda asked, "What about me?" I hesitated a moment and added "and wife."

Ensign and Mrs. Hall

Kingsville South Field

After picking up my still meager belongings at Pensacola, we drove to Kingsville, arriving late in the evening. The heat from the dusty red sun setting in the west was stifling and  confirmed what I had suspected. Kingsville was indeed the end of the earth. I was glad Linda was with me.

Training Squadron Seven

When I checked into Training Squadron Seven, VT-7, the rumor mill was rampant with the news that South Field was soon to close and VT-7 would move to a new training base at NAAS Meridian, Mississippi. The rumor turned out to be true. Our class was the last class to start Basic Training at Kingsville and would be the first class to graduate from Meridian.

At South Field we flew the North American T2J, "Buckeye." The T2J was basically a jet powered T-28 and retained the same straight-lines characteristic of North American built aircraft. The Buckeye was powered by a single J-34 engine housed in the lower fuselage directly beneath the straight wing and fed by dual intakes located below the front cockpit. The nose was pinched on the bottom to accommodate the intakes. The pudgy shape of the fuse-lage deserved its "pregnant guppy" nickname. The engine

VT-7 T2J NAAS Kingsville, Texas

exhaust was near the trailing edge of the wing beneath the extended fuselage that faired into the empennage. The horizontal stabilizer was located halfway up the vertical tail. A large dorsal fin extended from slightly above the horizontal tail to the aft end of the canopy. The large canopy provided excellent visibility with the aft, or instructor pilot's, seat raised above that of the student. A banana shaped tip tank was affixed to each wing tip. In recent years, the T2J was converted to a two-engine airplane and for good reason. On a hot day in Kingsville, Texas or most any other place, it used a goodly portion of the runway for takeoff and wasn't about to win a drag race with any vehicle.

My entry into the world of jets was nothing less than a touch of Heaven. In many respects, operation of the T2J was simpler than the T-34. The engine either started or it didn't. Once it was running the only engine control was the throttle; you moved it forward to go fast and back

Overhead view of the T2J

to go slow. There was no longer any concern for combinations of manifold pressure and rpm or whether you moved the throttle or propeller controls first or second. For the jet, exhaust gas temperature (EGT) was the primary concern and that wasn't usually a problem unless you were experiencing a malfunction. The only new control was for the speed brakes. The T2J's simplicity, however, did not negate the requirement for procedural crutches like those we used in the T-34. For example, in the break, as you roll into the turn, you retard the throttle, open the speed brakes, and at 165 knots drop the landing gear. This sequence became: flop, chop, pop, one six five drop.

Flying jets was not easier just because of fewer engine controls. The lack of engine torque made takeoffs, stalls, go-arounds and most acrobatics easier to fly. During most of the flying there was little or no requirement for rudder pedal inputs. I loved the quietness of the jet. I loved the freedom from combinations of "stick and rudder." I loved the smoothness with which it responded. I loved its speed.

It was sheer delight to play tag with the towering cumulus clouds that formed most every afternoon around Kingsville. I loved to fly directly at the top of a bulbous white cloud, pull the nose up and roll inverted over the top and savor the sensation of speed as the puffy gray-white moisture skimmed rapidly across the top

Out climbing Texas thunderstorms?

of the canopy. It wasn't unusual to find developing clouds boiling upward faster than the T2J could climb. Clouds are an integral part of the pilot's world. They can be fun playmates, but an angry one can damage an airplane or terminate a pilot's life.

An accident is always a sobering experience but even more so when you actually see one happen. While at Saufley Field, a student and instructor were killed in a T-34 accident at a remote field. At the time, the impact was minimal because I didn't know either of them. A couple of days later, however, the wreckage was returned to Saufley on a flat bed truck and sat out in full view of the flight line for a day. Most of us were drawn to it, as if it held a lesson for all of us, for indeed it did. Mortality, for all practical purposes, is a taboo subject for a group of young dedicated aviators. It will always happen to the other guy. The crumpled mass of metal meant a failure on someone's part. It also emphasized the old adage, "While aviation is not inherently dangerous, it is inherently unforgiving of error." This axiom is especially true of Naval Aviation where the margins for error are so very small.

One of the many requirements in the Training Command was to spend time in the Control Tower observing the controllers and if possible being useful. One morning several of us were in the Tower at South Field when the entire atmosphere was instantly electrified by a radio call from a student who was clearly in serious trouble. The first call was a highly excited, "Gasp, gasp, South Field ..., South Field Tower, gasp." All other radio transmissions ceased immediately. All controllers and listening aircraft concentrated on the frantic student. Mayday! Had to be the next call. After a long pause, "South Field Tower, gasp, this is..." The transmission took another long break. We immediately assumed the worst. Everyone in the Tower waited tensely, scarcely breathing lest they miss an important clue. Would he be able to get out enough information for us to know what was about to happen, to whom and where? Again the agonized voice penetrated the attentive silence, "South Field Tower .. This is..Ah..Ah pause, Victor Tango." The student gasped several more times and the transmission stopped. The Tower Chief's hand poised nervously over the crash alarm. Someone had the presence of mind to grab the clipboard on which the aircraft were logged airborne and when they returned. If he could only get out his tail number, we would at least know who was in trouble. The radio came to life again, "Gasp, gasp, South Field Tower, gasp, gasp, this is Victor, gasp, Victor Tango Two, gasp, Zero One, gasp (another long pause) for takeoff."

For a brief moment everyone remained static and silent. Nervous laughter finally broke the uncanny silence. It was the lone T2J holding short of Runway 21. The student was obviously having trouble talking against the constant positive pressure in the T2J oxygen mask system. It is different. When you relax and open your mouth, it fills your lungs with oxygen and you have to forcibly exhale, kind of like breathing in reverse. To talk, you have to force your words against the pressure. While unusual, it normally only takes a couple of flights before you get used to it. The Tower atmosphere returned to normal. We were relieved that one of our fellow future Naval Aviators was not in trouble.

One day while I was on Tower watch, two flight instructors, one of whom was the Maintenance Officer, were assigned to ferry one of the T2Js to Pensacola for its periodic major maintenance period. The Navy called these periods PAR for Progressive Aircraft Repair. We called it PAR for "Paint and Return," for most often the aircraft came back mechanically worse than when it left, but it always had a beautiful new paint job.

It wasn't often two instructors got to fly together, so we were especially watchful in the event they elected to give us a show on takeoff. We noted that on takeoff the airplane stayed on the runway longer than the other airplanes but we thought they were only gathering more speed for a steep pull-up or some other maneuver. To our dismay, the nose of the aircraft never rotated. The T2J went off the end of the runway considerably faster than takeoff speed and immediately burst into a huge fireball. We saw two ejection seats exit the airplane but only one chute and only briefly.

A hush settled over the Tower as the crash alarm sounded. We stood aghast, staring at the rising pillar of oily black smoke buoyed aloft by the deadly orange flames beneath it. We comforted each other in that we had seen two ejection seats exit the aircraft. We had indeed seen two ejection seats rocket from the ill-fated aircraft but only one parachute. The pilot made it. The Maintenance Officer was killed. He did not separate from his ejection seat. It was later determined that the tiny striker pin that activates the seat separation mechanism had been inadvertently left out of the seat. One man's error had cost another man's life. I was rapidly becoming aware of how strongly my life depended on the efforts of others. We pre-flighted our ejection seats more carefully after the accident.

Within a week of the accident, one of the more popular students in my class taxied too close to a parked T2J and scraped wing tip tanks. Both T2Js burst instantly into flames, accompanied by the same ominous pillar of angry black smoke. No one was hurt but we learned to hate that column of smoke. It was synonymous with disaster. The Navy ultimately stopped practicing crash drills during daylight hours because of the adverse reaction to that rising, boiling, angry, black cloud.

We completed the transition, precision acrobatics, and basic instrument phases of our training at Kingsville and relocated to the newly completed NAAS Meridian, Mississippi. The downside was that Linda and I experienced our first military-imposed separation after being married less than three months. As a point of fact, I was deployed twenty-five of the last thirty-six months of my active duty tour with the

Solo flight at NAAS Meridian

Navy. The upside was that I completed the rest of my basic training in a beautiful new facility on full per diem. Not bad pay for a new Ensign.

Hurricane Causes Pensacola Exodus

Shortly after we arrived at NAAS Meridian, a major hurricane was predicted to come ashore in the Pensacola area. All flyable Training Command aircraft were evacuated to Meridian. It was a veritable field day for an avid airplane

Hurricane evacuation from Pensacola to NAAS Meridian

watcher. The field was closed to all training flights as most of the ramp space was occupied by visiting aircraft. It was an impressive sight to see so many aircraft in one place.

Tip Tank on the Star

After spending all of my military flight training trying to stay far away from other aircraft in the sky, the day finally arrived when my instructor introduced formation flying. Following an extensive briefing with another student and instructor, the two instructors joined up soon after takeoff and flew in formation to the training area. It looked so easy. I was excited. I kept looking at the other airplane and thinking, *Wow!* I look like that. I had never been so close to another airplane in flight, even when Bobby and I had not too successfully attempted to fly formation in the Aeronca at Northfield.

Once in the training area, my instructor moved out slightly and carefully explained the sight picture I should have, "Put the leading edge of the tip tank of the other T2J in the center of the white star on the fuselage and keep it there. It will put us on the proper bearing. We'll worry about the lateral distance later. You've got it." For several seconds (probably only one or two) the two airplanes flew along in perfect formation. Slowly the other airplane began to pull slightly ahead, I added power and nothing seemed to happen, so I added some more power. The other airplane started to drop behind, slowly at first and then more rapidly. I pulled off a lot of power. The airplane quickly reversed and started moving forward with ever increasing speed. In addition I started to bob up-and-down as I sashayed fore-and-aft. My natural instinct was to move away from the leader's wing as I alternately got further forward and further back with every cycle. I couldn't believe flying formation was so difficult, the instructor had made it look so easy.

Early student formation flying

It wasn't long before the instructor did the inevitable, "I've got it, follow me through now," he said, as he eased us back into position. I rested my hands lightly on the controls and could feel him making nearly continuous small stick and throttle inputs, but I couldn't tell why, for we never seemed to move out of position. I couldn't figure out what he was looking at to get the information he was using to make the corrections. He gave me the airplane again. The result was the same as before, only this time it took me a little longer to get out of position. To myself, "Man, if flying formation straight-and-level is this difficult, I'll never be able to make a turn." We practiced straight-and-level for a while longer and even though I improved slightly, I really didn't have the picture.

My instructor took the controls and we assumed the lead. My hands were sweaty and cramped from holding the controls so tightly. As the other T2J joined on our wing, I felt myself leaning away from the wing man as if a couple of inches movement inside the cockpit was going to make a difference. The instructor flew as I relaxed and watched

the student in the other Buckeye repeat almost identically what I had done a few minutes earlier. My instructor began to call the relative motion before I even noticed any movement at all. Finally,

Wow! I look like that!

just by watching and listening, I began to pick up the relative motion earlier and easier. I was anxious to have another try.

It was exciting to fly so close to another airplane. It was like looking in a mirror and liking what you see. I could easily project myself into the other airplane. It was gratifying to know what I looked like. It reminded me of my early experience with flying when I visualized myself as being external to the airplane watching it fly over the earth. Formation flying allowed me to experience flying from both perspectives, inside out and outside in.

We reversed course and changed the lead. Again I started off over controlling the throttle and ended up too far away. The instructor moved us back into the proper position. He told me to stay on the controls but relax as he talked me through the changes in relative motion as he had done when the other student was flying wing on us. Without realizing it, I transitioned to flying the airplane. Either it got easier or I got a lot better, for the relative movement slowly settled down and I could hold an acceptable position for several seconds at a time.

The instructor took the controls and requested a gentle turn to the right. He explained as he demonstrated, "Since we are on the right wing, we will hold exactly the same relative position to the other airplane in a right turn, as we did while flying straight-and-level. This means that as the other airplane rolls into his turn we will have to descend and then climb back up as he rolls out." Again it looked so easy when the instructor did it.

As we rolled level he gave me the controls and requested another right turn. My automatic response was to bank away from the other airplane and pull ahead, not exactly great formation. The instructor coached me down and back. Once I was in position I held it pretty well. Even when lead announced he was rolling level, I was late pulling up and adding power to match his roll out. Although I felt I got back into the level flight position quickly, the instructor indicated I was still too far away from the leader.

The two instructors flew the T2Js into the break in a much tighter formation than we students were allowed to fly. I could have easily reached out and touched the tip tank of the other Buckeye. I loved it. In the debrief, the instructor said I did about as well as most of his students on their first formation flight. In other words, I had not exactly set the world on fire and there was lots of room for improvement. I was especially tired that night, but more in love with flying than ever.

Instructors fly formation

On my second flight something in my brain clicked. I was able to perceive the relative motion well before large displacements developed. I could actually hold a pretty good parade formation position during straight-and-level flight. I still had to caution myself to anticipate starting down when lead called for a right turn but quickly found, with a little anticipation, I could hold a respectable position during the roll-in and roll-out from the turns.

Left turns, when you are on the right wing, seemed a lot more natural to me. First of all, the other aircraft is banking away from you making it feel like you have more control over your destiny. In the turn, you essentially hold your altitude and match the lead airplane's bank angle. It presents an interesting perspective of the leader's airplane, for it looks like you're flying underneath him in the turn. I caught onto left turns much quicker than those to the right. We practiced turns and straight-and-level flight with the instructors making all lead changes. I was quite relaxed and getting better by the minute. Formation flying was really fun!

On the third flight we practiced cross-unders and flew formation on both sides. It was apparent that the smoothness and steadiness of the lead aircraft had a profound effect on the ability to fly good formation. We students worked as hard when flying lead as we did when flying on the wing. After the instructors were gone, we held our own informal debriefs and were quite candid with each other.

Once we had mastered the basics of flying formation, including cross-unders and lead changes, we tackled the more difficult problem of "How to get two or more airplanes together in the first place." By all means the rendezvous and join-up are the most demanding and dangerous part of formation flying and require the greatest amount of judgment and skill.

As always, when we first started practicing break-ups, join-ups, and rendezvous', the instructor demonstrated the first one. We flew along together and the lead aircraft "kissed off" and started a left or right, sixty degree bank, one hundred eighty degree turn. When the leader was approximately thirty degrees off the nose, we made a similar one hundred eighty degree turn so as to end up in trail. To start the rendezvous, the leader would commence a thirty degree bank, level turn and you essentially turned inside of him trying to keep your nose pointed in front of his, primarily varying bank angle to maintain a constant bearing as you closed on the leader. In the final stages of the join-up, you adjust power so as to pass slowly below and behind the leader.

The hard part, joining up

The rendezvous is complete when you get stabilized in the parade wing position.

The initial tendency was to get too close, too fast, pull off too much power, and end up "sucked." We have all seen, and made, large bank angle excursions during rendezvous. Safety rule number one was: no matter what else you did, always keep the aircraft ahead of you in sight. Nothing panics a lead aircraft more than watching a rapidly closing wing man wrapped up in a steep bank trying to salvage a poorly executed join-up. The old adage, "If I can't see you, you probably can't see me," is absolutely true.

Running rendezvous' were a lot simpler to fly, but harder to judge. As the name implies, a running rendezvous does not use a turn to affect the join-up. You simply drive up behind the lead aircraft using a speed advantage to catch up. The problem is that the closure rate is difficult to judge and the only indication of closure is the change in size of the lead aircraft. It is like what you observe as you approach another car from the rear. Running rendezvous' are great in the daylight but horribly dangerous at night and therefore seldom used.

On my last dual formation flight, a check ride of course, I scared myself with a rapid-closure join-up and, from the instructor's write-up, him too. It started out okay but I picked up

HAPPY SIGN *for VT-9 and VT-7 students is the arrow drawn by flight instructor signifying an "UP" flight after final check at Meridian.*

First graduates from NAAS Meridian

a rapid closure rate as I approached the lead aircraft and rather than throw in a large bank angle, I elected to dissipate the closure rate during the cross-under to the parade formation position. I passed rapidly under and *much* too close to the lead aircraft but surprisingly ended up in a near perfect parade position, the latter being the only redeeming feature of the rendezvous. We both knew it had been a dangerous maneuver. The instructor gave me a "below average" on join-ups and recorded: "As Number Two, made a fast, close, join-up bordering on Unsat. Other join-ups average."

Gunnery at Forrest Sherman Field

Upon completion of the formation phase of Basic Flight Training at Meridian, we returned to NAS Pensacola, Florida for Air-to-Air gunnery and Carrier Qualifications. We were now the "big boys" on the block and enjoyed the same envy I had amply heaped upon the flyers of those red-and-white jets as they whistled overhead, tantalizing and inspiring us during our Pre-Flight Training. Linda joined me and we

VT-4 T2J Flight line, Forrest Sherman Field, NAS Pensacola

enjoyed the Florida sunshine and being newlyweds. It was a happy time.

At VT-4, we flew gunnery first. The VT-4 Buckeyes were fitted with a yellow gun pod slung under each wing. The guns generally fired in a forward direction but their well-known inaccuracies provided our primary excuse when the banner didn't show any hits. In ground school, we learned gun sight and gunnery theory. In flight, by far the greatest

T2J with a gun pod under each wing

amount of flying was devoted to learning how to correctly fly the gunnery pattern so that, first, we didn't run into each other; second, we didn't shoot each other down; and lastly, we shot our bullets at the banner and not at the tow plane.

We always flew as a flight of four. Once we located the tow plane with its banner streaming behind it, we attempted to set up a tilted race track pattern with an airplane at each opposing corner. As the Number One aircraft pulled off the target, Number Two

A flight of four for gunnery practice

should already be rolling in. If all went well, the pattern orchestrated itself in a singsong:

"One in."

"Four off."

"Two in."

"One off."

"Three in," as the correct rhythm was established. We practiced arming and safetying the guns and tracking the target. Oh, I failed to mention another very important requirement, namely not to fly into the banner.

At last the day arrived when "live" ammo was loaded into the gun pods. It was exciting to see the red, "REMOVE BEFORE FLIGHT," cloth streamers dangling from the blackened yellow gun pods. Prior to taxi, we carefully recorded the color code of our ammunition so we could count the hits we were sure to get on the banner. The head of each bullet is coated with a color that wipes off on the banner as it penetrates the heavy cloth. Real ordnance men followed us as we taxied the trainers to the arming area and pointed them away from inhabited areas. An instructor always led the flight and was anxious to show his three charges how well he could shoot. We students were equally anxious to demonstrate our "top gun" techniques. The mental attitude of the flight was decidedly different when flying with loaded guns.

The instructor's T2J lifted off and started a lazy left turn over the calm blue Gulf. The three of us followed at the proper interval, joined up quickly, and tucked in close. Number Three and I were on his right wing and Number Four on the left. The tow plane already had the banner streamed when we entered the warning area.

We rendezvoused with the tow plane and climbed to the perch position in right echelon formation. Excitement abounded, but not so fast, first we had to establish the pattern and make several "cold" runs before we could blast the banner to smithereens. The instructor rolled in.

"One in."

T2Js in right echelon formation

We three students continued straight ahead. As soon as the instructor's T2J started to reverse its turn, I rolled hard left and dove toward the tow plane and banner.

"Two in."

"One off."

"Three in."

"Two Off."

"Four in."

"Three off." We made two more complete patterns. It felt good.

"One in. Cleared to fire."

"Two in." Look out banner your life is just about over.

"One off."

Increase the "g" ... where are you going gun sight pipper? Come on ... more "g"... track, track ... too late ... too close! DAMN, WATCH THE BANNER!!!

"Two off," safety the guns. Good grief, I never even armed them." Climbing back to the perch, "Get it together, Warren."

"Two in." Guns armed, increase the "g"... track, track ... easy, easy ... trigger now. BRAT-T-T-T-T-T, too far out on that run, up and over the banner, turn to parallel.

"Two off," guns safe. Settle down. That really shook the airplane didn't it? Back to the perch position. Keep the rhythm. "Two in," track, track, slowly ... easy, wait ... W-A-I-T, now, BRAT-T-T-T-T-T, still shakes the airplane. Over the banner, parallel. Climb back to the perch. Out loud, "Squeeze the trigger slowly, like this, BRAT-T! GOOD GRIEF, you could have shot down Number One. Set the safety you idiot."

"One off, two more firing passes, Over."

"Two."

"Three."

"Four."

"Two in," track, track, squeeze, BRAT-T-T-T-T-T, hold it steady now, BRAT-T-T-T-T. "Two off," Good run, I bet I sprayed the banner that time.

"Two in," last pass, more "g", track, good, hold the pipper right on the bull's eye, my best tracking yet, good, squeeze, nothing, squeeze again, drat, out of ammo.

"Two off." Back to the perch for rendezvous.

Back at Sherman Field we were impatient and excited, as we eagerly awaited the return of the tow plane with its precious telltale banner. We fell all over each other as we unfolded the banner on the ramp. H-m-m-m-m lots of red holes, the instructor did really well. Several green holes, one black, where are all the orange holes? Disappointing. Wait--two orange holes up near the front close to the top, not exactly top gun. Oh well, just wait until tomorrow.

We had a Flight Surgeon that was going through flight training with our class. He was the owner of the one black hole on the first flight. Following our second live gunnery flight, during his post flight inspection, a ground crewman found a slightly jagged hole in the vertical tail of Number Three's T2J. There was little doubt where it came from, as it was clearly outlined in black. It could easily have been mine.

While my gunnery continued to improve, I never did consider myself a great gunner. The few live firing flights were over much too soon, and we moved on to Carrier Qualifications.

Carrier Qualifications

We flew our Carrier Qualification training flights early in the morning to take advantage of the stable air and low winds. Our Field Carrier Landing Practice (FCLP) was conducted at, of all places, Eglin Air Force Base, a few miles east of NAS Pensacola at a landing strip known as Site Six. The outline of the landing area of an angled carrier deck was painted near the left edge of the approach end of the runway with a mirror landing system set up next to it.

Basically the mirror landing system consists of a vertical concave mirror that reflects a yellow source light at a pre-selected angle. Centered on either side of the mirror are two horizontal rows of green datum lights and vertically along the sides of the mirror are red

The mirror landing system

flashing lights the Landing Signal Officer (LSO) can use to signal the pilot to wave-off. What the pilot sees in flight is a slightly oval yellow light reflected in the mirror. The proper descent angle is achieved when the yellow light or "meatball" is in line with the two rows of green datum lights. If you are above the desired glide path, the "meatball" will appear above the datum lights or below if you are low.

Two rhythms were important. The first concerned the FCLP traffic pattern and the second the actual flying of the carrier approach. We attempted to set up and maintain a left-handed, six hundred foot traffic pattern with equally spaced airplanes. Ideally, one trainer should touchdown every thirty to forty seconds. As you turn from the base leg to final, the yellow "meatball" should appear on the mirror, at which time you report your call sign, call "ball" if you see it, or state "Clara" if you don't, and give your fuel state. You fly the airplane to place, and keep, the "meatball" centered between the green datum lights.

During the carrier approach all Navy jet airplanes fly angle of attack rather than airspeed. This technique places the wing at the optimum lift coefficient at all times. The scan pattern we were taught was "meatball," lineup, and angle of attack. I continued to parrot that phrase during most carrier approaches as I descended along the glide slope. Oh, another thing, it was absolutely mandatory on touchdown to immediately place the throttle full forward for maximum power in the event you missed the arresting wires. Of course, there were no wires to stop the airplane during FCLPs but

T2J in FCLP pattern

the proper habit pattern was created for the shipboard landings.

Carrier landings differ from normal runway landings in that there is no flare associated with a carrier landing. You fly "meatball," lineup and angle of attack all the way to touchdown. Your concentration should be so riveted on the "meatball" you literally shouldn't know when you are going to touchdown. I always use my Navy training as the excuse whenever I make a harder than desired landing in any airplane. As we had done during the gunnery phase, we flew in flights of four, but now usually as all students. We took turns leading the flights. Since it was only a short flight from Forrest Sherman Field to Site Six, we always arrived there with too much fuel to actually touchdown. We flew low approaches to an LSO directed wave-off until we were light enough to land. Yet another important habit pattern was formed, those flashing red wave-off lights signaled a mandatory go-around, you didn't even dare think about questioning them. Once I figured out that flying the "meatball" was akin to flying formation with another airplane, FCLPs were relatively easy and a lot of fun. The "unfun" part of FCLPs was the fact the LSO recorded and graded every pass and debriefed each approach in excruciating detail. Our egos soon adjusted to the "hard," no make that "firm," Navy touchdowns. However, most of us, relished a soft, "Air Force" final landing back at Pensacola.

Each of us was afforded the opportunity to stand with the LSO and observe other students fly FCLPs. I was amazed how much the tail of the airplanes shook and twisted as they flew steadily onto the runway. I'm convinced the LSO worked harder than most of the students during these

USS Antietam departs for Carrier Qualifications, November 1961

periods. It is an awesome responsibility to decide when a student is ready to go to the ship. Since we worked with the same LSO during most of these periods, he got to know us pretty well.

As students in Pre-Flight, we had often watched the Navy's Training Carrier, the USS Antietam, make its way toward the Gulf of Mexico. I doubt any of us fully understood the excitement we would some day experience around and on her flight deck. I know I didn't. I'm certain when we signed up, none of us fully comprehended what Carrier Aviation was all about. We dreamed of the excitement but never weighed the risks involved. On the weekends we often walked along the pier where the USS Antietam was berthed and marveled at the enormity of the stately steel-gray ship. None of us were prepared for how dramatically that enormity would shrink when viewed from the cockpit of our T2Js. In retrospect, I'm surprised none of us ever made an attempt to get a tour of the Antietam when it was berthed.

It was as if it were a sanctuary one dared not enter until he had completed the "rite of passage." The "rite" being that first Carrier Landing.

After weeks of FCLPs, the day before we're going to "Hit the Boat" finally arrives. If my fellow classmates were like myself, not a one got any sleep that night. I tossed and turned and rehearsed every procedure. I tossed and turned and rehearsed every call. I tried to remember those items on which I had only been briefed and had not yet experienced, not the least of which was the catapult takeoff. We had concentrated so much on the landing, little thought had been given the catapult or "Cat" shot.

While time has the magic quality of being able to speed up or slow down to match a given set of circumstances, it nevertheless continues to march and the morning of that long-awaited day finally dawned. "Dawned" is correct because it was a very early show time. We were once again briefed that we would make two touch-and-go landings and four "traps" or arrested landings. At the briefing, the LSO tried to bolster the confidence of his less than confident charges. We would follow him to the ship after a thirty minute delay. I was in the second flight. Until today, most of us had paid little attention to the tailhook other than to make sure we ducked underneath it as we pre-flighted the airplane (mostly because it was filthy black from the jet exhaust). It was sure different today, you would have thought it was the only part of the airplane that needed a pre-flight. The flight to the ship was strongly reminiscent of flights to the gunnery area. It was a beautiful fall day but for some reason the Gulf seemed more green than blue and surprisingly cold and uninviting. As we lined up astern of the ship, I could see three T2Js in the pattern.

The huge Aircraft Carrier which awed us when docked at NAS Pensacola, seemed a miniature toy floating in the Gulf. Was this really possible? We broke left over the ship and established the proper interval on the downwind leg.

USS Antietam with a deck full of T2Js

The wind was about ten knots and formed small scattered and irregular white caps on the green water below. With the gear and flaps extended, the 600 foot pattern and airspeed checks seemed comfortably familiar. As I passed abeam the Aircraft Carrier on the downwind leg and turned left base to final, all familiarity ceased. I promptly lined up on the extended churning white wake of the ship, only to discover the runway was pointed off to my left and seemed to have no length at all. The "meatball" appeared briefly on the mirror and exited rapidly off the top. "Foxtrot Two Four, no ball, uh, Clara, fuel state three point two." A calm and familiar voice

"Meatball," Lineup, Angel of Attack

replied, "Roger, you're a little high and lined up left, ease it down and move it to the right of the wake." I saw the yellow light and called, "Ball." OK now, "meatball," lineup, angle of attack. It's going low, why is it so hazy all of a sudden, lots of rough air too, must be smoke and turbulence from the ship. The ball sank even lower. The LSO cautioned, "Give me a little power now." I was so totally preoccupied with the water, the ship, the wake, and how different it all looked from what I had envisioned it would, that I almost forgot to fly the ball. The LSO came on the radio, "WAVE-OFF, WAVE-OFF, NICE PASS, give me another one like that next time, only get your lineup earlier and fly the ball." As I passed over the ship I couldn't believe the landing area could possibly be that small, surely it was half the size of the one we had practiced on at Eglin. I began to settle down a little as I turned downwind for the second pass.

As I crossed over the wake and lined up on the tiny runway, the "meatball" came into view very near the center of the datum lights. I must stop calling it a runway because there is precious little distance to run. "Foxtrot Two Four, ball, two point nine." Aloud to myself, "meatball," lineup, angle of attack; "meatball," lineup, angle of attack; just like at Eglin, feels good, Wow! What caused the ball to go up so fast. Power off, good grief, look at it start down, power up just as the LSO called: "A little power now." He should wave me off any moment now; "meatball," lineup, angle of attack, Woomph, touchdown, I TOUCHED DOWN! power, POWER, full throttle, WOW! "Thump, thump, thump," my heart was talking louder that I could. Now that was

Ball centered, lineup good

something! From the ship: "Foxtrot Two Four start your turn downwind." I DID IT! I DID IT! Watch your altitude.

"Foxtrot Two Four, ball, two point five." Concentrate now, "meatball," lineup, angle of attack. There goes the ball high again, ease the power back, going low, GOING LOW, P-O-W-E-R! Woomph, touchdown, WOW! Throttle, THROTTLE. Turn downwind. To myself, "You know, the ship is getting a little larger now, there's even a helicopter off to the right."

On the downwind leg after my second touch-and-go, Pri-Fly called: "Foxtrot Two Four, put your hook down, confirm, Over!" I grasped the hook handle in my right hand and gently, but with authority, lowered it full down, after all this was my first time. I stared at the handle long enough to ensure the red light went out. "Roger, hook down," I

First time with the hook down

called. It would be the last time they would make that call. From now on, turning final with the hook up would cost me a bottle of the LSO's favorite liquor.

This approach took on a whole new meaning. "Foxtrot Two Four, ball, two point zero." OK, this one is for real. "Meatball," lineup, angle of attack; there's still an airplane in the landing area, "meatball," come on, lineup, watch your airspeed, come on M-O-V-E..., he's clear.

LSO, "You're going high, ease it down."

"Meatball," lineup, Woomph! Grab, snap, Oomph! The T2J shook, the nose weaved back-and-forth and bucked up-and-down as the Buckeye came to an abrupt shoulder strap cutting stop. There was

T2J snags a number 3 wire

no time to remind myself to place the throttle full forward; me, the throttle, the stick, my knee board and especially my eyeballs were all flung violently forward in the cockpit. My left hand shook as I pushed the throttle as far forward as my arm and strength would allow. The airplane shuddered under the full thrust being restrained by the arresting wire firmly grasping the tailhook. I'm sure there was a Taxi Director out there somewhere giving me signals, but all I remember is someone on the radio saying, "Son, you can pull the power back now, you can't make this ship go any faster." Power to idle. What now? Heart pounding. There's the Taxi Director. Hook up. **WOW, THAT WAS INCREDIBLE!**

Follow the Taxi Director, damn he's impatient, forward and right, toward the catapult. Let's see, what am I supposed to be doing now? Look at your knee board. Follow the Taxi Director. I need a couple of moments here, slow down, follow the Director, check the knee board, oh yes, flaps and trim; trim? trim? Set five degrees nose up. Follow the Taxi Director, I wish he'd slow down, line it up, just do as he directs, over the shuttle, a little further, the Director passes me off to the Cata-pult Officer. There's a lever in front of the throttle here some-where. Power up on the Catapult Officer's signal, trim checked at five degrees nose up (we used a trim setting of zero for take-

An impatient Taxi Director

offs from the runway), throttle full forward, grab the throttle lever, head back. Salute the Catapult Officer, which hand am I supposed to use? Right one I guess. Salute, pause.. WHAM, swish, the airplane is literally thrown into the air. I was pressed against the seat a lot harder than I expected. O-O-o-o-w, I guess I didn't hold my head back hard enough. I finally had control of the airplane about 300 feet in the air. Not so calmly to myself: "I've got it now Lord, thanks." Now I know why we were required to use the five degrees nose up trim; there was no chance the airplane was going to descend. I was definitely NOT prepared for the acceleration of the catapult shot. It all happened so fast, too fast.

Pri-Fly, "Foxtrot Two Four, start your turn downwind and check your altitude, you're going high." The image of the roller coaster at Buckroe Beach flashed through my mind. Hook down. Left base. Turn toward final. Cross the wake. There are several T2Js on the deck now. "Foxtrot Two Four, ball, one point six." Concentrate, "Meatball," lineup, angle of attack. Thud, oomph, nice landing. This could get to be fun. Taxi Director, right on cue. Throttle back, hook up. Follow the Director.

Now I remember what I was supposed to be doing after the first landing. The LSO had carefully briefed us, "When coming out of the landing area and prior to lining up on the catapult, it is VERY important to check all the airplane and engine instruments to make sure everything is OK." I was amazed to find the airplane still had instruments. On the first landing I was so excited, as long as I had an airplane beneath me it must be OK. I gave it a much more careful check this time. I even had a moment to watch the airplane in front of me take his "Cat" shot.

Better prepared for second Cat shot, maybe?

My turn; lineup, over the shuttle, passed off to the Catapult Officer. I'll press my head back a lot firmer this time. The Catapult Officer gives me the two-finger turnup signal. Power up, head back, harder, and salute. OH MY God!!! I started moving slowly down the catapult. I jammed on full brakes when... Wham, the catapult fired. The full brakes didn't slow me down even one knot. What was that all about? I realized that out of the corner of my eye I had picked up the relative motion of the ship moving through the water, I hadn't been moving along the catapult at all. The most I had done was leave two black skid marks parallel to the length of the catapult track, adding to the rubber deposits already there.

I'm beginning to feel like a real Naval Aviator, this *IS* fun. Hook down, cross the wake, h-m-m-m, green and white, its kind of pretty. With considerably more confidence, "Foxtrot Two Four, ball, one point two." "Meatball," that must be the

Catapult shots are FUN!

spud locker just below the round down. Lineup, angle of attack; OK remember now, the meatball will go a little high as you hit the ship's burble or "rooster tail" and then settle in close. "Meatball," lineup, angle of attack. Easy with the power. Touchdown, power up, power off. Hot damn, I beat the Taxi Director that time. OK, OK, hook up, out of the landing area. Follow the Taxi Director.

These Carrier landings aren't so difficult. My confidence soared as I approached landing number three. I called the ball and kept it centered with very little effort. So little that I relaxed just enough to get behind the airplane. In close, the LSO called for power and I over reacted. The T2J sailed over all four wires. I touched down but there was no comforting tug. "Bolter, Bolter, Power." I got the message loud and clear, never ever let your vigilance down on a Carrier landing, no matter how comfortable you feel. I concentrated harder during the next approach and the landing felt good.

Gee, there are lots more people on the deck now. Where did they all come from? Look at all the different color jerseys. Over the radio, "Foxtrot Two Four, you're bingo after this launch, rendezvous overhead for the return to Pensacola, acknowledge, Over."

"Foxtrot Two Four, Roger."

"You'll be number five in a flight of seven, Over."

"Roger." The pace sure has slowed down, I wish I could get another landing, nope, better leave well enough alone. Over the shuttle, power up, salute. For the first time, I noticed how much the T2J squats and groans under the stress of the acceleration of the catapult launch. It almost sighs as it leaves the deck. I smile, grin is probably more appropriate; for there is no doubt that I have to be the greatest Naval Aviator in the world.

The rendezvous over the ship was perfect. All seven aircraft aboard. Will we

Carrier Qualifications complete, headed for home

ever impress the troops back at the field? The formation looks great as we turn toward the runway, good lead; he's being smooth and gentle as we lineup in right echelon for the left break. I concentrate on keeping a nice tight formation. H-m-m-m-m looks like we might have overshot the center line of the runway a little. About a quarter-mile from the runway while attempting to correct for the overshoot, the leader turned into the flight. It's more than we can handle; everyone went a different direction. The seven world's greatest Naval Aviators could not have had a more ignominious ending to their near perfect Carrier Qualification flight. We finally got ourselves regrouped and reorganized somewhere on the downwind leg for landing. Hook not required for this landing but I reach over and ceremoniously pat the hook handle anyway. I made as soft a touchdown as possible, just to feel how nice it can be.

The Crew Chief shared my enthusiasm as I shutdown the engine and climbed down the side. I walked around the Buckeye, affectionately touching its wings and tip tanks and carefully inspected the tailhook. I smiled at the greasy imprint of the arresting wire on the hook. It's a ritual aviators everywhere find irresistible. Somehow I failed to mention to the Crew Chief

A "real" Naval Aviator?

that both main wheel tires probably have flat spots on them. It was my last flight in the T2J.

I doubt if anyone remembers the LSO's debriefing, I know I didn't. The adrenaline level was too high as each of us described only perfect approaches and landings. Another major milestone completed. We would leave for Advanced Flight Training in a few short days. It was time to celebrate. My log book reads: Carrier Qualified USS Antietam, November 21, 1961.

As is true for a lot of firsts, that first Carrier Landing leaves a lasting memory. It is what separates the land-to-air aviators from the sea-to-air Naval Aviators. It is a well-deserved distinction.

Linda and I packed our things and once again made the drive from Pensacola to Kingsville for Advanced Flight Training in the F9F-8 "Cougar" in VT-21.

Swept Wings

The F9F-8T was the two-seat trainer version of the Grumman F9F-8 "Cougar," an airplane I had always thought was especially nice looking. The somewhat thick swept wing blended into the fuselage and a large trian-

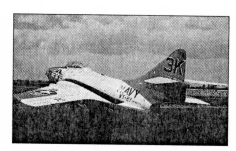

VT-21 F9F-8B single seat Cougar

gular fillet faired the trailing edge of the wing into the small circular exhaust at the tail. The highly swept vertical tail rose in a natural curve from atop the fuselage and contained the swept horizontal stabilizer. The trainer version was not as sleek. It had a bulbous fuselage and large canopy that ruined the shapely contour of the forward fuselage of the basic Cougar. For Carrier operations or ground handling, the wings folded vertically from outboard the triangular engine intakes located in the wing root. Two large blow-in doors behind the canopy

VT-21 F9F-8T Cougar trainer

provided additional air to the engine during ground and high-power operations. The single J-48 centrifugal-flow jet engine had a peculiar characteristic sound. When accelerated on the ground, it made a sustained honking noise.

The F9F-8 had its oddities

In engineering parlance, the F9F-8 was an order of magnitude more complex than the T2J and had equally better performance. On my first takeoff, the Cougar accelerated rapidly, was airborne and climbing through 1,000 feet while my brain was still lumbering down the runway. I was impressed, my instructor was not, as he reminded me to raise the landing gear before we exceeded its airspeed limit. The F9F-8 was unusual in that it used spoilers rather than ailerons for roll control. As the spoilers moved, the disturbed air on the wing made a noticeable swishing sound. The fact that rolling moments were achieved by destroying lift was particularly noticeable in the landing approach. If you were high, you could move the stick rapidly left and right, stair stepping downward by alternately destroying the lift on opposite wings. The downside (pun intended) was that you could get yourself low through overly aggressive use of the spoilers.

The Cougar was highly stable and made an excellent instrument platform. Conversely, it felt heavy during high "g" maneuvering and lacked the power to sustain elevated "g" turns without a significant loss in airspeed. It was, however, a great airplane for fledgling Naval Aviators to make their first excursion into the "Fighter Pilot's World." Like other Grumman "Iron Works" machines, the F9F-8 was a strong, well-built airplane. It was a good thing, because they suffered considerable abuse at the hands of inexperienced pilots whose egotism and inflated view of their capabilities greatly exceeded reality. Once we soloed the F9F-8T, we were allowed to fly the single seat F9F-8B, a real treat because it was the first airplane we got to fly that an instructor didn't check us out in first. I enjoyed flying the "B" more than the "T," it made me feel like a real fighter pilot.

The aggressiveness with which we flew was a strong function of the aggressiveness of the individual flight instructors. Some instructors were much more fun than others and let us do four-ship acrobatics and occasionally attack other flights in the training area. One afternoon our flight of four was tail chasing through the hazy Texas sky, when an authoritative voice on the radio demanded, "Tango flight, state your position, Over." Wanting to demonstrate my heads-up knowledge of where we were, I quickly replied, "Tango flight is on the zero seven eight radial, nineteen DME off the Alice TACAN, Over." Strange no reply. In less than three minutes we were bounced by four other orange and white Cougars. Our inexperience was no match for the initial advantage achieved by the new arrivals. We were trounced. In the debrief, I was admonished for giving away our position and graded "below average" on headwork.

Tears of Failure

By far the longest and most demanding part of the Advanced Training syllabus was the instrument portion. My primary instructor was Marine Captain Carr. We worked well together. Without exception, the most critical check ride in the entire flight training syllabus was the instrument check ride in the Cougar. Continuation in the program depended on its satisfactory completion. We all sweated it and looked forward to its completion but not the thought of taking it. As this important milestone approached, I did not feel I had done as well in the instrument syllabus as I had hoped and my confidence was low. Luckily, my check ride was scheduled with LCDR Cleland who was noted for his fairness. He gave me the proposed flight routing the day prior to the flight and I worked diligently to get prepared. It was not a complicated flight.

That morning, I briefed LCDR Cleland on the departure, en route segment and arrival at Kingsville. I was somewhat nervous as I pre-flighted the aircraft and strapped in. LCDR Cleland made the start and taxied to the active runway. Once cleared, he aligned the airplane on the runway for takeoff, instructed me to raise the instrument hood, and gave me control of the brakes. The instrument hood in the F9F-8T is a canvas covering attached to a half circle ring that stows in front of the aft cockpit instrument panel. To raise the hood you lift the ring and slide it back until the canvas completely blocks out all forward and side vision. To drop the hood you reach up and back and push it down and forward.

Later, following a fluky accident, a cloth handle was sown on the left forward canvas to allow the hood to be lowered by reaching forward with your left hand. The ejection seat handle is a "U" shaped handle that extends forward from the top of the seat over your helmet. The handle is attached to a canvas face curtain, which protects your face as you pull the handle downward for ejection. As the story goes, an F9F-8T was nearing the end of a hooded instrument approach and the rear seat pilot was instructed to "pop" the hood for landing. When he reached up for the hood he inadvertently stuck his arm through the ejection handle and explosively exited the airplane as he lowered the hood. Unfortunately he bumped the throttle to idle as he departed. The instructor saw the rear seat pilot eject, felt the engine start to unwind, surmised an engine failure, and ejected as well. The perfectly good, but now pilotless, F9F-8T crashed at the end of the runway and was destroyed. The accident investigation revealed the embarrassing story. Shortly thereafter all instrument hoods were modified.

Back to the check ride. The first maneuver was an instrument takeoff (ITO). Basically, as you accelerate to takeoff speed you try to keep the heading indicator (RMI) pegged on the runway heading. It is not a difficult maneuver and since you can't see outside you really don't know whether you go down the center line or not. At takeoff speed you rotate the nose approximately four degrees up and the Cougar flies off the ground. Properly executed it is a great confidence builder. The takeoff was without comment. Confirming a positive rate of climb, I raised the gear, and at 140 knots raised the flaps. I contacted Air Traffic Control (ATC) and provided my estimate for the Alice TACAN. ATC did not yet have radar coverage in our area thus verbal position reports were required. The departure went as planned. We crossed the Alice TACAN within a minute of my original estimate. I recalculated the Brownsville estimate and reported it to ATC. As we reached cruise altitude, I relaxed a little.

The first hint of a problem occurred inbound to Brownsville. The TACAN bearing pointer broke lock twice and spun several times but the distance seemed okay. I was so psyched up it was easy to convince myself that the instructor was giving me an instrument failure as part of the check ride. The bearing reacquired, seemed to point in the right direction, broke lock, reacquired not quite forty-five degrees to the right of course, broke lock, spun, and again pointed to Brownsville. No longer relaxed, I tried to figure out whether there was a problem or not. Over Brownsville and during the turn toward Beeville, the attitude indicator failure flag came on. This was not totally unexpected, although I would have preferred it not happen in the turn. While attempting to transition to partial panel flying (flying without all instruments working) in the turn, I over banked, let the nose drop, lost altitude and overshot the outbound heading. I pulled back on the stick to stop the altitude loss and over banked in the other direction. I chased the sensitive turn needle from one side to the other, it wouldn't settle down. It was awful. I went from nearly five hundred feet low to over five hundred feet high and continued in an unusual attitude for several seconds. When I finally got the airplane under control I knew I had exceeded the altitude limits for a successful check ride, which meant I had blown the most important flight check in the Advanced Flight Training curriculum. To make matters worse, the TACAN needle was now spinning continuously and I couldn't figure out where

Not my day

we were. I made the ATC report based on my pre-flight estimate to Beeville but wasn't sure I was actually heading toward it. I remembered there was a UHF/ADF station at Beeville but I didn't have the frequency noted on my knee board. Already overloaded flying partial panel, I pulled out the map and tried to find the ADF frequency at Beeville. As I stared at the map, my instrument scan broke down again and the Cougar started a slow descending turn to the right. I caught it after a twenty degree heading change and a loss of three hundred feet. I refocused my attention on flying the airplane and still didn't have the frequency. I reacquired the preplanned heading and altitude but for all practical purposes I could have been anywhere. More properly dividing my attention between flying partial panel and map reading, I found the ADF frequency but lost altitude again while leaning over to dial it on the radio. Even with the frequency set, the needle still didn't point. "Damn," I had forgotten to select the radio to the ADF position. Sometime during these gyrations the instructor mercifully gave me back the attitude indicator but the TACAN never did reacquire lock. I switched the UHF/ADF and the TACAN to Beeville but both needles continued to rotate. I couldn't believe on top of busting every altitude limit, I had also managed to get completely lost. The only thing for sure was that we were fifty-three miles from Beeville, headed in that general direction, and I was totally distraught over having busted my first and most important check ride.

The instructor told me to "pop" the hood and pointed out Beeville in the distance about ten degrees left of the nose. I took his word for it for I could barely make it out through the tears. He took the airplane and tuned in the Alice TACAN with no better results than I had with Brownsville and Beeville; distance but no azimuth. He tuned the Kingsville UHF/ADF. We could hear the identification signal but again the needle would not point to the station. It wasn't a real problem because we could see Kingsville in the distance. He called ATC, canceled our IFR flight plan and turned toward home. We flew on in silence, or at least for me, agonized silence. LCDR Cleland made a VFR letdown and landed.

Captain Carr was waiting for us as we taxied in. Since we were back early, he knew the check ride had not gone well. He put his arm on my shoulder and walked with me toward the hangar. His kind and genuine concern overwhelmed me and I started to cry. He explained that failing a check ride was not the end of the world nor the end of the program and that I would get another chance. I knew I had let him down.

LCDR Cleland (most assuredly with Captain Carr's coaching) was better than a Santa Claus. He allowed that I had not done well, had busted the altitude limits for an acceptable check ride but was going to give me an "incomplete," rather than a "down," because of the dual instrument failure. It was a nice way of telling me that I had gotten a "down" but leaving my bruised ego intact. He recommended one more simulator period

Instrument simulator

before reflying the check ride. I was able to get two simulator periods the next day and rescheduled for the check ride the following day. In the simulator I concentrated on flying partial panel and passed the second check ride with flying colors.

Welcome to SAC

A reward for successfully passing the instrument check was to get to fly a supervised cross-country. It would be my first time outside of the Kingsville training area. Most people wanted to go to Pensacola and I was no exception. Unfortunately, it was hurricane season and the weather was too risky to chance getting a much-needed training airplane stranded in Pensacola. Captain Carr suggested we go west to Marine Corps Air Station (MCAS) El Toro, California. Of course it just happened to be where he was stationed prior to coming to Kingsville. It sounded great to me. I did the flight planning and we launched off for sunny California.

Our first stop was Biggs Air Force Base at El Paso, Texas. I had thought the runway at Byrd Field in Richmond was huge as I approached it in the Aeronca Champ, that was before I made the approach to Biggs. The runway at Biggs was at least twice the size of Byrd Field's and half again as long as the one at Kingsville. I really felt like one of the Big Boys as I taxied onto the huge concrete apron of a major Strategic Air Command (SAC) base, complete with a follow me truck and a second escort vehicle with flashing red lights. I changed my mind when we shutdown and climbed down the side of our trainer and came face to face with the muzzles of two loaded rifles wheeled by tough looking, no nonsense, Military Police. One policeman directed us to the dark blue military van with the flashing red lights while the other confiscated our helmet bags from the trainer. I didn't quite know what to make of it all and was glad Captain Carr was along. Few words were spoken but there was no doubt somebody thought we were up to no good. We were driven to a blue and white trailer where an Air Force Major demanded to see our military ID cards. We produced our green ID cards, which only seemed to partially satisfy the Major. Next he wanted to know, where we were from, and why we had arrived at Biggs without a flight plan. At last a clue, either Kingsville Operations had failed to activate our military flight plan when we took off, or ATC had not passed the information to Biggs advising them of our impending arrival. We gave the Major the Autovon phone number for Kingsville Operations. He phoned. Kingsville had activated the flight plan but the information never made it to El Paso. I was relieved that the Air Force was relieved. Once we made it through the security check, things moved at a rapid pace. We were escorted to Transient Alert, where we arranged for fuel, and to Base Operations where we filed the second leg from El Paso to El Toro.

We were soon on our way. It was hard to believe El Paso was hotter than Kingsville but it was. I soon found out why the runway was so long. We used most of it to get airborne and even then barely maintained a minimum climb rate. The mountains to the west loomed larger and larger with every passing second as the straining Cougar struggled to gain altitude and speed.

We had hardly checked in on the ATC frequency when we were told to contact Biggs' Base Operations on UHF frequency three seventy two point two. Captain Carr said it before I did, but I was thinking the same thing, "What the hell have we done now?" He made the call, "Biggs' Ops, this is Tango Three Two Seven, Over."

"Roger, Tango Three Two Seven, after your takeoff we found a tire carcass on the runway, we believe it came off your airplane, Over."

"Roger Biggs, thanks, we didn't notice any problem but we'll check it out when we get to El Toro, Over." Now I was really glad Captain Carr was along.

We talked it over. The only thing unusual about the takeoff was the long takeoff roll and that wasn't an anomaly because it matched the computed takeoff data. If we had blown a tire we should have at least felt a swerve but we had rolled straight. We concluded we probably didn't have a problem but couldn't explain how we could leave a tire on the runway and not know it. Perhaps it happened at liftoff and we never felt it. As a precaution we decided to request an arrested landing at El Toro. ATC forwarded our request. The rest of the flight was uneventful.

When we arrived at El Toro, the midfield arresting gear was rigged and hordes of crash equipment were standing by. To my surprise, Captain Carr allowed me to make the landing, although I'm sure he was on the controls and closely monitoring every input. Had I been the instructor, I would have been. He instructed me to touchdown about five hundred feet short of the cable and roll into it. We made radio contact with the Crash Crew on the ground who told us no LSO was available to help us, that we were on our own. We lowered the gear and flaps and made a low approach to let the ground crew get a look at our wheels and for us to get a feel for the approach. As we turned downwind and lowered the hook, the Crash Crew relayed that our right wheel looked strange. We had no idea how to interpret that observation.

On the second pass, I concentrated on holding the landing approach angle of attack and Captain Carr coached me on the altitude. We touched down "on speed" and very near the right distance from the wire. The hook grabbed the cable and tugged the Cougar to a stop. It was a lot softer than the T2J landings on the USS Antietam. The crash trucks immediately converged on the airplane. As we shut down, a small but amused crowd, most of whom seemed to be shaking their heads or rubbing their chins, gathered around the right wheel. The airplane appeared to be level from the cockpit.

We were equally amused as we rounded the nose and saw the right wheel. We did not have a flat tire, as we suspected, but we had in fact left the tire's entire rubber carcass on the Biggs' runway. There was not an ounce of rubber remaining on the wheel. An experienced Apache Indian could not have performed a more perfect scalping. The tire looked like a large ragged ball of white string.

Burning Up the Desert

Flying low level or "Oil Burner" routes in the Cougar was fun. We students spent hours cutting and pasting strips of sectional charts together, carefully crafting them into knee board sized flip charts covering each leg of the low-level route. There was one major problem. There were very few identifiable landmarks in the desert surrounding

Kingsville. From two hundred feet at four hundred knots the entire area looks like a sandy tan blur. With my extensive cross-country experience in the Aeronca Champ, I was really looking forward to this phase of training. I quickly learned, however, that holding a good heading and constant airspeed was the real secret to success, because most turning points were made on time rather than by visual identification of a landmark.

There was one major railroad track that traced a nice straight north-south line in the sand toward Brownsville. It was the one prominent landmark that figured in most of the designated low-level routes.

Although we never flew low-level at night, I had this devilish idea that I wanted to fly down that track and meet a train head on. The Cougar had a single light that shone forward. I could imagine the stories that would result from the high-speed ghost train that haunted the rail line between Kingsville and Brownsville. All in all, I did quite well on these flights and absolutely loved racing low across the desert at a high rate of speed

Air-to-Ground

We had our first introduction to air-to-ground weapons delivery in the Cougar. By this time I felt very comfortable in the airplane and it seldom took me by surprise anymore. We jumped back and forth from the single seat "B" model and the two-seat "T" model. Of course, we all enjoyed the "B" model because it lacked the often critical instructor looking over your shoulder. As always, when we were introduced to a new facet of flying, we first had to learn to fly the prescribed pattern before we actually dropped or launched a rocket.

It was obvious from my first couple of instructional flights that dropping a bomb from a fast moving aircraft was not as easy as it looked in the movies. We were using fixed gun sights for our weapons delivery and it was quite a chore to make the dive angle, airspeed, altitude, pipper placement (aim point), and lateral lineup all come together at the right

Dropping bombs, not so easy

altitude and spatial positioning to make a bomb fly the proper trajectory to impact a target. I was convinced that once an iron bomb departed the aircraft it refused to obey the laws of physics. In fact the bombs do meet both the letter, and intent, of the laws of physics. It is just that they react to atmospheric disturbances, crosswinds or any unwanted pilot input at launch with the same faithful fidelity.

We flew forty-five degree bomb drops and twenty degree rocket launches. Both were fun. The rocket runs were easier to fly and much more impressive to watch. As I flung myself at the ground, I easily transformed myself into the Bridges of

Toko Re scenario. Again we flew as flights of four with a pre-scribed pattern around the target. In typical Navy style we always made left hand roll ins on the target. It was critical to arrive over the roll in position, on speed and on altitude, otherwise achieving a proper dive angle and airspeed at the drop altitude was nearly impossible. Just as we used rules like; don't fly into the banner during air-to-air gunnery, the cardinal rule in air-to-ground was; don't, under any circum-stances, underfly your "pullout" altitude. To do so may or may not reduce your longevity to zero, but it would most certainly get you a "down" (unsatisfactory flight). This was not an easy rule to follow because your brain keeps telling you that the closer you are to the target, the better your chance of hitting it. You also know that if you can make just one more correction, a "bull's eye" will be your reward. As they say, "You only get target fixation once in your life, but it lasts forever." Not a good idea for longevity.

In the early stages of air-to-ground you spend an inordi-nate amount of time scanning the altimeter, as it is critical. You quickly figure out that you have to move the aiming point of a fixed gun sight in the wrong direction to achieve the proper lateral positioning of the pipper. Because the pipper is below the target, to account for the gravitational trajectory of the bomb, if you are lined up left of the target you have to make a right turn to correct for the displacement, but when you do, the pipper moves to the left until you roll out wings level. Sounds complicated doesn't it? Believe me, at first it is, and it takes some practice to anticipate the proper roll out point. As you track the target, the pipper moves up the run-in line until it intercepts the target. If all goes well, the pipper ends up over the target when your aircraft is at the proper dive angle, airspeed, and altitude and you will get a bull's eye. As we had seen in air-to-air gunnery, the instructors were quite good at it and we students improved with practice.

Enlisted men stationed in wooden towers surrounding the target area followed the aircraft trajectories and called out our dive angles over the radio. When we started dropping practice bombs, they also called out the location of the puff of white smoke from the impact of the bomb. We all strained our necks to locate the tell-tail smoke.

The rocket launches were flown at a shallower dive angle and easier to aim, but most of all, they streaked out in front of the aircraft in a violent stream of gray-white smoke and you could usually see them impact the target. It was great fun. I didn't like the idea that you only got an average score, so I tried to keep a log of my individual impacts. Air-to-ground weapons were fun and I would likely have enjoyed being an attack pilot, but my fighter pilot dream was still alive and intact.

Carrier Qualifications in the Cougar

A swept wing airplane, by its very nature, is much draggier at a high angle of attack than is a straight wing aircraft. This meant the Cougar required higher power settings and had a greater susceptibility to rapid decelerations than the T2J. Consequently, there was a tendency to decelerate or lose airspeed anytime you pulled the nose up without anticipating the requirement for increased power. When I started flying Carrier approaches in the Cougar, I tended to start out low on the glide path, fly a flat approach, and end up high in close. It took a while before I figured out the obvious; mainly to hold a higher power setting early in the approach, establish a stabilized centered ball and fly it all the way to touchdown. It always felt like I was carrying too much power, but even then, it was never enough. I had already learned that it was much better to error on the "high" side, for both the ball and power.

Earlier I talked about the Cougar using spoilers rather than ailerons for lateral (roll) control where bank angles were achieved by destroying lift on the down going wing. In the carrier landing approach you had to pay particular attention not to use excessive lateral inputs, especially in close to the ship, because you could find yourself creating additional sink rate while trying to get lined up. The spoiler problem complicated glide path control, especially if you were having lineup problems. Fortunately the Cougar was highly stable and tended to hold its trimmed speed quite well.

In the Cougar, I used the same approach to the carrier landings that I had in the T2J, namely reciting the familiar "meatball, lineup, angle of attack" during the approach. I enjoyed the Field Carrier Landing Practice and was excited about taking a higher performance aircraft aboard ship. This, of course, was before I knew about night carrier landings.

While we were in the Field Carrier Landing Practice phase, the training squadron experienced a highly unusual accident aboard the Antietam. Like most jet aircraft of that time, to work on or remove the jet engine from the Cougar, it was necessary to unbolt and remove the entire tail section. For the F9F-8, the tail section disconnected just aft of the wing root and was rolled away on a dolly. The bolts connecting the tail section to the rest of the fuselage absorbed the force of the arrestment.

During Carrier Qualifications, a F9F-8 made a normal landing, but when the hook engaged the arresting wire, the tail section separated from the rest of the fuselage. The entire front end of the airplane careened off the end of the angle deck and crashed into the sea taking the pilot with it. The tail section remained on the deck attached to the arresting wire. Yet another data point that reminded me that this was a dangerous endeavor that needed to be taken very seriously.

Cougar snags a wire with late lineup

To digress, yet another senseless accident occurred at Kingsville while I was there. A Navy, TV-1, the Navy version of the Air Force T-33, had undergone major repairs at the field and was going out for its first test flight following the maintenance. On takeoff roll, the airplane departed the runway to the left and one of its tip tanks crashed into the Duty Crash Truck, killing three Crash Crewmen in a huge holocaust. The accident investigation revealed that the ailerons had been connected in reverse, causing the pilot to lose control on takeoff. Another accident that never should have happened.

I approached the USS Antietam in my F9F-8 with considerably more knowledge, experience, and confidence than I

Carrier Qualifications in the Cougar

had several months ago in the T2J. Carrier Qualification in the Cougar occurred on March 19, 1962 with two touch-and-goes and three arrested landings.

Tigers

The Naval Air Training Command demonstrated its confidence in its flight training program by letting us fly the single seat Grumman F11F "Tiger" in the final phase of Advanced Training. All the other aircraft we had flown had a dual cockpit trainer, which allowed an instructor pilot to fly with us and declare us safe for solo. It was a real ego trip to strap on my first afterburner-equipped, high-performance, supersonic fighter before I had pinned on my "Navy Wings of Gold." The F11F Tiger was a continuation of Grumman's Panther and Cougar line of Naval fighters. It was the first supersonic aircraft in the lineage. Its most notable feature was the use of the "area rule principle" to improve its super-sonic performance. It also lacked the blended body contours and thick wing of the Cougar. Its thin swept wing extended from the middle of the coke-bottle shaped fuselage without a noticeable fairing. The earlier F11F models had a stubby nose but the ones we flew had the latest elongated nose that greatly improved its looks.

VT-23 Grumman F11F Tiger

The F11F Tiger had a relatively short fleet career and was replaced by the F8U Crusader. It was, however, a wonderful aircraft to fly. It was by far the best formation aircraft I would ever fly. It was obvious why the Navy Blue Angels flight demonstration team flew them for so many years.

I had thought the performance of the F9F-8 Cougar was a big improvement over the T2J Buckeye, and it was, but the first time I selected the afterburner in the Tiger, my concept of "high performance" took a giant leap. The old cliché of having a "Tiger by the tail" was most appropriate. What a fantastic feeling to be pressed back against the seat with the airspeed indicator winding up and the runway whizzing by in a blur. Look out sky, here I come, grinning from ear to ear. Of course the ever present, and critically watchful, instructor was nearby, albeit in that beautiful orange and gray Tiger tucked in on my right wing. I negotiated the course rules and proceeded out over the thin white line of sand that defined the Texas coastline. Occasionally, and affectionately,

VT-23 Instructor trails student's F11F

I touched parts of the cockpit to ensure myself that this was not simply a dream.

Aligned along the pre-briefed course, I checked the fuel, announced "Burner now," and shoved the throttle outboard and forward. After a small hesitation, the huge mass of fuel pouring in the afterburner ignited and the Tiger leapt forward as it had on takeoff. The fighter accelerated rapidly forcing me back against the seat. The Mach meter climbed steadily toward that mystical and magic Mach 1. Visions of shock waves, transonic drag rise, and the changes in the aerodynamic equations I had studied at the University flashed briefly through my mind. I was about to have the experience of a lifetime. I would soon fly faster than the speed of sound. The acceleration slowed slightly as the Mach meter approached Mach 1, and it required a slight dive, but the Tiger and I were soon supersonic. A new Chuck Yeager was born. I started a left turn with the instructor stationed a little further out now. Interesting, my supersonic Tiger was not as agile as the subsonic Tiger and the forces required to hold level flight in the turn were noticeably heavier. It was the instructor who reminded me, much too soon, to come out of burner before I ran out of gas. I hesitated for a moment trying to imprint this incredible experience in my mind. I deselected afterburner and was quickly subsonic again. "Say your fuel state Hotel Two Four?" It was time to head back to Kingsville and practice landings with this fantastic machine. Surely life could not get any better than this.

Simulated Air-to-Air Combat

For a fledgling fighter pilot, flying air-to-air combat against the instructor or other students was by far the most fun. We were given considerable free play and allowed to try different tactics and maneuvers we thought might work. Of course we were no match for the instructor pilots but we took great delight in besting our fellow classmates. Pilot "ego" is the critical factor in simulated air-to-air combat, just as your "life" is the critical factor in the real thing. You will try anything not to be the one who is shot down. In actual combat, coming in second is simply not an option for a fighter pilot. It means you are probably dead or someone's prisoner. It is indeed a competitive business in which you bet your life.

Energy management is the essence of air-to-air combat. While aggressiveness is important, it is usually the smoother pilot who is capable of exploiting the envelope of his aircraft without wasting energy in rough ham-fisted maneuvering that comes out ahead. Several tenets are vital to success: Foremost is the requirement to keep your adversary in sight; second is to know the strengths of your own aircraft; third is not to get suckered into playing your opponent's game; fourth is to know the capabilities and especially the weak-

Power to burn, lots to learn

nesses of your opponent's aircraft; keep your energy up; be decisive, as he who hesitates is lost, and last but not least, know when to break it off. Always remember that running out of gas and crashing is a kill for the enemy.

It is amazing how good you can get at making your aircraft do what needs to be done without having to think about it. You soon find that you can maneuver through complex attitudes and rapidly changing situations with relative ease. Of course the movies make it look a lot easier than it really is. They fail to capture the effects of the high "g's" and physical exertion the pilot experiences. In the movie "Top Gun," Tom Cruise always ended up with his hair neatly combed and with hardly a drop of sweat on his brow. A good air-to-air engagement can be quite exhausting but equally as exhilarating when you come out the winner or totally devastating if you lose. During some rather violent maneuvers, one of my Training Command classmates experienced a catastrophic engine failure in his F11F and was forced to eject from his disabled aircraft. It was the most serious airborne mishap any of us suffered during our training.

Air-to-Air Gunnery

We flew high-speed gunnery, which I found difficult, less for the maneuvering requirements, but mostly for the difficulty of seeing the tow plane and keeping tract of the other planes in the flight. The gunnery pattern was huge. Tracking and firing runs required a steep high-speed, nearly Mach one, dive toward the tow plane. In the hazy environment off the Texas coast, the tiny gray tow plane, at least for me, would simply disappear. This is not a good thing when you are hurtling through the sky at a tremendous speed and trying to track a tiny tow banner while trying not to collide with the banner, tow plane or fellow aviator. While it was kicks and I enjoyed it, if those conditions were representative of the real world, I once again proved I was not going to be a great gunner. As always, things improved with practice, and the two live firing gunnery sessions were over much too soon.

Wings of Gold

The nineteen flight syllabus in the F11F passed quickly and my classmates did quite well. Most important, we had completed our flight training and earned those coveted "Wings of Gold." Only three of my pre-flight classmates who had entered the jet pipeline received their wings at the same time I did. Kingsville, Texas was so remote that there were very few visitors at our "Wings" awarding ceremony. It was May 4, 1962. Linda proudly pinned on my wings and there would never again be a more proud Naval Aviator. We had a big party at the NAAS Kingsville Officer's Club that night.

As always, good old teetotaling Warren was an excellent designated driver.

Within two days we had once again packed our household goods, said good-bye to friends and started the long

The coveted "Navy Wings of Gold"

trek across the country, this time to Virginia. Four of the graduating couples rendezvoused near Houston for one last dinner together before we scattered our different ways. Only one other classmate had orders to Demons, most were assigned to A4D Skyhawk Squadrons.

Survival School and POW Training

My ultimate orders were to report to Fighter Squadron 101 (VF-101), the F3B "Demon" Replacement Air Group (RAG) training squadron at NAS Boca Chica near Key West, Florida. En route I was required to attend the Arctic Survival and Escape and Evasion (E&E) Training Course at Brunswick, Maine and the Instrument Refresher Course at NAS Jacksonville, Florida. Larry Barringer was headed for North Carolina and planned to drive to Maine. He agreed to pick me up in Richmond on the way. Larry was a Naval Academy graduate and a good friend who had provided me considerable "Navy" guidance over the past year and a half.

The ten day course at Brunswick included six days of Arctic Survival and four days of Escape and Evasion training. Albeit early May, there was still plenty of snow around and after being in Kingsville, Texas, Maine felt like the Arctic. The first six days were a piece of cake compared to the last four. We had the usual classroom lectures and tried out the latest Arctic survival gear. We even cooked beef jerky, which we were allowed to carry with us during the Escape and Evasion training.

The military had not been impressed with the performance of its Prisoners of War (POWs) during the Korean War and had started a training program to better educate its personnel as to what to expect and how to organize themselves in a POW situation.

Early on the first day of the E & E training, we were paired up with a classmate, driven to a pre-arranged location, and deposited out in the woods. Our instructions were to use evasive tactics to arrive at a pre-designated checkpoint at an appointed time the next day. My partner was a young seaman. He was a nice kid but not in particularly good physical shape. He won my admiration for sheer guts as we negotiated some really difficult terrain. We were in trouble almost immediately. We didn't know it at the time, but the drop-off point did not correspond to the position we were given on our map. It took several arduous hours before we figured out we were not where we thought we were, and lost even more time trying to determine where we really were. Our progress was soon halted by the looming darkness. We rolled out our sleeping gear on the edge of a small clearing surrounded by towering pine trees. We went to full alert as we heard something smash against a nearby tree, followed shortly by another and yet another. After our hearts settled down, we were treated to a beautiful aerial display by a group of flying squirrels gleefully gliding between the trees. It was a delightful diversion from the strenuous day we had just completed. It was not a restful night. We knew we had to be on the move as soon as it was light enough to negotiate the rugged terrain.

Breakfast consisted of beef jerky and a dry crumbly high-protein survival bar from the survival kit that had the consistency and taste of sawdust. Before the sun even thought about peeking over the horizon, we continued our trek, being especially careful because we knew aggressor forces were known to be in the area. We were making our way along a ridge line in some deep forestation, when my partner slipped while climbing over a downed tree and let out a less than stealthy string of profanity. Within ten minutes we found ourselves face to face with two aggressors. In the real world, we would have been prisoners of war; instead they took our names and let us continue on our way. The "capture" resulted in a substantial reduction in our course completion grade. We finally made it to the designated checkpoint but long after the appointed time. We soon discovered that we were not the only "good guys" who were late.

While pondering what we should do next, we saw some of the bad guys drive by the checkpoint in a jeep but they didn't stop. It was obvious from the map that they were on a road that dead-ended in about half a mile. We combined forces and barricaded the road with a fallen tree to prevent their return. The jeep slowly approached and stopped at the blockade. It was interesting to watch their apprehension, knowing that they were somewhat at our mercy at this time. They began to undo the barricade and invoked the old "School Situation" rule by shouting for us to show ourselves, which we did. There were considerably more of us there than we even knew ourselves. Almost no one had made it to the checkpoint on time. We were given the coordinates for the next checkpoint. It was a much easier task when we started out from a known location.

When we arrived at the next checkpoint, there was, in fact, a "good guy" van waiting to pick us up. As soon as everyone had checked in, we happily clamored aboard the van and started back to the training center, or so we thought. Spirits were high. We had driven only a mile or so when the van was violently attacked amidst a deafening flurry of gunfire. Chaos reigned. The driver of the van was killed, complete with realistic bloodshed and the entire van load taken prisoner. We were shackled and roughly herded into the back of an open enemy truck. After a short, bumpy ride, we were unloaded into a barbed wire stockade. In spite of the cold, we were completely stripped and all our possessions confiscated, including the few precious rations we were carrying. The prisoner clothes we were issued were no match for the cold spring weather we were experiencing, but we made the best of what we had.

For the next two and a half days we were subjected to a myriad of physical and psychological events to see if we would break under the strain. They were very effective in breaking us in either or both categories. The aggressors were well trained and we were tired, hungry, and psychologically off-balance. Chains of Command were rearranged, selective interrogations were performed, people were placed in coffin boxes and wet holes in the ground, and all were required to perform strenuous, meaningless, manual labor. I decided to become an addicted smoker. I let it be known that I was willing to do anything for a cigarette. For the most part it worked. It was the one thing they tormented me with the most.

As a group we made two escape plans only one of which worked. Fortunately, I was selected for the successful attempt. It required a major group effort. It became obvious from our first attempt that there were collaborators in our ranks, which was especially difficult because you couldn't figure out whom to trust. Mistrust of your own is tough to handle. It is betrayal at its worst. The escape occurred from a small work party, with the help of a riotous diversion by the majority of the prisoners. The escapee, me, had to negotiate a lengthy escape route to reach a "safe" haven. I was chosen because of my physical conditioning and small size. The escape was considered successful and I was rewarded with food. Even in the elation of having successfully escaped from the compound, I broke into sobbing tears as I was offered food. The only thing that kept most of us going was that we knew the imprisonment would be over in two more days. In the real situation, that would not have been the case. We all have our limits. My partner was taken from the compound the evening of the first day. His feet were severely blistered from the boots he had worn during the trek through the woods and needed medical attention. I admired his perseverance throughout the ordeal.

Larry and I were glad it was over. We stopped briefly in New York City for a decent meal before we continued south toward Virginia and North Carolina. The food was expensive and, even with our past hunger, not very good. Our stomachs had shrunk enough that neither of us could finish the meal. To add insult to injury, when we were less that ten miles from my house, we were pulled over by the Virginia State Police for speeding. Fortunately our military ID cards got us out of a jam. Larry dropped me off at my house in Richmond and continued on to North Carolina.

Instrument School

Linda accompanied me to Jacksonville for Instrument school, and my first exposure to a "fleet" training school. In retrospect it wasn't too different from the training command but it was obvious that the shiny Wings of Gold received a higher degree of respect and expectation. In other words, I was expected to already know how to fly and did not have to be trained. It was indeed an instrument "refresher" course. It made me work even harder to prove my right to wear the wings. I never looked forward to instrument school until I was about halfway through the course. New airway procedures were covered in academics, concluding with the annual written instrument exam.

Comfortable with Instrument School F9F-8T

Climbing into the backseat of the trusty F9F-8T, Cougar was deja vu. When the canopy slid forward and clunked into place, the instructor started, taxied, and lined up the airplane on the runway center line, after that, the rest of the flight was up to me. Every flight started with a hooded instrument takeoff (ITO). Once takeoff clearance was received and the engine had reached full power, I released the brakes and concentrated on keeping the heading pegged on its current value as the airspeed built up to rotation and takeoff speed. At altitude, the first task was to work on improving my instrument scan. It always amazed me how quickly my scan deteriorated when I had not flown instruments for a while. Increasingly complex patterns were flown. Constant-heading and airspeed climbs and descents were followed by constant altitude and airspeed turns and reversals, and various combinations of the above, including airspeed changes. I was pleased with how quickly my instrument scan improved and how accurately the patterns could be flown. It was personally satisfying to be able to correlate all these variables precisely to the rotation of the second hand of the clock, anticipating changes in altitude, heading and/or airspeed to effect each change to the second. We ultimately did increasingly complex acrobatics under the hood, which were great confidence builders. Probably the most fun, and likely the most important, was properly reacting to "no attitudes barred" instructor-induced, unusual attitudes. Some instructors were more innovative than others. Typically the instructor would maneuver the aircraft for several seconds, and not necessarily gently, to induce vertigo and then leave the airplane in some unusual attitude from which I had to recover. At one time or another, most of us screwed up the unusual attitude of being straight-and-level, because it was an unusual attitude to find yourself in during unusual attitude recovery training. I always found this part of the training particularly challenging but rewarding and fun. The last part of the flight was more mundane, but especially important because it included standard instrument procedures such as holding patterns and approaches. Figuring out how to enter and exit holding patterns was always problematic for me, not unlike my difficulties with determining the correct entry for VFR runways.

Enter the Demon

Upon completion of the instrument refresher training course, Linda and I continued down the Florida coast to Key West and Fighter Squadron VF-101, the Replacement Air Group (RAG) for the F3B, "Demon," an airplane I had only seen fly once in an air show at the Naval Air Test Center. The Demon had a terrible reputation as a fighter, and had easily earned the reputation of "Ensign Killer." Originally designed as an all-weather, supersonic, single-seat fighter using the Westinghouse J-40 engine, the early F3B barely had enough power to fly, much less achieve the supersonic speed for which it was designed. Several of the early Demons never flew. They were shipped by barge directly from the McDonnell plant at St. Louis to Navy Technical Training Schools

The McDonnell F3B Demon had its problems

to be used as maintenance training aids. The F3B was later redesigned around the Allison J-71 engine.

My first "close" encounter with an F3B actually occurred during the instrument refresher training at NAS Jacksonville when I discovered a moth-balled F3B on the repair ramp. Compared to the other fighters of its day, the Demon was a large airplane and this particular one was completely covered with white plastic preservative, making it look remarkably like a gigantic white whale. From ground level the cockpit appeared to be at least fifty feet in the air. How did one climb up there without getting a nosebleed or needing an oxygen mask? I was aghast at the thickness of the wings and the large engine exhaust nozzle sticking out the rear of the fuselage. It looked as if the engineer who designed the wing had never heard of supersonic flow and the one who designed the fuselage had obviously been given the wrong dimensions for the engine. The engine was at least three feet longer than the fuselage structure designed to house it.

While the J-71 engine provided sufficient power to fly, the F3B was only supersonic in a dive and then barely to Mach 1.3. The J-71 engine also proved to be highly susceptible to icing in the clouds. So while the Demon could legitimately claim the supersonic label, it was anything but all-weather. Several modifications were incorporated into the engine to achieve all-weather operation, all of which reduced its already limited power. The engine had two serious problems; a tendency to compressor stall in the 83 to 87% rpm range, and an exceptionally high afterburner nozzle failure rate. Incorporating a series of bleed valves that opened anytime you were in the stall sensitive rpm range, with an associated loss of thrust, of course, solved the compressor

The F3B Demon in full afterburner

stall problem. During our training, we were often cautioned to avoid this rpm range.

The approach to the afterburner nozzle failure problem was a novel one. If the nozzle failed in the fully open position you were in real trouble. Depending on your weight, there may not be enough power to stay airborne. Consequently, designed into the J-71 was the ability to select "emergency" afterburner should the nozzle fail open. Normally afterburner could only be selected and maintained at 100% rpm. The "emergency" afterburner position allowed you to maintain and modulate the afterburner over the entire throttle range. The good news was that you had sufficient power to fly, the bad news was that the engine guzzled fuel at such a prodigious rate, you weren't going to fly for very long or go very far. One of the numerous engine checks required prior to takeoff was to select the "emergency" afterburner switch to the ON position, advance the throttle until the afterburner lit, accelerate to 100% rpm, and then bring the throttle all the way to idle. This check looked and sounded awful. The engine howled and growled and flames shot out the back as the throttle was retarded. One of my Squadron mates set fire to his aft fuselage when he was unable to deselect "emergency" afterburner. When he realized what was happening, he shutdown the engine, lost electrical power, and was unable to contact the tower to have them scramble the fire trucks. Tower personnel had grown accustom to seeing fire come out of the back of F3Bs, and never considered notifying the crash crew when they saw the flames. It looked normal to them. Fortunately the airplane was not severely damaged.

To say the Demon was *under-powered* is a gross understatement. It was the only airplane I knew of that, if the brakes wouldn't hold the airplane on the runway at full power, you didn't fly, because the brakes were bad. My first takeoff in the Demon was a major disappointment. It didn't even have the performance of the F11F Tiger I had flown in the training command. What a let down it was to go to a fleet squadron and fly a lesser machine!

The view from the spacious cockpit was superb but a little disconcerting at first. The canopy wrapped around in such a manner that it was possible to see downward, creating the illusion of descending. I spent the first few flight hours resisting a strong inclination to climb. My first landing was as comical as my first takeoff had been disappointing. We had been so thoroughly cautioned about avoiding the engine rpm range between 83 and 87%, that I was reluctant to retard the throttle enough to land. The LSO finally

LTJG Hall "Demon Pilot," 1963

got tired of me making low approaches to the runway and said, "Son, if you intend to land that airplane before it runs out of fuel and lands itself, you've got to take off some power." To my pleasant

Reluctant to land

surprise, the engine didn't stall or quit or do unusual things and I finally did get it on the ground.

The Sparrow III Missile

The primary reason the F3B remained in the fleet as long as it did was because of its radar guided Sparrow III missile system. At the time, the Sparrow III was the only missile capable of attacking a target head-on.

Demon with four Sparrow III Missiles

The Sparrow III guided on the reflected energy from the launching aircraft's radar and was indeed impressive. During one of our Operational Readiness Inspections (ORIs), we fired six missiles against Delmar targets, (Styrofoam targets about the size of a person), and impacted the target with five of them and the sixth was declared a lethal near miss. This was truly impressive since the Sparrow III had a proximity fuse, which meant it only needed to get near the target to destroy it. The missiles we were using in the ORI did not have explosive warheads but actually flew through the target.

The Demon had a rig that attached to the underside of the left wing that held the red Styrofoam target in place when it was not deployed. A reel was attached to the underside of the fuselage from which you could reel out over three miles of thin wire to provide separation between the tow plane and the target. We also towed Delmar targets for the ship's anti-aircraft gunners to practice against. None of us relished that mission but it had to be done.

When conducting live firings of the Sparrow III, we always made head-on attacks. The pilot in the tow aircraft breathed a lot easier when he saw the firing aircraft disappear beneath him with a radar lock on the target. The clearance to fire was granted once the tow plane and firing aircraft passed each other.

Radar Intercept Training

We used the F3B's radar system to lock onto the target to provide the missile its homing signal. It was necessary to maintain the radar lock until the missile reached its target.

We spent hours and hours in the F3B simulator chasing intermittent green blips across a circular screen learning the finer points of operating the radar and how to conduct an intercept once we detected a target. The radarscope was located on

F3B cockpit, large and roomy

the upper right side of the instrument panel and had an extended rubber boot to shield it from the sun. Radar intercepts were flown on autopilot while the pilot looked at the radar and controlled the airplane with a small "joy stick" located on the right console. This procedure worked fine as long as the autopilot worked fine. The radar intercept was primarily a mental exercise to determine target drift angles, closure rates, etc. and preferably guide the airplane to meet the simulated intruder head-on for a Sparrow III launch. The real fun began when you abandoned the radar and

VF-101 "Grim Reapers" F3B

attempted to achieve the ultimate fighter pilot goal of being at your opponent's six o'clock position for a Sidewinder missile launch. Once we mastered the art of radar flying during the daylight, we entered a period of extensive night flying.

Beware the Thunderstorms

Flying out of Key West on a clear night is quite an experience. The hundreds of shrimp boats operating with their incandescent gas lanterns below and the stars above, made it feel like you were flying in a sphere with stars all around. I always imagined this must be what it would be like to fly into deep space. I was particularly susceptible to vertigo, especially when the autopilot disengaged in some unusual attitude. Key West, however, is not always blessed with clear nights and even those that were, often harbored towering thunderstorms that sporadically and brilliantly lit up the

A typical Key West thunderstorm

black sky. Linda and I often watched the thunderous "fire-works" in the distance, there wasn't much else to do in Key West.

Thunderstorms were not just a nighttime phenomenon. The Squadron kept a close eye on all thunderstorm activity near the field, and was quick to issue an aircraft recall if it looked like the weather would deteriorate below minimums. Flying out of Key West was not unlike being on board the Aircraft Carrier. The nearest military divert field was Homestead Air Force Base some 110 miles to the northeast. During one such recall, I arrived at the airfield minutes after a huge thunderstorm had passed overhead, dropped tons of water, and proceeded to station itself at the one eighty degree landing pattern position to watch how we neophytes would handle the erratic winds and wet runway. The heavy rain made it difficult to see the runway and hard to judge the landing pattern. I found myself closer in toward the runway than I intended, wrapped up in a steep bank angle, and a lot faster than I would have liked. Because of the early recall, the airplane was also heavier than usual. I splashed down on the runway, did minimum aerodynamic braking, lowered the nose and applied the brakes. The harder I braked, the faster the Demon hydroplaned down the runway. I was well beyond the point where I thought I could stop or get airborne and fast running out of directional control and ideas. Fortunately, it was another of those times when I instinctively did the right thing without the time to reason it out in my mind. I slammed the hook down barely in time for it to grab the chain link overrun arresting gear. I ended up quite a bit left of center line but luckily not in the greenish blue water only a few hundred feet in front of me. I received great accolades for my actions. It is amazing how often one gets an atta-boy for having screwed up whatever it was they were trying to do and has to recover from their own mistakes. I suspect the thunderstorm was disappointed that I didn't end up in the sea. The old adage that the superior pilot is the one who uses his skills to avoid situations that require superior piloting skills to extricate himself from is certainly true.

St. Elmo's Fire

Under certain atmospheric conditions an airplane can build up excessive static electricity, especially around the nose and forward canopy. The discharge of the electricity manifests itself as rapidly moving lines of celestial green light casting an eerie glow around the airplane known as Saint Elmo's fire. The Demon was highly susceptible to St. Elmo's fire. The first time I saw St. Elmo's fire, it really got my attention. I found I could place my hand near the windscreen and actually change the pattern of light. Saint Elmo was a common companion around Key West.

All-Weather Fighter Pilot

We flew hours and hours of intercept training, most of it at night. Every flight ended in a full instrument approach to NAS Boca Chica. We got real good at night formation and I could figure out and accomplish head-on and crossing intercepts in my sleep. The less than sterling performance of the Demon all but guaranteed that any target we were likely to shoot at would be several thousand feet above us. Consequently we spent lots of time practicing pitch-up maneuvers and launching a missile with the nose thirty to sixty degrees above the horizon. Now this is lots of fun and quite easy on a nice VFR day, but we were training to be all-weather interceptor pilots. At night, in the clouds, or under the hood, a high nose up attitude maneuver almost always ended up requiring a recovery from a self-induced unusual attitude. I was particularity susceptible to vertigo, especially if the autopilot disengaged during these steep maneuvers, which was most of the time. The instrument training at Jacksonville paid off.

Early in our training, we learned to respect the rapid rate at which the Demon gobbled fuel. It was an important and life saving lesson. In the few day flights we flew, we were able to hassle (practice air-to-air tactics) with the instructors and our classmates. The lack of engine thrust was immediately obvious and, when maneuvering, begged for the use of afterburner, which in turn, rapidly depleted our already short fuel supply. It was a real "Catch 22." The Demon had excellent handling qualities and, when properly flown, was quite maneuverable, especially at lighter weights. Its full span leading edge flaps could be used to increase your turning rate at low speeds. It was not an airplane that liked to be manhandled; smoothness was the secret to keeping your energy up. When chasing, or being chased by, another airplane, continuous knowledge of your angle of attack is critical. Air-to-air fighting was clearly not the forte of the Demon, but as I would quickly find out when I got to VF-31, a pilot in a fighter squadron is expected to be a fighter pilot, and that's what I wanted to be. The air-to-air practice proved challenging, invaluable, and fun. You certainly learned a lot about flying, about your airplane, and about yourself, the latter likely being the most important lesson.

We were heavily into the last phase of our training, Field Carrier Landing Practice, when the Cuban Missile Crisis hastened the completion of our Demon training in the Florida Keys. Virtually

VF-101 F3B in the FCLP pattern

overnight, the Boca Chica Naval Air Station was converted into a formidable attack base to defend our vulnerable southeastern coast. The rapid buildup was impressive. Fighter and attack airplanes, with all their associated equipment, amassed on the field. It was suddenly a very busy airport and the F3B training squadron was only in the way. Since our training was nearly complete anyway, we were ordered to fly our airplanes to NAS Cecil Field at Jacksonville, Florida. Typical of the speed with which the other airplanes had arrived, we were told around noon that all training airplanes would be gone by fourteen hundred hours that day. Of course I volunteered. A quick phone call home alerted Linda to pack some clothes and have some money for me when the military truck arrived to collect my bag, for I'd be taking off for Cecil Field in two hours.

Carrier Qualifications in the "Demon"

We completed our Field Carrier Landing Practice at Cecil Field and our Carrier Qualification aboard the Aircraft Carrier USS Lexington. Ten day and six night landings were required. We nervously and impatiently waited at Cecil Field until our "Charlie" (arrival) time at the ship was determined. It wasn't difficult to arrive at the

Demon over the ramp

ship at landing weight because the Demon was always fuel limited. Flying the meatball with the Demon was fairly easy as long as you stayed ahead of the airplane. Not only was the F3B underpowered, it also had a sluggish, no, make that a horribly slow responding engine. Early on, I learned that you really had to anticipate the requirement for power and to error on the high side, shades of my early experience with the, "Don't go below 87% rpm rule." I decided that since I was never going to fly the perfect approach, I would decide which direction to error and that was high and fast.

The Demon had an engine thrust indicator (#7 on panel illustration, next page) located on the instrument panel high and to the left of the radar scope. For most practical purposes, it was useless. One day during Field Carrier Landing Practice (FCLPs), I noticed that whenever the thrust reading went below 5,000 pounds, the airplane decelerated rapidly and I had better add power and soon. Ultimately I managed to include the thrust gage in my scan and am sure it helped keep me safe.

My day Carrier Qualification in the Demon was not particularly memorable for being either good or bad. We

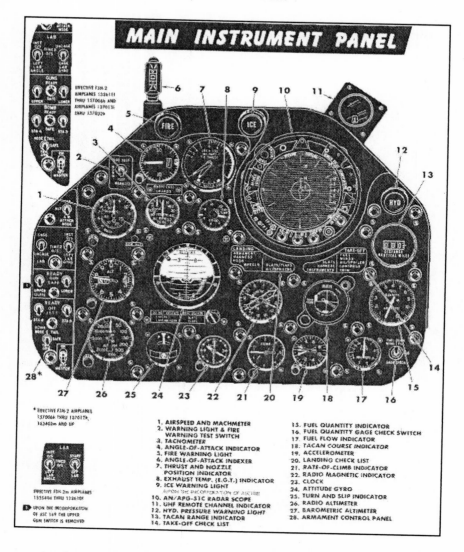

MAIN INSTRUMENT PANEL

1. AIRSPEED AND MACHMETER
2. WARNING LIGHT & FIRE WARNING TEST SWITCH
3. TACHOMETER
4. ANGLE-OF-ATTACK INDICATOR
5. FIRE WARNING LIGHT
6. ANGLE-OF-ATTACK INDEXER
7. THRUST AND NOZZLE POSITION INDICATOR
8. EXHAUST TEMP. (E.G.T.) INDICATOR
9. ICE WARNING LIGHT
10. AN/APG-51C RADAR SCOPE
11. UHF REMOTE CHANNEL INDICATOR
12. HYD. PRESSURE WARNING LIGHT
13. TACAN RANGE INDICATOR
14. TAKE-OFF CHECK LIST

15. FUEL QUANTITY INDICATOR
16. FUEL QUANTITY GAGE CHECK SWITCH
17. FUEL FLOW INDICATOR
18. TACAN COURSE INDICATOR
19. ACCELEROMETER
20. LANDING CHECK LIST
21. RATE-OF-CLIMB INDICATOR
22. RADIO MAGNETIC INDICATOR
23. CLOCK
24. ATTITUDE GYRO
25. TURN AND SLIP INDICATOR
26. RADIO ALTIMETER
27. BAROMETRIC ALTIMETER
28. ARMAMENT CONTROL PANEL

made three catapult shots and three arrested landings and did what was called "hot-refueling," i.e., kept the engine running while the flight deck crew refueled the airplane through its single point refueling receptacle. After my third

Hot-refueling at the base of the island

landing they taxied me aft of the ship's island to refuel. Parked barely three feet off the safety line delineating the landing area, I had a front row seat from which to observe a flight of A4 Skyhawks that had arrived for their initial Carrier Qualifications.

My eye was drawn to one of the Skyhawks that seemed to be having more trouble than the others. Since my radio was tuned to the LSO frequency, I could hear all radio calls and LSO instructions. The one call that electrifies any Carrier pilot, and causes his heart to leap, is the LSO's staccato call, with ever increasing urgency and volume of, "power, Power, POWER" for you know an airplane is dangerously low and settling at the ramp. Amid one such call, the approaching A4 hit the ramp shearing off all three landing gear; luckily the

A4D in Carrier Landing configuration

hook caught a wire and dragged it to a stop right in front of me, resting squarely on its two under wing fuel tanks. No fire, no smoke, it just sat there about three feet shorter than a normal A4. Obviously it was going to need a lot of power to taxi out of the landing area. The speed and precision with which the flight deck crew surrounded the airplane and extracted the pilot was impressive. Within minutes, the "Cherry Picker" (Navy slang for crane) lifted the airplane and cleared the landing area. Carrier Qualifications continued as if nothing untoward had happened.

My memory of the six night landings is as vivid as the memory of the ten day landings is hazy. As I climbed into my Demon on the ship that first night, my concept of a "black night," darkened a hundred, maybe even a thousand fold. A Carrier deck, with only its red lights illuminated, qualifies as one of the darkest places in or out of this world. The darkness was oppressive. Until now the area around Key West had seemed black at night, but it didn't compare with the near total blackness of the mildly pitching deck of the USS Lexington that night. It was frightening. The darkness was the bogeyman from my youthful dark closet; the monster lurking behind the rustling tree beside the dark road; the center of the rock lined well, fifty feet down to the black water below; it was all my fears come true at once. The blackness paled the memory of the white wooden roller coaster at Buckroe Beach. Even the familiar glow of the red instrument lights in the cockpit provided little consolation. Every nightmarish story regarding the dangers involved in night Carrier operations raced and re-raced through my mind reverberating with increasing and terrifying intensity. The stark reality I had failed to imagine as I dreamed of becoming the "Superman" in the small yellow Navy trainer faced me at this moment. The basic Cro-Magnon response of fight or flee took on a new meaning. It was fright and flight combined. I was scared to death and willing to admit it. Unsuccessfully I tried to push the reality of the blackness toward the back of my mind and set about preparing for my first night catapult launch. Although all my Demon training had taken place in the vicinity of Key West, and included hours of flying over black water, there was no comparison with this. The inky blackness continued to flood my consciousness. A quiet private conversation with God, "Lord, if this is the end, may I please come to be with You," was my final consolation.

As I followed the waving ghostly yellow wands skillfully manipulated by the Taxi Director, my mind slowly responded to the task at hand. Once on the catapult, the wands extinguished, and again, total blackness, not a single light in front of me. The seat of my pants registered the slight heave of the deck, but my eyes could not perceive any motion. The world no longer existed. I imagined how a sailor during Columbus' time must have felt with his "flat earth theory," as he sailed slowly toward the nonexistent black horizon, knowing any moment that his tiny ship might fall off the edge of the Earth into the black abyss beyond.

The Catapult Officer's green wand flashed to life and started to revolve rapidly in a small circular motion. With calculated reluctance, I pushed the throttle full forward, carefully checking each instrument as the J-71 slowly spooled up to 100% rpm, hesitated for a moment and selected full afterburner. "Make sure everything is perfect before you touch that navigation light switch," I cautioned. "Unfortunately, everything looks okay." I pressed my head hard against the headrest, took a deep breath, and flipped the navigation light switch to "on." The Catapult Officer's green wand made a large vertical three-quarter circle, touched the deck, and disappeared into the black. In an eternity of less than a second, the enormous steam-generated force of the catapult pinned me against the back of the seat as it accelerated me into the black nothing ahead. My full attention, and trust, was focused on the red glow of the dimly lit black and gray attitude indicator in the center of the instrument panel. My life depended on its flawless performance. My internal accelerometer judged the acceleration along the catapult as normal. My brain admonished in a slow rhythm, "Fly those instruments, fly those instruments." When the acceleration stopped, I rotated the nose ten degrees up, tried to hold the wings level, and without looking, reached for the landing gear handle and lifted it up.

As the altimeter climbed slowly through 300 feet, I deselected afterburner and at the Radar Controller's request, started a gentle left downwind turn. My heart was racing.

For the moment, the intimidating blackness went unnoticed, as my eyes had not wandered from the more comfortable familiarity of the tiny round instruments behaving quite normally in front of me. Only after leveling off at 600 feet on the downwind, did I dare risk a glance to my left in hope of catching sight of the Carrier. No such luck. "Fly the instruments; Check your heading; Come left another fifteen degrees; Fly the instruments," I created my own airborne guidance. As incredible as it seemed, it was even blacker out here than it was on the ship. I sneaked another peak outside. The red light on the Lexington's mast was barely visible but I had no idea how far away it was or in what direction it was steaming. The Fox Corpen (the course of the ship) was only a notation on my knee board. It was impossible to judge distance. Again my brain cautioned, "Fly those instruments, Believe those instruments."

With welcome relief, the headset interrupted my singular concentration, "Alpha Delta One Zero Seven, turn further left heading one seven five degrees, perform your landing checks, Over." The ship's Radar Controller sounded calm and professional. I relaxed a micro degree, slowed down, extended the gear, checked the fuel, and dropped the hook. Three tiny green lights advertised the gear was down and the lack of a red light in the hook handle confirmed its extension. The radar controller continued, "Alpha Delta One Zero Seven, turn left heading zero six zero, say your fuel state, Over."

Trying to appear calm, "Alpha Delta One Zero Seven, forty two hundred pounds." With my heart pounding faster than the airplane was flying, I didn't fool anyone, least of all myself.

"Alpha Delta One Zero Seven, come further left, heading three three zero degrees, the ship will be one mile at your twelve o'clock, Over."

"Alpha Delta, One Zero Seven, Roger." As I rolled out on heading I sneaked another peek straight ahead. He was right; there was a small white light with an even smaller red light suspended above it. Unfortunately the lights had no shape, no direction and no motion. They were merely two small pinpricks of light in a black, black sphere of intimidating nothingness. While I now believed in the light at the end of the tunnel, I never expected it to be so small nor so far away. There wasn't going to be enough fuel to fly that far. I modified my normal instrument scan to include an occasional peek over the nose to reassure myself that the light at end of the tunnel was still in front of me. Fortunately it was. The Radar Controller announced, "Alpha Delta One Zero Seven, half mile call the Ball." I acknowledged, took my eyes off the instruments, and tried to make sense of the tiny pattern of lights ahead. The green datum lights of the mirror were clearly distinguishable but there was no definition to the runway lights. I focused my attention on the mirror and guessed at the lineup. As the yellow meatball appeared between the two lines of green lights, I eased the power and the ball abruptly disappeared low. "Power, Power," I made my own LSO call. As the meatball reappeared, I let it ride a little high and made my call, "Alpha Delta One Zero Seven, ball, four thousand pounds." The response was the familiar and friendly voice of the VF-101 LSO. He didn't have to ask if my hook was down as the steady angle of attack indexer lights relayed that information. "One Zero Seven, you're a little high, start it down. Your lineup is good," he stated.

Small consolation, I agreed with him and liked the "little high" part, but my lineup was not at all obvious. Gradually the center line lights separated into individual points of light but provided little additional information. I was surprised at how slowly I seemed to be gaining on the ship, for the landing area didn't seem to be getting any bigger. LSO, "A little power now; hold what you've got." In the last few hundred feet, the runway lights exploded in one rapidly expanding motion and accelerated toward the airplane. I was lined up slightly right but it all happened so fast, it was impossible to correct in such a short time. The meatball slid rapidly left and high as the F3B slammed onto the deck. I felt that lovely, firm, hard tug as the arresting wire dragged the Demon to a stop with the engine still responding to my request for full power.

I had made my first night Carrier landing. It was exhilarating but terrifying. It had all happened so fast. I was powerless to know what I had done, right or wrong, but there was little time for reflection. The Taxi Director's yellow wands impatiently signaled hook up, and start a right turn out of the arresting gear. If I thought my heart was racing following the catapult launch, that was only a slow trot compared to what it was doing now, even with the relief of knowing I was safely aboard. I still had to do this five more times. There was no doubt night Carrier landings were *NOT* going to be my favorite thing! The radio interrupted my thoughts as a stern voice commanded, "Alpha Delta One Zero Seven, turn your lights off."

We all use the term "Pucker Factor," and I can't think of a situation where the term is more appropriate than in a night Carrier landing. Pucker factor is not a simple term, but a combination of many things. We all know the margins for error in any Carrier landing are small, and an accumulation of small errors can easily and quickly create a situation from which recovery is nigh unto impossible. With the unforgiving nature of Carrier Aviation, the result can mean disaster. We also know that the information available at night is dramatically less than during the day. At night you always make an instrument approach to a visual landing on a tiny landing strip which seems even smaller, because it is only three short rows of lights which show little relative motion until you are almost on top of them. Pucker factor is what you feel when you know you are betting your life on doing a nearly perfect performance, with less than perfect information, in a harsh environment, with anxiety at its peak, when you don't feel comfortable because you don't fly enough at night to feel comfortable, or proficient, and on top of all that, you're scared to death. That's what pucker factor means to me.

While I was taxiing onto the Starboard Catapult, one of my classmates launched from the Port Catapult. It was fascinating and exciting to watch the yellow-red afterburner

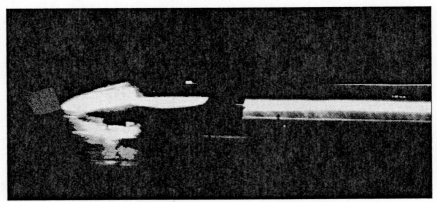

Night launch of a Demon in full afterburner, 1964

plume, accented with faint blue and yellow diamonds, hurtle down the catapult into the inky blackness. I hoped that whoever it was shared some of my fright. The persistent yellow wands again beckoned me forward. I was now sorry I had reveled in the launch of my classmate, as it had destroyed a goodly portion of my night vision adaptation. I felt the nose wheel start its climb over the aft end of the catapult shuttle and added a little power to help it along. As the wheel dropped over the front lip, I jammed on the brakes to keep from rolling too far forward. In the seat of my pants I was aware of the nose strut bobbing up-and-down, but again there was no visual sensation to accompany the feeling. As the cable was attached to the catapult hooks located at the root of each wing and the shuttle moved forward to take up the slack, the Demon creaked in protest. "Please airplane, I've got enough to worry about without your complaining."

A deck man holding a lighted red board with black grease penciled numbers on it appeared to my left to confirm my aircraft weight. It was close enough. I acknowledged with a thumbs up. Those numbers are used to set the catapult pressure for the launch. I was still checking the settings of my flaps and slats when the rotating circular green motion of the Catapult Officer's wand signaled it was time to advance the throttle for my second night catapult launch. I wasn't about to be rushed. Even if I couldn't see it, I was determined the black world would turn at my speed.

Once again the tiny circular dials indicated the engine was functioning fine at 100%. I pushed the throttle outboard and forward into full afterburner, momentarily envisioning the yellow brilliance of the previous Demon's afterburner, and checked the gages. Still OK. I pressed my head back, stared at the attitude indicator and flipped the navigation light switch to "on." Slightly more than a second went by; no kick in the butt; no rapid acceleration; no anything; nothing! I desperately wanted to look to my left to see if the Catapult Officer had actually given the launch signal but dared not take my eyes off the attitude indicator. "Something must be—;" The catapult fired in midsentence. I overshot the desired ten degree nose up attitude by a couple of degrees but the airplane was lighter now and it didn't seem to mind. I coached myself to stay on the instruments for I now knew there was absolutely no information to be gained from looking outside. My heart was again racing as I deselected afterburner, leveled off, and turned downwind. The Radar Controller promptly started giving me vectors for my second approach.

I was only slightly more comfortable as I turned final toward the ship. The tiny lights of the ship didn't seem any larger or better defined than on the first pass; they only served to emphasize the incredible blackness. When the yellow meatball appeared on the mirror, I stopped it between the green lights and called, "Alpha Delta One Zero Seven, Ball, three point two."

"Roger ball," the LSO responded.

I started chanting my familiar, "meatball, lineup, angle of attack," but I may as well have been saying, "meatball, angle of attack," for I still couldn't discern my lineup.

"Zero Seven, you're drifting a little left," interrupted the chant.

I corrected to the right. A little closer in, I began to perceive the relative motion of the runway lights. It was apparent I was now overshooting to the right. As I concentrated on the lineup, the meatball drifted above the green datum lights.

The LSO reacted, "You're moving right and going high, bring it down some. That's good. Hold what you've got. A little power now." Almost immediately the hook grabbed a wire and snatched the Demon to a stop. This time I remembered to turn off the navigation lights as I raised the hook. The Taxi Director was already waving me out of the landing area.

There were two airplanes in front of me to launch, allowing a few moments to ponder the first two landings. There had to be someway to get my lineup sooner. In close I was making too many, and too large corrections, too late. Let's see, my fuel is 2900 pounds, "Bingo" fuel is 2000 pounds, looks like only one more landing before I'll have to refuel, that is, if they get me launched soon. The flight deck seems a little less dark now; ghostly figures scurry around the airplane in front of me. Yellow wands wave aircraft onto both catapults simultaneously. Even in the darkness, or more correctly, especially in the darkness, the flight deck continued its organized orchestration. "Well, what do you think One Zero Seven, are you ready to give it another try?" I asked aloud over the intercom. "It looks like you're holding up okay, let's do it," I said, answering my own question.

The third catapult launch was only slightly more comfortable. At least I didn't feel rushed and captured the ten degree nose up attitude right on. My heart, however, continued in overdrive. This close to "Bingo" fuel meant that if I didn't get "trapped" (catch a wire) this pass, I'd have to go to NAS Cecil to refuel and probably wouldn't get my six landings tonight. I was here now, with a good airplane, and the landings seemed to be getting easier. Mostly I didn't want to go back to square zero and start the "fright" all over again on another black night.

A different controller's voice gave me a heading downwind and explained it would be an extended pattern because an F8 Crusader had boltered and was a mile and a half ahead of me. I couldn't resist sneaking a peek to make sure I agreed with the distance. There was a tiny white light ahead but I had no idea how far. "Concentrate on your own airplane, Warren." Continuing to talk to myself, "I've got to get my lineup sooner and anticipate the burble. The airplane is definitely flying me, rather than the other way around, and I'm still getting too rushed near the ramp."

Continuing downwind, the controller announced, "Alpha Delta One Zero Seven, come left heading three one four, the Crusader is off your left wing tip, you're behind him."

"Alpha Delta One Zero Seven, heading three one four."

On final, I rechecked the gear, flaps and hook. The ship was so far ahead, it was barely visible. "Fly the instruments until you get closer." I relaxed slightly as the well-trimmed Demon continued toward the dimly lit ship.

"Alpha Delta One Zero Seven, half mile call the ball, Over."

"One Zero Seven, Roger ball, two point two, Over."

"Roger, ball," the LSO acknowledged.

I concentrated on the tiny runway center line and continued talking aloud to myself, "Get your lineup early, angle of attack, lineup, meatball. OK, the ball should start up about now, anticipate, good, add a little power or you'll get slow, lineup, meatball, lineup, lineup, lineup looks good, ball a little high." Wham! The Demon hit the deck and snagged a wire, throttle up, throttle back, lights off, hook up, "Not bad." Still scary. Heart continuing to race.

Pri-Fly instructed, "Alpha Delta One Zero Seven, you'll be spotted aft of the island for hot refueling, say your fuel state, Over."

"Roger, One Zero Seven, fuel one point nine," I replied, and dutifully followed the waving wands. The Demon was no sooner chained to the deck than the fuel quantity gage started to increase. It stopped at 4,700 pounds. My weight would be 28,360 pounds. There was barely enough time to self-critique the three landings before the ever impatient yellow wands beckoned me forward and smartly passed me to another set of wands near the Port Catapult.

There were fewer airplanes on and around the ship now. As always, the Demons were the last ones leaving the pattern. As the nose wheel dropped over the shuttle, the lighted red board with the grease-penciled weight appeared, it was close enough, i.e., slightly high. The catapult shot surprised me a little because the airplane felt noticeably sluggish on rotation. "That small increase in fuel shouldn't have made that much difference." I turned downwind feeling a little more confident. The brief respite had apparently helped. I followed the Radar Controller's directions and called the ball with four point two thousand pounds of fuel. My ability to ascertain lineup had improved but was still not great. In close the ball went slightly low, I added power, no change. "You're a little low Zero Seven, bring it up," the LSO instructed sternly. I was also a little slow so I added a lot of power, too much. Over the deck the meatball disappeared rapidly off the top of the mirror. I touched down but there was no comforting tug from the wire, throttle full forward, BOLTER.

"BOLTER, BOLTER, POWER," the LSO screamed.

I was way ahead of him. If I could have pushed the throttle any further forward, any faster or any harder, I guarantee I would have. The engine was still spooling up, as the white runway lights disappeared in a flash beneath the nose. For a moment I just sat there staring straight ahead at the inky blackness, waiting for my brain to catch up with my galloping heart. My first coherent thought was, "Shit." My second thought was a bit more constructive, "Get on those instruments and NOW!" My heart established a new record high for beats per minute.

The controller's voice helped calm me down, "Alpha Delta One Zero Seven, come left, heading, one four zero." The sound of my heavy breathing echoed loudly in the earphones as it was magnified by the inter phone system. As I called the ball, the LSO commented, "Zero Seven, nice pass, last time you had a little too much power over the ramp. Fly the ball all the way to touchdown. You were lined up nicely." His calm confidence synergised my own.

I started my landing approach ritual, this time aloud but more softly, "Meatball, lineup, angle of attack, lineup, a little left, move slightly right, looks OK, going a little high, a little power off, put it back on, put it...not too much." Wham! Rapid deceleration. "That's got to be a number three wire." The last two landings, while not perfect, were safe enough.

Barely airborne, Pri-Fly called, "Alpha Delta One Zero Seven, your signal is Bingo, I repeat Bingo, Navy Cecil Field bears two eight seven degrees, forty-seven miles, Over."

Gear up, out of burner.

In my calmest tone of voice, "Alpha Delta One Zero Seven, Roger, Bingo." I was fully Carrier qualified in the F3B. I wonder what that's worth?

The 10,000 foot runway at Cecil Field looked like miles and miles of super highway, no hook required this time. The Ready Room was a jubilant place. Four new Demon drivers had passed their most difficult test and wouldn't even have it spoiled, for the LSO wouldn't debrief us until tomorrow. At the BOQ, exhausted, but much too excited to sleep, I called Linda in Key West to let her know it was over and to share my elation.

My orders were to Fighter Squadron Thirty One, VF-31, one of two Demon squadrons stationed at NAS Cecil Field, Jacksonville, Florida. We had even arranged to rent a house from one of the VF-101 instructors, LCDR Ernie Waller. As usual, Linda drew the task of ensuring our household goods were packed and shipped. She followed me to Jacksonville a week later. The next time I saw her, Hal Seaman, Larry Barringer, and I passed her going in opposite directions on Normandy Boulevard. It was one of those, "Hey guys, I think that was Linda we just passed," and it was.

Fighter Squadron Thirty One

I reported to Fighter Squadron Thirty One (VF-31) on November 12, 1962. VF-31 traces its lineage to one of the Navy's oldest Fighter Squadrons, Fighting Squadron One-B (VF-1B) which was commissioned on July 1, 1935 and served on the Aircraft Carrier Langley (CV-1) flying the Boeing F4B-4.[1] The original Squadron insignia was the shooting stars.

Felix the Cat Insignia on Boeing F4B-4

In 1964, VF-31 was once again flying the F4B, this one known as the Phantom II and built by McDonnell Aircraft Company. The 141 knot maximum speed of the original F4B-4 wasn't much faster than the landing speed of the F4B Phantom II. We proudly proclaimed our heritage in our Ready Room with photos of both aircraft coupled by the slogan, "Progress: F4Bs 1935 to F4Bs 1964."

The "Felix the Cat" insignia actually preceded the commissioning of VF-1B and is one of the oldest insignia in the Navy, joining Naval Aviation in late 1928. Credit goes to LT Emile Chourre who drew cartoonist Pat Sullivan's "Felix the Cat" with a lighted bomb in his paws as the insignia for VB-2B (Bombing Squadron Two B, Battle Forces).[2]

VF-1B was redesignated VF-6 on July 1, 1937 and subsequently VF-3B on July 15, 1943. The VF-3B Squadron Commander, LCDR Lou Bauer, "unofficially" adopted the famous "Felix the Cat" emblem as their Squadron Insignia. Unknown to Bauer, the Felix Insignia had been officially designated to a new VF-6 Squadron. This dilemma wasn't fully resolved until October 1945 when VF-6 was decommissioned and even then the Felix Insignia did not "officially" belong to VF-3 until July 26, 1946.[3]

VF-31 Demon lives up to the Squadron Motto, "We Get Ours at Night"

VF-31 was commissioned on August 7, 1948 with the officially sanctioned "Felix the Cat" insignia. The Felix Insignia included the original shooting stars emanating from Felix's feet up until late 1958, when they were removed. Felix naturally engendered the nickname "Tomcatters" but even that was not our official call sign, which was the unimaginative, and not well liked, "Bandwagon." The Squadron Motto was appropriately, "We Get Ours at Night," which meant we stood a lot of night alert duty on the Carrier. As for me, approximately one third of my Carrier landings were night landings.

VF-31 first saw combat in the Korean Conflict from the Aircraft Carrier USS Leyte (CV-32) flying Grumman F9F-2 Panthers. VF-31 transitioned to the McDonnell F2H Banshee in 1953, the McDonnell F3B Demon in 1956 and the McDonnell F4B in 1964.[3]

Unfortunately, the Squadron's early experience with the Demon mirrored the tragic development of the Demon as a fleet aircraft. In June 1957, President Eisenhower was aboard the new "Super Carrier," USS Saratoga to observe fleet operations. Jack Tefft, the Squadron Commander, and a young Ensign, Tom Aldrich, were launched in their Demons to intercept an Air Force B-52 bomber. Both aircraft disappeared off the Saratoga's radar as they were vectored toward a moderately heavy thunderstorm. Commander Tefft's engine quit and he ultimately ejected at 10,000 feet about 150 miles off the Georgia coast. After a harrowing and uncomfortable night, he was found by a search airplane and picked up relatively unharmed. Unfortunately Ensign Aldrich did not fare as well. He had also ejected and was found still in his open parachute but one of his legs was severed and he had bled to death. Two weeks later, another VF-31 Demon had a similar engine failure, this time over land. The pilot parachuted to a safe landing. The Demon was clearly a fair-weather bird. Jack Tefft's replacement, Commander Geoffrey King, was also killed in a crash at sea.[4]

In 1958, VF-31 provided fleet air defense for the Sixth Fleet in the Mediterranean during the Lebanon crisis and participated in the Cuban Missile Crisis in 1962. Fortunately, the Demon was never called upon to fire its weapons in anger.

The most notice-able difference of being in a Squadron was that, while I was definitely treated as the new kid on the block, at last I was no longer a student. It was refreshing. I liked the other pilots and felt at home.

The Squadron's Commanding Officer

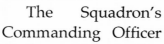

CDRs Creaseman & Pierozzi

(CO) was Commander C. Nello Pierozzi, an ex-Blue Angel, with the looks and personality we all ascribe to the members of that august flight demonstration team. Jess Creasemen was the Executive Officer (XO).

Protocol

An important event in every young Naval Officer's life is the requirement to pay a personal visit to the home of his Commanding Officer and leave his calling card. Ideally it occurs within the first week or so of reporting to the Squadron. It is carefully planned in advance and precisely timed. Linda and I read and rehearsed the etiquette requirements carefully spelled out in the Naval Officer's Official Guidebook and were quite nervous about the whole thing. We arrived in the Pierozzi's neighborhood a half-hour early, parked a couple of blocks away and timed our arrival at their doorstep to the second. Nello and Marsha were so warm and friendly they quickly made us feel at ease. I carefully slipped my calling card into the conspicuous silver tray on the buffet. We enjoyed the visit but ensured that we left after precisely the proper interval of time. We were invited back when tradition and formality were not an issue. They were a lovely couple. It was great to have a father figure for my first Commanding Officer.

Bingo

In less than three weeks after becoming a member of VF-31, the Squadron deployed aboard the USS Lexington to support the Cuban Missile Crisis. My first night Carrier experience as a "real" fighter pilot occurred about eighty miles south of Cuba. The night launch and flight went just fine. The landing, however, did not go as well. The airplane carried a full ordnance load, making the maximum fuel weight for landing considerably less than what had

USS Lexington cruising south of Cuba, 1962

been available during the Carrier Qualifications. The night was equally as black south of Cuba as it had been off the east coast of Florida. It was also my first night experience trying to meet a given "stack" time with the other airplanes holding at different altitudes and distances aft of the ship. It was a clear night and airplane lights were all over the sky. It took nearly a sixty degree bank turn for me to try to hit my departure point on time, and still I was twelve seconds late. "Bandwagon One One Two, departing, squawking, lights bright and steady, hook down," I reported.

The controller replied, "Roger Bandwagon One One Two."

Descending through 5,000 feet, I made the mandatory call, "Bandwagon One One Two, platform, Over." This call primarily served to remind the pilot of his altitude and increase his awareness of the approaching water. I leveled off at 600 feet at about the same time the CCA (Carrier Controlled Approach) Controller gave me a heading correction for the ship. I extended the gear and flaps, checked my fuel weight, and mentally calculated what airspeed an "on-speed" angle of attack indication should read. The cross-check of angle of attack and airspeed was close enough. I set about flying the instruments until the controller instructed me to call the ball.

This would be the heaviest weight and fastest landing speed for a night landing for me. I called the ball as it passed through the green datum lights and went high. I was anticipating a high power setting and had too much power. As I reduced power, the ball immediately went low. "Settle down, Warren."

The LSO advised, "You're a little low, bring it up."

I eased back on the stick to correct the low ball and promptly got a high angle of attack chevron indicating I was slow. I added power to correct for the low ball and slow speed and almost simultaneously entered the rooster tail of the ship and the ball went high. I took off some power. Concurrently the LSO hit the red wave-off lights and broadcast, "Wave-off, Wave-OFF, WAVE-OFF." I pushed the throttle full forward and transitioned to instruments as I overflew the landing area. "Great start, settle down now and remember to fly, meatball, lineup and angle of attack."

The controller broke my train of thought, "Bandwagon One One Two, continue up wind, I'll call your turn."

"Bandwagon One One Two, Roger."

"Bandwagon One One Two, turn left heading zero niner five, you'll follow a Skyhawk at your eleven o'clock, Over."

I turned downwind not feeling as confident as on the first approach. On the controller's cue, I executed the hundred and eighty degree turn back toward the ship, picked up the ball and stopped it very near the center of the datum lights. As I made my radio call, the ball drifted slightly high, I eased the throttle back and it sank slightly low. "Easy now," half talking to myself and half to the meatball. "Meatball, lineup, angle of attack." The ball drifted high again. "I'm surprised the LSO is so quiet." In close, my control of the ball seemed even more erratic than on the first pass. The ball never fully settled down to my satisfaction. Anticipating the rooster tail, I eased the power momentarily and added it back, plus a little more to preclude settling at the ramp. I obviously overdid it. I touched down as the ball exited off the top left side of the mirror.

"Power, Power, Bolter, BOLTER," was the urgent reply from the LSO.

As the controller picked me up again, his instructions were different than what I expected, "Bandwagon One One Two, your signal is Bingo, I repeat Bingo. Guantanamo bears zero one eight degrees, eighty-five miles, Over." I checked my fuel and started to argue with his instructions, there was enough fuel for at least two more passes. Half heartedly, and with a downward inflection, I replied, "Bandwagon One One Two, Roger, Bingo." Turning north, I raised the gear followed shortly by the flaps.

I now had a whole new set of problems. I admit to not being egotistical enough to believe a divert was not possible but surely not likely. I leveled off at 10,000 feet, went on autopilot, which fortuitously was working fine, and started digging through the map case to find the approach plate for Guantanamo Bay, Cuba, when the ship called, "Bandwagon One One Two, confirm your hook is up, Over."

"Bandwagon One One Two, Roger, the hook is up," I replied, while reaching over and lifting the hook handle. To myself, "Nice call ship, nice call." I finally located the approach plate, checked the TACAN frequency for

Guantanamo, and dialed it in; fifty-nine miles out with plenty of fuel. Luckily, the weather was good. They should be landing toward the east. I rechecked my knee board for the special instructions we had been given regarding landing at Guantanamo. My mind dwelled on the reason for being bingoed with plenty of fuel. I wonder how long it will take to get refueled and back to the ship?

"Fairfield, Bandwagon One One Two is switching to Guantanamo Tower, Over." My knee board instructions were not very explicit. All I had written down was: try to takeoff and land within the field boundary to avoid overflying Cuban territory. "Let's see. Landing to the east will require a fairly tight right turn and a short final to keep me clear. I'm sure glad I've got plenty of fuel. What a way to start my fighter pilot career, diverted on my first night launch. Actually a 9,000 foot runway won't be so bad. Remember you've still got to fly back to the ship tonight. I wonder what time they'll want me back?"

I broke my singular concentration, made my first radio call and waited. "Guantanamo Tower, Bandwagon One One Two, thirty-one south for landing, Over." No answer.

"Guantanamo Tower, Bandwagon One One Two, Over."

Finally, "Roger, Bandwagon One One Two, say your position and type of aircraft, Over."

Good! "Bandwagon One One Two is a Foxtrot Three, twenty-eight south for landing, Over."

"The active runway is zero nine, call abeam for landing, the mid-field arresting gear is rigged, confirm your hook is up, Over."

I patted the hook handle, "Tower, Bandwagon One One Two, hook is up, I'll call abeam with the gear."

Outside the perimeter of the base, it was pitch black. Visions of camo-clad, Cuban guerrillas clustered along the fence with large guns and bandoleers of bullets crisscrossing their chests waiting to shoot at me, flashed through my mind. When the approach lights came into view, I was aimed at the end of the runway but almost ninety degrees to it. I dropped the gear, checked the indicators and called the Tower,

"Guantanamo Tower, Bandwagon One One Two, right base, gear down, full stop, Over."

"Cleared to land, wind one one zero, ten knots, call the gear."

I was still in a thirty degree right bank, desperately trying to get lined up, when the extended runway lights disappeared under the nose. If there was ever a steep turn to final this was it. The touchdown was Carrier-landing firm. I wasn't proud of it, but then not too many things were going right on this flight anyway. As I taxied to parking, my conscience eased a little, for there were at least three other aircraft with the distinctive Alpha Charlie (AC) markings on their tails parked on the ramp. Mine would not be the only airplane from the Lexington at Guantanamo that night.

At base operations, there was a message waiting: "Charlie time for F3B Bandwagon One One Two, eleven fifteen (a.m.)" The courteous female sailor at the desk inquired, "Sir, if you'd like transportation to the BOQ, I'll get the duty driver to take you over." As I started to answer, I heard the unmistakable high pitch sound of an F3B taxing on the ramp. "Excuse me, I'll be right back." I waited at the door as the Demon shut-down and LCDR Bill McGrath climbed down the side of the fuselage, onto the wing and slid off the flap onto the ground. I would even have a Squadron mate to share my red face when I returned to the Lexington tomorrow. The duty driver took us to the BOQ.

The return to the Lexington the next day was without incident. The LSO carefully explained that the flight deck had begun to pitch significantly and everyone agreed that, with my inexperience, it would be best to divert me to Guantanamo while I still had plenty of fuel. I appreciated their concern for my safety. However, I didn't get off quite that easily. The LSO pointed out that even though the ball will go up-and-down as the ship pitches, I was overcontrolling the airplane all the way down the glide path, and didn't have it sufficiently under control to attempt a touchdown on the first pass. The second pass was better but not great. While definitely safe, I had too much power, leveled off in close, and overflew all four wires. It was a humbling but good lesson for me. Always be prepared for the worst, it can and will happen.

Contrail in the Sky

When I was flying out of NAS Cecil Field, the large areas of Positive Controlled Airspace, as we know them today, did not exist. All you had to do to signal you were ready to engage in a dogfight was to make one circular contrail over the field. It acted like a giant magnet. Airplanes from miles away were irresistibly drawn to the wispy circle, ready and eager to accept the challenge. Since no one knew or even cared who started it, everyone seemed to be chasing everyone else. We created our own theory of chaos. I have seen as many as ten aircraft, including four different types, practicing "Top Gun" maneuvers over Jacksonville and Cecil Field. You couldn't

Contrail in the sky; join the fray

get away with that kind of uncontrolled flying today. It was
great fun and good training but you didn't dare join the
fray in your Demon until light on fuel, otherwise you were
guaranteed to get shot down by an F8 Crusader, or even
worse, by an attack weeny in a lowly A4 Skyhawk. At the
lower fuel weights, the Demon turned quite well as long as
you had the afterburner to sustain the "gs." In addition, you
could augment the already high lift capability of the thick
Demon wing by selecting half flaps that also extended the
large full-length leading edge slats. Just as the leading edge
slats on the Skyhawk were a good indication of how close it
was to the stall, I can only imagine how much information
the Demon slats provided our adversaries.

The air-to-air training was outstanding. You quickly
developed a strong situational awareness and a rapid
visual scan while trying to keep your quarry in sight, not
get shot down by someone else, and most important, not hit
another airplane in the fracas. The nearest I ever came to a
midair collision was during one of these gaggles. While in

A Demon at a Crusader's six o'clock

an ever-tightening right-hand descending spiral, and very close to getting an F8 Crusader in my gun sight, an inverted Grumman F9F-8B, Cougar, flashed by my canopy between me and the F8 I was tracking. My heart leaped upward as I counted the rivets around the blow-in doors aft of his canopy. I have no idea who he was chasing, or who was chasing him, which at the moment was probably no one, for it looked like he had spun out and was no longer in control of his airplane, as gravity took command and sucked it downward. He was definitely going down faster than the Crusader and I. It broke my concentration long enough for the F8 to ease his turn and descent rate, and get his nose started upward, allowing him to take advantage of his superior thrust to weight ratio. As soon as I recognized the Crusader's nose was starting upward, I knew I was on the defensive. My best bet was to clean up the flaps and slats, drop the nose further, and try to increase the vertical separation between us. There was no way I was going to turn the corner and climb with him. Once again I proved something I already knew, the F3B was no match for an F8 in a dogfight, especially if the F8 pilot knew what he was doing, and this one did. I continued my screaming descent and headed for Cecil Field, exercising prudence over valor once again.

To the Bone Yard

I had the opportunity to deliver a retiring VF-31 Demon to the Navy's aircraft bone yard at Litchfield Park, Arizona. We didn't get to fly cross-country very often because of the lack of servicing and parts available for the few F3Bs remaining in the Navy inventory. The only remaining Demon Squadron on the East Coast was VF-13 aboard the USS Shangri-la, CVA-38. I RON'd (Remained Over Night) at El Paso, Texas International Airport, avoiding Biggs Air Force Base, where I met a VRF-31 ferry pilot who was delivering an F9F-8 Cougar to Litchfield Park. VRF-31 was a Squadron that specialized in ferrying airplanes around the country. He convinced me I was wasting time and fuel and, in general, complicating my life by filing IFR and having to make all those position reports, and that he flew VFR all the time.

Knowing full well that I was violating Squadron policy, I followed the sage old Lieutenant's advice and filed a VFR flight plan. I struggled off the El Paso runway, relishing the fact that I wasn't going to have to do all those calculations required to make the standard FAA reports at every checkpoint. The early part of my flight plan took me along the Mexican border. As if to teach me a lesson, the same navigation equipment that had worked perfectly inbound to El Paso refused to lock on to a single station along my route of flight. I had only taken a cursory look at the mid-level winds and had not bothered to calculate a single anticipated heading. I didn't even have a sectional chart with me, and if I had, the whole world below was one huge expanse of red desert with precious few discernible landmarks.

I relearned a lesson I already knew; namely, that I have never been able to break the rules and get away with it. This time I knew I was going to be in big trouble when I got back to the Squadron. I anticipated that Mexican Air Force T-28s would show up any minute to deal with my intrusion into their sovereign airspace. I fully expected to be embroiled in a full-blown International Incident. I tried every frequency I could find, except for Guard channel, to contact any FAA Service Station that would talk to me. I decided I had better confess early before I got even further in trouble. No such luck, no one would answer my calls. I pressed on, erring as far north as I dared go to avoid Mexico, wherever it was. I worked out an IFR flight plan just in case I ever got in touch with the FAA or a Military Command Post. I was over thirty-five minutes into the flight when the TACAN needle made a half-hearted attempt to lock onto Cochise. If the indication was anyway reliable, I was clearly not in Mexico, that in itself was some relief. In a few more minutes the DME and bearing pointer achieved a steady lock on. I was at least twenty miles north of my intended track. I managed to talk to Prescott radio on UHF 255.4 and filed my IFR flight plan. I was cleared to Flight Level 260 and instructed to contact Albuquerque Center for my IFR clearance. I relaxed for the first time since leaving El Paso. I had learned a good lesson the hard way. Fortunately it would be my secret. I was happy to get to Litchfield Park. It would be nice to take the airlines back to Jacksonville and let someone else worry about the navigation.

I never heard of an F3C

When I arrived at Litchfield Park with my retiring Demon, I was welcomed with open arms. I thought this a little strange but I soon found out that Litchfield was tasked with delivering an F3C (a highly modified F3B) to the Naval Air Technical Training Center at Memphis, Tennessee. They were short of "Demon Drivers" and a live one had just dropped in out of the big blue sky. That F3C was the worst looking airplane I had ever seen. It looked like it had been parked in the desert for twenty plus years. Not only was the paint all but faded away, there were external pipes running the length of the fuselage that I never did find out what they did, and likely didn't want to know. The cockpit looked like they hadn't even dusted out the cobwebs and I was certain there was at least one rattlesnake hiding in there some place.

VF-31 F3B in preservation at Litchfield Park, Arizona

They asked if I would mind flying the F3C to Memphis for them. In all honesty, I did mind. The airplane had flown exactly one flight and on that one, the pilot had to make an emergency landing back at Litchfield with a massive after-burner fuel leak. I was even more skeptical now. I spent some time in the cockpit, only to find there was a single UHF radio for communication and a single low frequency ADF receiver (the poorest of the poor) for navigation. After just taking the advice of the VRF-31 Ferry Pilot, and losing all my navigation aids en route to Litchfield, I knew for sure I didn't want to deliver this abortion of an airplane.

With typical fighter pilot machismo, I agreed to deliver the airplane, provided I could do a local test flight to satisfy myself it was safe to fly. Actually that was only one of my motives. I wasn't sure I knew how to navigate with the single ADF. I was spoiled by TACAN that gave me the bearing and distance to the station.

The mechanical part of the flight test went fine, i.e., the engine ran, the afterburner lit, the gear and flaps went up-and-down and the pressurization worked. I knew that much in the first ten minutes. The rest of the flight, I worked on tuning and tracking with the ADF. It seemed to work okay, and while not exactly elated about the prospect, I concluded that I could probably find my way to Memphis, provided the weather wasn't too bad. It looked like I could make Dyess Air Force Base to refuel and from there I could make Memphis.

The flight from Litchfield to Dyess Air Force Base was uneventful. The ADF proved accurate and my confidence was soaring. The Air Force ground crew at Dyess couldn't believe the Navy operated any aircraft in the perceived condition of this one. They were convinced the Navy had run out of money, or that I had stolen it from some museum's used aircraft lot. Never the less, they serviced the dingy Demon while I filed a flight plan to Memphis. The Memphis weather, while not great, was acceptable. As I was accustomed to seeing in Florida weather forecasts, isolated thunderstorms were forecast in the Memphis area at the time of my arrival.

In typical Demon driver fashion, I came out of afterburner soon after takeoff to conserve as much fuel as possible. It was the longer of the two legs. Up until about two hundred miles from Memphis, the flight was great. Slowly the ground below began to fade in a thickening gray-purple haze and the forecast thunderstorms started to pop up in increasing numbers along my route of flight. Unseen lightning flashed red inside the clouds and occasionally sharp jagged white lightning charged toward the ground. Still I was not particularly concerned because, at best, the thunderstorms were scattered and my fuel pretty close to my fuel plan. Closer to Memphis, the lightning delighted in creating excessive static on the single UHF radio and to my dismay, the ADF decided it liked the thunderstorms better than the tuned ground stations. The ADF needle did its share of just spinning around and delighted in pointing out the strongest thundercloud in the area. In my imagination, time slowed down and the fuel burn rate went up in direct proportion to the increasing number of thunderstorms racing me to the Memphis airport. I made my next to last position report with a lot less confidence in my estimated time of arrival at the next navigation fix. I contacted Memphis and got the latest weather report and, while it could have been better,

Memphis was well above landing minimums. As my luck would have it, the Precision Approach Radar (PAR) was out of service, therefore a radar-guided approach was not an option, but then the airport was "officially" VFR. My problem was not the clouds but finding the airport in the haze. I had practically memorized the ADF approach to the airport, but that wasn't much help as the Memphis ADF signal was no match for the highly charged thunderstorms. Navigating solely by heading and time, I started my descent. I entered the haze south of the field outbound on the first leg of my mostly guess work teardrop approach. When I made the right turn back toward the field, or at least where I believed the field to be, if the visibility was the predicted three miles, I would have eaten my helmet. Hoping for the best, I continued to descend. At the legal VFR ceiling of 1000 feet, the haze reduced with an attendant improvement in visibility. I rapidly scanned the horizon, squinting hard, hoping to improve my visual acuity. I stopped my descent at the 600 foot minimums and was prepared to go around if I didn't see something recognizable as an airport. I knew, however, that I would really be lost then, since I only had a vague idea of where I was now. About twenty degrees to the left of the nose was a relatively clear area. I turned slightly left and "voila" there was an inviting gray concrete runway. I immediately pulled the power to idle, extended the speed brakes, flaps and gear almost simultaneously. Slowing down was something the Demon did very well. I called the tower about two miles out and landed straight in. The Memphis ground crew wasn't the least bit phased by the way the Demon looked, as they had obviously encountered other Navy aircraft as hideous as this one. I am likely one of a

Reserve crews, casual, but good

handful of Demon drivers that can claim flight time in an F3C, for whatever that's worth.

I hitched a ride back to Jacksonville in a Navy Reserve P2V Neptune. The Reserve crew seemed a lot more casual than the Active Duty crews but flew better. They treated me like a special guest and let me ride most of the way in the clear panoramic Plexiglas nose. We flew low and slow. It was a wonderful view. Linda picked me up at Navy Jacksonville.

Dependent's Cruise

It was customary to do a one-day Dependent's Cruise prior to departing for the Mediterranean. Family support is vital as the long separations are particularly stressful on everyone. It was important for the loved ones left behind to have an appreciation for what it was we would be doing during the deployment. Linda came along, but with the motion of the ship, coupled with her pregnancy, she didn't feel very good most of the time. The Ready Room never smelled, nor felt, as good as it did that day, until possibly the next Dependent's Cruise.

One cold wife

This particular cruise almost turned into a disaster. One of the events was to rendezvous with a Tanker and conduct an underway refueling. Part way through the fuel transfer, the Tanker almost ran into the side of the Carrier. It was close enough that as the Tanker rapidly disappeared under the overhang of the starboard flight deck, the Saratoga sounded the collision alarm. The two ships came within a very few feet of hitting each other. It was a very tense few seconds as the refueling ceased and the two ships miraculously maneuvered to avoid a collision. It was obvious that flight operations were not the only dangerous activity we engaged in.

Refueling demonstration nearly a disaster

"See the World" at last

I was excited, apprehensive, looking forward to, and dreading a seven-month cruise to the Mediterranean. I was excited about "Joining the Navy and seeing the world," apprehensive about leaving Linda alone and not quite three months pregnant, looking forward to some exciting flying, and putting into practice what I had diligently trained for, but dreading the long separation.

The time leading up to the departure passed quickly. The Squadron's preparations for the deployment reached a peak about two weeks prior to the ship's departure. It was complicated by the requirement to get the flight crews Field Carrier Qualified. The entire Air Group needed day and night FCLPs. There were simply not enough night hours to fit everyone in. It was not unusual to have a three or four o'clock in the morning night FCLP period scheduled at Whitehouse Auxiliary Airfield. During the Squadron's wives indoctrination, the remark had been made that a high percentage of pilots involved in accidents had not eaten properly before the accident. Linda had taken this seriously and dutifully got up at all hours of the night or early morning to ensure that I did not fall in the unfed category. I probably didn't appreciate it as much then as I do now.

In the midst of these operational requirements, Linda and I strived to spend as much time together as possible. The social structure of the Squadron was especially active to promote a bonding between the wives who would be left behind. The adage that "Being a Navy Wife is one of the toughest jobs in the World," could not be truer. I never fully appreciated the strength and fortitude demanded of Linda at that time. If I were her, I would have been frightened to death.

We had precious little time off during the feverish push to get everything ready for the deployment. Linda and I managed a memorable day trip to Silver Springs. The impending absence made the time very special. Linda was more beautiful than ever as the early signs of motherhood stirred within her. We were

"Early Motherhood"

very close. In our own way, we tried to store up enough loving to last until we could once again share it in person.

"Close It Up"

We flew the Demons from Cecil Field to Mayport Naval Air Station to be hoisted aboard the USS Saratoga. The small airfield barely handled the hundred odd aircraft assembling on its apron. The competition between Squadrons started with the fly-in. As the aircraft flew into the break above the critical eyes of the ground and air crews collected below, none other than perfect formation was expected. I was tail-end Charlie in our flight of four Demons. LCDR Ken Cornell calmly said, "Close it up guys, let's look sharp." The three of us took him at his word and tucked in closer than the turbulence from the midday Florida sun really allowed. Every small bump rippled down the formation being amplified

"Sir, were you having engine trouble?"

by each successive machine. I was determined to hold the perfect position no matter what. Both hands were working overtime but I hung in there. We executed a near perfect ascending fan break, with all four aircraft rolling and pulling up simultaneously, achieving the desired separation by each successive pilot pulling less "gs" in the break.

The Plane Captain complimented me on the formation, paused a moment and asked, "Sir, were you having engine trouble?"

"No," I replied, "Why do you ask?"

"Well, Sir, your airplane was the only one puffing black smoke as you all came into the break. I've never seen a jet do that before. I was sure something was wrong."

I must have been pumping the throttle rapidly from idle to 100% rpm to stay in position. Unfortunately, or fortunately in this case, the old J-71 engine couldn't respond that fast, so it was probably all for naught. Anyway, we did VF-31 proud and that was the whole idea. The airplanes were hoisted aboard the next day.

Off to the Mediterranean

On the day of departure, the drive to NAS Mayport was quiet, touching, filled with love but hovering on the verge of tears. Linda and I mostly made small talk about whether I had everything I needed and what she should do about "baby" things. We avoided the painful subject of separation until we had arrived, and stood among the large emotionally charged crowd gathered in the shadow of the USS Saratoga. We held each other tightly and tears began to flow. Still we avoided the subject.

"I love you Linda. I think I had better go now."

"Good-bye, Honey, I love you and I'll miss you."

I kissed her hard, climbed the boarding ladder, saluted the Officer of the Deck, and disappeared into the gray interior of the Saratoga; home for the next seven months. I tossed what little remaining gear I had brought with me on the desk, lay down on the bunk and, in pensive silence, stared at the mattress springs above. I wasn't sure I wanted to go, but deep down inside I really did. I hoped Linda understood, but then how could she?

"Get up Warren, you're not the only person going on this cruise, get your ass in gear," I prodded. Several of my squadron mates were gathered in the Ready Room, including my roommate, Jim Carnes. Jim was talking to Ensign Pat Rogers, another one of our ground pounders (non-aviators), so I joined them. It was also Pat's first cruise.

I decided I'd better go up on the flight deck, just in case the Captain needed my help getting underway. From the catwalk, I peered down on four of the world's smallest tug boats nuzzled up against the port side of the bow of the Saratoga. There was simply no way those tiny boats were going to budge this behemoth of an Aircraft Carrier. I needn't have worried. With lots of white

USS Saratoga departs Mayport

water churning up from their screws, they carefully eased the Carrier out into the harbor channel. Once the Saratoga was headed in the right direction and under its own power, the tugs joined up on either side like little ducklings following their mother across a pond.

They escorted the Carrier until it passed through the jetties of the St. Johns River, tooted their whistles and retreated to their familiar habitat. We were on the way to the Mediterranean. It was March 29, 1963.

The Ready Room

The pilot's Ready Room is the hub, the heart, the control center, the briefing room, the movie theater, the social center, and the living room for the Squadron. Each flight crew member is assigned a number that represents his official rank within the Squadron. Yes, a few days difference causes there to be rank differences, even among Ensigns. Seating is arranged by rank and suitably marked by the respective officer's helmet hanging over the owner's seat.

The Officer of the Day (OOD) sits at a desk in the front of the room and keeps the flight schedule up-to-date as missions are flown. During flight operations, the front of the room is reserved for flight crew briefings. Above the OOD's desk is

LT Fleming briefs a flight

a television set known as the PLATT where an aft-looking camera mounted in the flight deck landing area shows the airplanes during their approaches and landings. Along the far wall is a chart where the pilot's landing performance is dutifully recorded for all to see.

After flight operations are completed, the Ready Room becomes the theater. It is the OOD's responsibility to procure the best possible movie aboard the ship, or endure the wrath of the highly critical and vehemently vocal audience assembled for the evening's entertainment. Movies were passed between ships and between Air Group Squadrons, and Ship's Divisions. You could always tell when some interesting, i.e., usually sexy, part of the movie was about to occur because the film would start to chatter and skip from the abuse the film had taken from being rewound and shown, rewound and shown, rewound and shown, and ..., you get the idea. All movies were subjected to suitable running commentary from the highly participative audience, often making even bad movies enjoyable.

The Mailman

Most people believe the most important aircraft on an Aircraft Carrier are the fighters and bombers, but they would be totally wrong. The most important aircraft on the ship is known as the COD (Carrier Onboard Delivery) aircraft. The COD delivers the parts and replacement personnel, but most important, it brings the mail, the movies, and the cookies from wives and girlfriends, not necessarily the same person.

The COD looks high!

Most of us watch the PLATT when our Squadron aircraft are landing and only tacitly observe the other aircraft, except for the COD. The COD pilot gets more impromptu and unsolicited pseudo LSO help than does any other pilot flying aboard the ship. Mail call is a major event eagerly anticipated by all. Dean Padrick, one of the few bachelors in the Squadron, clearly held the record for the most mail received, but not from a brooding covey of females as one might expect. Dean received more junk mail than the rest of the Squadron combined. His mailbox was always cluttered with colorful advertisements and get rich quick schemes.

The two Fighter Squadron Ready Rooms are located on the O-3 level, i.e., just below the flight deck, providing the quickest access to the flight deck to facilitate launching the alert fighters should the need arise.

The Flight Deck

The flight deck of an Aircraft Carrier qualifies as one of the most dangerous work places in the world. The potential for instant death lurks in every spinning

The Flight Deck: crowded and dangerous

propeller, every air-hungry jet intake, every high velocity flaming exhaust, in the tons of volatile fuel and explosive ordnance handled daily, and in the high kinetic energy of every catapult takeoff and arrested landing just to name a few. The Navy attempts to reduce the risk through technology, organization, and training, but in the end it boils down to the individual performance of the men and boys who are willing, or in some cases reluctant, to accept the awesome and challenging responsibility of the job.

There are few situations where so many life-critical functions must be performed perfectly every time to prevent a disaster. For example, when an airplane is connected to the catapult shuttle for launch, a cable attaches the airplane to

One man's error, another man's life

the flight deck to keep it from moving down the catapult until sufficient steam pressure is attained to ensure the proper end or flying speed is achieved. A small dumbbell shaped metal fitting is used to connect the cable to the airplane. This fitting is appropriately called the "holdback" fitting and is different for every airplane. One of my fellow VF-101 classmates, LTJG Joe Janiac, was killed when an A4D, Skyhawk, holdback fitting was used for his F3B. His Demon was towed down the catapult and fell nose first off the bow with too little airspeed to fly. One man's life for another man's error.

The flight deck, while dangerous, is also a place of art and beauty. Myriads of multicolored shirts identify the various functions of the men wearing them. Precise choreographies accompany the launch and recovery of aircraft. As they work, men lean into thirty knots of wind, tilting at precise angles to balance the constant pressure of the wind against their bodies. The pageantry extends the entire length of the flight deck. Airplanes rise and descend on the

A parade of Demons

elevators like props appearing and disappearing on a giant stage. Steam escapes along the Cat tracks creating artificial fog. Plane Captains mimic Morley's Ghost as they trudge slowly beside their moving aircraft with heavy tie-down chains draped over their shoulders, ready to secure their airplane to the deck the instant it stops.

The Aircraft Carrier

The Carrier itself floats in an ever-changing sea of blue, green, white and gray. Sometimes angry, sometimes placid and serene, the sea leaves no doubt that the mighty War Ship is always at its mercy and subject to its moods. The Carrier Pilots' world is controlled by the elements of the sky and the sea. A brilliant azure sky might be accompanied by a wildly pitching and rolling deck, or a dark ominous low ceiling may find the Carrier running firm and true. What's more, it can all change from the time of launch to the time of recovery.

When the period of the waves is short, the Plane Guard Destroyer climbs and dives into every wave. In an attempt to emulate the tiny gray machines escaping its big brother ahead, the Destroyer first tries to fly over the wave by

The Carrier rides on a sea of color

extending its bow well into the air, only to stall out and come crashing nose down into the sea, its bow disappearing in a geyser of white spray. The Carrier on the other hand rides these waves straight and true. When the period of the waves is long, it is the Carrier that climbs and dives into the waves, sending salty spray gushing over the bow, while the Plane Guard Destroyer simple rides up-and-down in a rhythmic ballet.

The Carrier never sleeps. Internally it is an uninterrupted symphony of high and low frequency vibrations and humming sounds, as various equipment turns on and off. You can forecast the surface wind by gauging the speed of the ship. If there is no wind, the entire ship shudders harmonically as the four giant screws churn the water to drive the ship at maximum speed. When the natural wind is high, there is only a low rumble as the ship moves just fast enough to maintain steerageway. I always enjoyed a trip to the fantail to watch the brilliant whites and greens as the agitated water

Plane Guard Destroyer, a welcome companion

emerges behind the ship. It holds the same attraction most of us have for flames in a fireplace.

Brightly colored aircraft tails identify the Squadrons to which they belong. Early in the cruise red, yellow, and white lines give precise definition to the flight deck, only to dim as the continuous flight operations take their toll on the deck's surface. Signal flags adorn the mast like colorful wash day clothing, relaying information to the armada surrounding the Carrier. The sense of color is heightened by the damp salty smell of the sea, interrupted by the pungent sulfur smell of stack gas, the occasional suffocating loss of oxygen from the expended kerosene of a jet engine, or the delightful oily whiff of burned Avgas.

Grow Up Fast

The Navy has a different approach to its Aviation Officers than does the Air Force. All Navy pilots and Naval Flight Officers are expected to hold a major non-flying job in the Squadron. My assignment in VF-31 was as the Aircraft Division Officer. I was in charge of the Airframe, Engine, Avionics and Personal Equipment shops and reported directly to the Aircraft Maintenance Officer. Fortunately the Navy learned a long time ago that the enlisted Chiefs could run the shops infinitely better than an inexperienced officer just out of college. This tenet certainly held true in VF-31 and my Chiefs, like Gunnery Sergeant Hustler in Pre-Flight, held my highest esteem. What I was not expecting, nor prepared for, was the fact that I would be responsible for all the personnel actions required. During my first year as a Naval Officer, I learned more about life, especially the bad side, than I had learned in the previous twenty-one years. I dealt with financial, alcohol, drugs, and marital problems. I handled disciplinary, and performance problems, not all of which were restricted to the younger enlisted men. In my youthful sheltered life, I had only heard that such things existed and had absolutely no experience to draw upon. I found myself setting up budgets to help get people out of debt. I talked to/counseled men old enough to be my father about marital problems. I defended people at Captain's Mast. I wrote letters to family members and tried to help people hopelessly addicted to alcohol. Like a father or "mother hen," I worried about each of them when we entered a new foreign port with its many unhealthy enticements. I discovered more about the negative side of life than I ever dreamed existed and did what little I could to make things better.

I actually enjoyed being with the enlisted troops and learning about the innards of an aircraft and even exercised some of my engineering education. Like most of us, more than anything, we like to be listened to and appreciated. I did a lot of listening. It was fun to climb around the aircraft and hang out at the engine test stand on the stern of the Carrier. Although young, these men gave their utmost to successfully complete the Squadron's mission. The Chiefs were as good as they came and deserved the reputation they had earned. The Navy was absolutely correct when they said, "It's the Chiefs that run the Navy."

Carrier Air Group 3

The aircraft complement, known as Carrier Air Group Three, CAG-3, was made up of two Fighter Squadrons, VF-31 and VF-32; two Light Attack Jet Squadrons, VA-34 and VA-36; a Light Attack Propeller Squadron, VA-35; and a Heavy Jet Attack Squadron, VAH-9. In addition to the Carrier Air Group aircraft, there was: a Photo Reconnaissance Detachment, VFP-62; an Airborne Radar Detachment, VAW-12, and a Rescue Helicopter Detachment, HU-2. At any given time, the Carrier was home to between eighty and a hundred aircraft.

CAG-3 aboard CVA-60, 1963–1964

The Aircraft

VF-31 flew the McDonnell F-3B, "Demon," an All-weather Interceptor.

VF-31 F3B Demon

VF-32 flew the Vought F8D, "Crusader," an agile Air-to-Air Fighter with limited radar and night capability.

VF-32 F8D Crusader

VA-34 and VA-36 flew the Douglas A4C, "Skyhawk," a small but highly effective Attack Airplane.

VA-34 A4C Skyhawk

VA-36 A4C Skyhawk

VA-35 A1H Skyraider

VA-35 flew the propeller driven Douglas A1H, "Skyraider," one of the finest Air-to-Ground Aircraft in existence at the time.

VAH-9 A3D Skywarrior

VAH-9 flew the Douglas A-3D, "Skywarrior" the Largest Carrier Aircraft in the fleet.

VFP-62 F8U-1P Photo Crusader

VFP-62 flew the Reconnaissance version of the Vought F8U-1P "Crusader."

VAW-12 E1B Willy Fudd

VAW-12, the Airborne Radar Detachment flew the Grumman E1B, affectionately known as the "Willy Fudd" or the "Stoof with a roof," a highly capable Airborne Radar Control Aircraft that greatly extended the radar capability of the Carrier. We Demon drivers spent many hours working with the Airborne Radar Controllers.

HU-2 HUP-1 Retriever

Last, but certainly not least in the eyes of all the pilots, HU-2, the Rescue Helicopter Detachment flew the Piasecki HUP-1 "Retriever," a tandem-bladed, single-engine Rescue Helicopter.

The Transit

The ten days it took us to cross the Atlantic were filled with hours of training and aircraft maintenance. By far, the largest number of lectures were devoted to vivid descriptions by the Flight Surgeon of all the horrible diseases we would contract should we even glance at one of the numerous "ladies of the night" who would proposition us once we made port. We were also provided political and protocol briefings on the various countries we would visit.

Most important, we accomplished a major portion of the required aircraft related ground training and completed the attendant exams. I would have much rather been flying, but we were clearly a captive audience. Compared to the tempo of operations we would experience once in the Mediterranean, the crossing was like leisure land, but I couldn't wait to get there.

Welcome to the Mediterranean

April 8, 1963 was a beautiful day. The bow of the USS Saratoga carved its way through the Straits of Gibraltar and into the Mediterranean Sea. It had been ten days since we left the Caribbean. I was scheduled for the second launch. It was great to be airborne again. I was beginning to feel more like a sailor (black shoe) than an aviator (brown shoe). Early in the flight, I did at least fifteen aileron rolls to savor the exhilaration of flying and to experience the power of turning the world upside down. The two Demons, alternated doing radar controlled air intercepts on each other and took a

USS Saratoga transits the Straits of Gibraltar

turn practicing dry refueling plug-ins with the duty A4C tanker. It was a great flight and I felt especially good about the landing. In other words, I wasn't dreading the LSO's debrief.

I entered the Ready Room all smiles and quickly surmised something was wrong. There was little talk and a lot of long faces. Two airplanes had failed to return from the first launch, an F8U-1P Crusader from the Photo Reconnaissance Detachment and an A1H Skyraider from VA-35. A search effort was being organized. It was a quiet, sad afternoon. Neither airplane nor pilot were found. The first of several solemn trips to the Forecastle to honor the memory of fellow Crew Members and render the "Navy Hymn:"

> *"Lord, guard and guide the men who fly*
> *Through the great spaces in the sky.*
> *Be with them always in the air*
> *In darkening storms or sunlight fair.*
> *Oh, hear us when lift our prayer*
> *For those in peril in the air."*

A Fine Roommate

Ensign Jim Carnes was one of four "ground pounders" (non-Aviator Officers) assigned to the Squadron. He was a big man; over six foot four and well built. We shared staterooms for the Demon cruise and most of the Phantom cruise until he left the ship and the Navy. A Junior Officer's state room is little more than a six by ten foot cubicle containing two bunk beds, two combination dresser/desks at the end of the bunks, two metal chairs, and a wash basin. All VF-31

VF-31 Officers, 1963: 1st row, L to R: Knaus, LT; Cornell, LCDR; Pierozzi, CDR; Creasman, CDR; Franklin, LCDR; Way, LT. 2nd Row: Regan, LT; Wood, LTJG; Rogers, ENS; Padrick, LTJG; Fleming, LTJG; Gore, LT; Mase, LTJG; Carnes, LTJG; Connor, LTJG; Seaman, LTJG; French, ENS; Bachman, LTJG; Green, LTJG; Hall, LTJG.

officer staterooms were located on the O-3 level, the level immediately beneath the flight deck. Our stateroom was located on the port (left) side of the ship and smaller than most, for the Number Two Catapult literally ran through our room. It was the Aircraft Carrier equivalent of the proverbial railroad track that runs through the house. To accommodate the catapult, the wall slanted upward at a sixty degree angle from about two feet above the right side of the upper bunk to the ceiling. Although I offered Jim the lower bunk, he said he preferred the upper. I was never sure why, for he could barely turnover and was surely unable to sit up in the bunk in other than a hunched over position. The catapult took some getting used to. The first test shot every morning was a guaranteed wake-up call and always came as a surprise. It was like being overtaken from behind by a low-flying jet you didn't know was coming. At the end of its stroke, the cata-pult shuttle is stopped with a resounding thud as it crashes into a water brake located in the bow of the ship. Retraction of the shuttle consists of several seconds of rattling metal sliding roughly over metal. While not as loud as the Catapult shot, it was considerably more irritating because of its duration.

Fleet Exercises

Joint exercises with the NATO countries and those conducted against the other Sixth Fleet Aircraft Carrier in the Mediterranean were the most fun. During one of the NATO exercises, while proceeding back to the Carrier after a rather uneventful mission, a glint off the water caught my eye, probably just a ship. "What the heck, may as well check it out." I rolled into a sixty degree bank and halfway through my three sixty degree turn, I discovered a flight of four Spanish, World War II, Hienkle 111 twin-engine bombers, with their distinctive rounded wings, chugging along no more than fifty feet off the water and headed directly for the Saratoga. Well

Spanish World War II Hienkle 111s

below the ship's radar detection capability, they hadn't been seen by any of the screening Destroyers or the Willy Fudd Airborne Radar Sentinel from the Carrier.

"Fairfield, Bandwagon One Zero Two has four bandits bearing two three one degrees, twenty miles, descending to investigate, Over." I started a descent from behind the finger-four formation. The mottled gray aircraft skimming low across the water looked like a scene straight out of a World War II movie. Estimating their speed to be about a 140 knots, I slowed, extended the flaps, and joined the center of the formation from behind. Several serene seconds passed before my presence was noticed. Three of the four airplanes moved laterally to give me more room. Heads popped up like corks in every window. What a contrast in aeronautical technology! Surely they were impressed with the Navy's radar detection capability when the proper term was LUCK. I waved, tapped the afterburner, pulled up, dipped my wing, and raced toward the Saratoga to make my "Charlie" time, proudly claiming four kills.

When I arrived overhead, the ship was experiencing its own scene from World War II. The Saratoga's flight operations were being totally disrupted by four, dark-blue, inverted gull-wing, Corsairs from the French Navy. The pilots were having the time of their lives. There had never been a more thorough buzz job. The Corsairs did everything but fly through the hangar deck openings and I'm sure if they thought they could have, they would have. Since they were not in communication with the ship, there was little we could do but wait until they were done. Saratoga's airplanes orbited overhead in clusters. As always, we Demon pilots were pressing for priority due to our low fuel states.

Where is Hal?

At night or in inclement weather, aircraft marshal aft of the Carrier on an assigned TACAN radial but at different altitudes. Your particular distance is obtained by adding fifteen to the first two digits of your assigned altitude. On a clear night, aircraft lights blink all over the sky. Individual departure times are used to establish the required landing intervals. We worked hard to depart the assigned fix to the second. It was considered highly unprofessional not to be on time. In the holding pattern, it was not unusual for me to alternate between full afterburner and idle power, with bank angles up to sixty degrees, depending on whether I was early or late.

One early evening, Hal Seaman and I flew individual Combat Air Patrol (CAP) missions with one of the several Destroyers in the Task Force. Most Destroyers had their own TACAN, so we often used them for positioning during these missions. The early takeoff meant we would get a twilight landing, something we dearly loved, because we got credit for a night landing for what was really a "pinky" landing,

A3D gets a "Pinky Landing"

i.e., while there was still enough light to see the water and perhaps the ship. Even the slightest hint of a horizon was coveted. Squadron Commanders normally rated these missions.

On this particular night, Hal departed the marshaling point "on time" and I departed "on time" behind him. Hal called "Platform" in front of me. I was surprised I couldn't see him, but didn't give it much thought. Evidently the ship was more surprised because they didn't have him on radar, and asked him twice to repeat his distance from the ship. Both times Hal came back with approximately the right distance. He was only a few miles ahead of me and well within visual range, but I couldn't see him. Maybe his white taillight was out? When the Radar Controller queried him the third time, Hal sheepishly admitted that he had forgotten to switch back to the Saratoga's TACAN, had marshaled on, and made his landing approach to the Destroyer with whom he had worked his CAP mission. Hal later confided that he had thought it unusual not to see any other airplanes in his marshaling area. Of course every airplane on the CCA (Carrier Controlled Approach) frequency knew what had happened and went out of their way to guarantee the rest of the Air Group knew about it. Since Hal was one of the Air Group LSOs, he was well-known and ribbed unmercifully for days about his "Destroyer Approach."

Suspended in Black

When there is no natural wind, the Aircraft Carrier must operate at high speed to achieve the required "wind over the deck" for launch and recovery operations. While normally

not a problem for launches (all but the Number Three Catapult are aligned with the axis of the ship), disturbed air from
the island and other protrusions on the ship create additional
turbulence in the approach path, and the angled deck causes
a right crosswind for landing. During daylight operations, a
fairly well established technique is to aim the nose of the aircraft at the notch where the angled deck intercepts the axial
deck and this keeps you pretty well aligned for most of the
approach. You still have to take out the crosswind correction
as you cross the ramp to achieve a straight-on engagement
of the wire. As always, it is a different story at night, when
it is difficult enough to determine lineup without the added
complication of a crosswind.

On this particular night, I was having more than my usual
difficulty with lineup. It wasn't until I was near the ramp
and the sudden rush of lights started to race out toward me,
that I realized I was pointed well right of the runway center
line. I made a late and apparently too large correction to the
left. I barely snagged the number four wire going smartly
right to left. When the airplane stopped, there was no visible
reference anywhere. I was suspended in a black, but happily
dry, nothingness. My adrenaline was always so high on any
night landing that any small anomaly was blown out of proportion. This night was no exception. Not knowing exactly
where I was, I wasn't about to retard the throttle until I was
convinced I was safe.

The airplane had stopped completely outside the runway
lights. I didn't realize it at the time, but the Demon is long
enough, nearly sixty feet, that it is possible for the nose
wheel to drop into the catwalk on an extremely off-center or
right to left engagement. I must have come awfully close. A

Taxi Director ultimately appeared in my peripheral vision, much further right than I had ever seen one before, and gave me the signal to throttle back. I slowly retarded the throttle and the retracting arresting wire pulled me backwards into a still dark, but recognizable world. It was a pleasant relief to be back from my short trip into the black abyss beyond.

Optical Illusion

Night formation, like a night Carrier landing, is difficult because of the lack of visual cues available during daylight flying. Naturally, the rendezvous and join-up are the most difficult and hairiest maneuvers to perform. Overshoots are common. While it is relatively easy to perceive the lead airplane's drift angle, it is hard to estimate his heading angle and your closure rate until very late in the rendezvous when you are often too close to make salvageable corrections. When flying multiple airplanes in night formation, the profusion of lights as the individual airplanes join up can also be confusing.

As an aid in holding the desired formation position once there, the Demon had four small rectangular yellow lights, one embedded in the trailing edge of each wing tip and the other two located on either side of the fuselage slightly aft of the engine intake. When you were in the proper position, the navigation light on the wing tip leading edge, red or green, depending on which side you are on, and the two yellow lights form a horizontal line and are equidistant apart. After flying formation for an extended period, I often experienced a confusing and highly disconcerting optical illusion at the whims of these lights. Most of the time, the lights lined up and even appeared to lay in the same vertical plane, although I knew the yellow fuselage light was a wing's length away. Occasionally the red or green navigation light would appear to jump from the wing tip to the fuselage, dwell there for a moment and jump back to the wing tip again. I was so programmed to react to any relative motion, that when the light moved I always made a control input, disturbing my formation position. I never admitted this to anyone for fear it was the result of some severe physiological malady that might keep me from flying.

Now It Works, Now It Doesn't

One night, the overhead fire extinguisher system in Hanger Bay II inadvertently activated, deluging all aircraft and personnel with thousands of gallons of sea water. We were fortunate, or unfortunate as the case may be, only one Demon was filled with water. What a mess! It took two weeks to clean and/or replace the damaged components, particularly those in the electrical and avionics systems. When the work was completed, I flew the maintenance test flight and found only two discrepancies: 1) the cabin pressurization system didn't follow the proper altitude schedule and 2) the radar was inoperative in flight.

The pressurization problem was traced to an improperly secured cockpit drain plug and the radar worked perfectly. The radar was signed off with the proverbial, "Could not duplicate, ground checks OK." On the next flight the pressurization worked as advertised, but the radar was again written up as, "Inoperative in flight." The Avionics Technicians checked the radar from stem to stern and couldn't

Sometimes you just don't get it right the first time

find anything wrong with it. By all rights it should be one of the best radars we had. After the fourth write-up and the third "Ground checks OK, next pilot check," we decided to replace the main radar unit.

When the technicians started to disconnect the transmitter unit from the airframe, they found a connector aligned with the fuselage that was slightly loose. Apparently the force of the catapult launch would pull the connector apart and the arrested landing would push it back together. Consequently, it always checked out perfectly on the ship but didn't work in flight. Once the connector was tightened, the radar was indeed one of our best. Just another gremlin in a highly complex system.

Roman Toga

During one of many stays in Naples, Jim and I had the opportunity to visit Rome. Jim enjoyed being a tourist as much as I did and we enjoyed traveling together. I always felt particularly safe when I was with him. Jim decided he wanted to buy his wife, Lu, a Roman toga nightgown. Surely there was no better place to do this than in Rome. We added an additional requirement to our quest, that it be modeled for us. Rather haphazardly we started visiting ladies apparel shops. In 1964, English was not as widely spoken as it is today. After several attempts at trying to communicate what we wanted, we would soon have the one sales clerk, usually a young female who had taken some English in school, surrounded by several other equally young females laughing and giggling as we described what we wanted. We would talk for a while and one of the assembled females would scurry off and come back with someone's concept of

a "Roman toga" night-gown, or at least what they thought we had described. We were surprised how little lingerie came close to looking like a toga or at least what we saw as a result of our ability to describe what we wanted. Even with the ones that came close, we never came close to getting one modeled. We had a grand time and met a lot of nice friendly people.

Me, Jim Carnes & Pat Rogers

A Dumb Idea

Lieutenant Vince Knaus and I also enjoyed flying and traveling together. In the Navy's constant quest to outwit the enemy, we were always seeking new ways to operate at sea with minimal electronic emissions from the ship. Since the Demon had the best airborne radar for its time, Vince and I were assigned the task of trying to locate and land on the Carrier, at night, without navigation aids or radio communications. Both were of course readily available should we need them.

We flew a two-ship air-to-air intercept mission and took on an extra thousand pounds of fuel from the airborne tanker. Vince, in the lead aircraft, easily located the Carrier on his radar and we flew toward it. The idea was to fly a daytime overhead recovery pattern in the black of night. At best, in retrospect of course, it was a dumb idea.

Vince broke left over the Carrier and ten seconds later I rolled into my 180 degree turn downwind. Flying on instruments while trying to keep track of Vince and the Aircraft Carrier was both taxing and dangerous. Soon after getting my gear and flaps down, almost simultaneously we realized this Aircraft Carrier was, at best, unusual. It had a small almost triangular flight deck pointing forward at the bow and similar shaped one pointing aft at the stern. The Carrier was not a carrier of aircraft but a carrier of cargo. It was a freighter, identity still unknown, but assuredly not equipped to handle two heavy weight Demons and their somewhat embarrassed pilots. If the freighter captain saw us, I'm sure he's still wondering what two airplanes were doing buzzing around his ship in the middle of the night. It was time to confess and request the Saratoga to turn on its navigation aids.

Amber Solaire

Amber Solaire was from Cannes, France and she was absolutely beautiful. Tall and thin, she had long slender legs, was beautifully suntanned and had a shape any model would love to possess. Dark brown hair framed her slightly oval face, curled underneath and rested lightly on her shoulders. Her expressive brown eyes sparkled, and when you were in her presence, they followed your every movement. I can't remember ever seeing her when her makeup wasn't immaculately applied or when her sexy red lips did not possess a slightly pouty come-hither smile. When I first met Amber she always dressed in yellow. Although it matched the Squadron patch, it didn't fit the red color assigned to VF-31 when aboard the USS Saratoga. Prior to the cruise, a number of JOs (Junior Officers) chipped in and bought her an entirely new wardrobe of red. Her favorite outfit was a red bathing suit complemented by a red drape across her right shoulder emblazoned with the VF-31 Squadron patch. I didn't speak French and Amber didn't speak English. Consequently, I knew very little about her other than that she was from Cannes, had modeled for a French cosmetics company, which had named a suntan lotion after her, or vice versa, and that she had been with the Squadron for over two years.

In the early 1960's, the Navy had not yet officially allowed females aboard combat ships. Amber Solaire was one of a very few exceptions in that she was allowed to deploy with the Squadron. Prior to the cruise, a Squadron

Officer was assigned to see that she was safely aboard and that all her needs were attended to. Much to the delight of the flight crews, her favorite spot on the Carrier was the Squadron Ready Room. During flight operations she stood at the doorway and patiently endured a friendly pat from departing crewmen and provided a friendly smile upon their return. She was as much a member of the Squadron as any of the assigned officers or enlisted men. She was so beautiful it was not surprising a certain jealousy developed among the other squadrons on the ship.

One night Amber disappeared, leaving only a cryptic note on the Duty Officer's desk indicating that: "She was leaving VF-31 for a better home." The Squadron was distraught over Amber's departure and the suddenness with which it had occurred. She was always so devoted to the Squadron, it didn't make sense that she would leave on her own. She had never done anything like this before. It was so uncharacteristic that the only plausible explanation was that she had been kidnapped. We were convinced a serious crime had been committed. An All Points Bulletin was issued for any information leading to the identity of her abductors and her safe return. Bulletins were broadcast during the morning report and daily notices posted in the plan of the day. Two nights later, a second note appeared in our supposedly "locked" Ready Room relating how much better life was in her new surroundings. There was neither signature nor hint of her abductors. Although the note was written in French, we doubted it was pinned by Amber herself.

It wasn't difficult to convince the ship's Captain, Captain Moore, that a major crime had been perpetrated on his ship. He took up our cause. There were only two possibilities.

The culprits could reside, in the Air Group or in the Ship's Company. The only clues were the two notes, and the fact that whoever it was had access to our locked Ready Room. Surely you couldn't hide a beautiful woman on a ship for any length of time before it was known where she was. The Squadron took up a collection and offered a twenty-five dollar reward for information leading to the identification of her abductors and the safe return of Amber to her rightful place. The ship was abuzz with rumors. If you were from VF-31, it was not unusual to be stopped in the passageway by interested persons seeking the latest information on Amber.

The sixth night out of Naples, and three days prior to dropping anchor at Genoa, Italy, another note appeared in the locked Ready Room. Thereafter a JO was "volunteered" to spend the night in the Ready Room to catch the phantom (bad choice of words) note bearer. It was no longer a laughing matter. We were increasingly concerned for Amber's safety.

In a last ditch maneuver, Captain Moore announced that all shore liberty at Genoa was canceled until Amber was safely returned to VF-31. Several false leads were received, none of which provided useful information. The $25 reward remained unclaimed. The threaten shore leave cancellation worked. The day prior to arriving at Genoa, an anonymous early morning phone call to the VF-31 Duty Officer announced that Amber would return at 1800 hours that evening, and that all VF-31 Officer Personnel should assemble in the Ready Room.

At precisely 1800 hours, a loud rap rattled the Ready Room door. Two JOs from VA-34 appeared in the doorway with "mop" rifles over their shoulders. Several seconds later, the CO and XO of the blue-tailed Attack Squadron appeared with Amber Solaire between them. Two more JOs armed with mops followed in quick succession. Amber looked awful. She was dressed in blue, sported a matted blue wig, but worse, she was unmistakably pregnant. From the size of her stomach, it was apparent she would deliver any day now.

Commander Pierozzi assigned LTJG Padrick and Ensign Carnes the task of caring for Amber and coming up with an appropriate response to Amber's kidnapping and inglorious return. The second day in port Genoa, we invited the officers of VA-34 to our Ready Room at 1100 hours. Several bed sheets were suspended on a rope across the front of the Ready Room. The very pregnant Amber calmly lay on a table beneath a white sheet. Commander Pierozzi welcomed the officers of VA-34 and introduced Hal Seaman who would narrate and explain the procedure. Hal intro-

Emcee Hal Seaman explains the procedure

duced "Dr. Ludwig Von Carnes." Enter Jim Carnes dressed in a white medical gown, supplied by the Flight Surgeon, his blue VF-31 beret pulled tightly down on his head, and billowing smoke like a straining steam locomotive from the largest cigar he could find. With a strong German accent, "Dr. Von Carnes" explained that the time for Amber to give birth had arrived. None other than the world-renowned gynecologist "Dr. Denio Padrick," who just happened to be attending a major medical convention in Genoa, would perform the delicate delivery. Enter Dean Padrick in green medical attire. Playing to an appreciative audience, Dean and Jim were great. They slapsticked their way through an elaborate pre-scrub procedure and a complete physical examination. Finally, to spare the audience the gore of the actual delivery, the sheet over Amber was raised until her elevated stomach was concealed. Dean was a riot as he explained the inner working of

Dr. Carnes, "The moment of delivery"

the female anatomy, and described all the things he came across as he searched for the baby. He missed his calling; he should have been a stand-up comic. At last he found what he was looking for. The attentive crowd was in stitches when, with a bang, a slap and a loud bawling, an inflated plastic Felix the Cat appeared feet first from behind the curtain. Contrary to the VA-34 boast, Amber had not become pregnant

Dr. Denio Padrick and Baby Felix

while in their care, but was obviously pregnant when she was kidnapped. Amber reappeared, dressed in red, smiling as usual, no worse for the wear.

It was revealed that this was not the first time Amber had been kidnapped. Amber was "officially classified as an Illegal Alien." Two slightly inebriated VF-31 pilots had kidnapped her off the streets of Cannes on the last cruise. You see, Amber Solaire was a paper covered plywood cutout advertisement for Amber Solaire suntan lotion. A good time was had by all. It was time to retire to the wardroom for lunch.

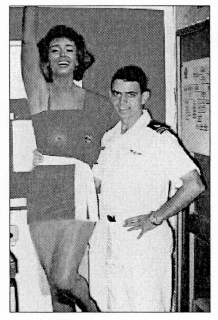

Amber back home

Who's The Boss Here?

The low stratus blocked the light of the rising sun effectively delaying morning. As I pre-flighted the dew-laden Demon, the unanticipated darkness accentuated the chilling cold. Everything was soaked. The Mediterranean was mirror calm. The only movement of air resulted from the motion of the Carrier as it maintained steerage knots through the smooth gray sea. The cockpit was cold and damp. Once the engine was started, the warm dry air from the air conditioner was a welcome addition to my environment. As I taxied onto the Number Three Catapult, low clouds reached downward and wiped across the flight deck with increasing frequency, occasionally extending all the way to the water, dropping visibility to near zero.

After carefully checking the engine instruments in basic and again in afterburner, I saluted the Catapult Officer, pressed my head firmly against the headrest, and focused my attention down the catapult track. I couldn't see the bow of the ship. The visible world ended partway down the Number Two Catapult, visibility was less than 150 feet. The catapult fired and halfway through the stroke I was still desperately trying to re-orient my thinking from its mind set of the relative ease of a day launch, with a well defined horizon, to the elevated anxiety of a night launch, with its total reliance on the flight instruments. I had not fully made the transition as the weight of the aircraft transferred from the landing gear to the wings and the outside world turned totally gray. Fighting for control, I was lucky the fog was less than 200 feet thick and was relieved to break out between cloud layers. I cleaned up the airplane and checked in on my assigned Combat Air Patrol frequency.

On climb out I penetrated a second layer of clouds at 4,000 feet and was on top at seven. After being airborne less than forty minutes, without explanation I was instructed to return to the ship and contact Pri-Fly on Channel 7. When I checked in, the Air Boss explained, "Bandwagon One Zero One, the ship has been transiting a fog bank for the last thirty minutes and is below landing minimums. We'd like you to descend in the vicinity of the ship and recommend a direction for the ship to steer to try to get us out of the fog, Over." I started down and was in the clear at 2,000 feet. When I reached the ship, the only visible part of the Saratoga was the top of its mast sticking out of the fog. It looked like the "up periscope" of a giant submarine. A dark trail of disturbed moisture traced the Carrier's passage through the fog.

From my vantage point, it was obvious that if the ship made a forty-five degree left turn it would clear the fog in less than two miles. It was the only time I would ever give an order to the Captain of the ship. The Captain accepted my "recommendation," for I observed the mast start moving left toward the clear sea. For lack of anything else productive to do, but mostly to ensure an early spot in the landing sequence, I set up a left-hand orbit about the slowly moving mast.

Airplanes collected overhead awaiting their "Charlie" signal for landing. I was the first airplane aboard. On roll out, the arresting wire stuck to the hook and the persistent pounding of the Hook Runner was not sufficient to break it loose. The Taxi Director signaled me to release the brakes so they could pull me backward to disengage the wire. As I rolled backwards the wire fell off the hook but when I hit the brakes to stop, the nose wheel cocked off to the left. In response to the impatient persistence of the Taxi Director to get me out of the landing area, I added a hand full of power and stood on the right brake. The nose swung rapidly to the right and the Demon accelerated across the safety line. I yanked the throttle to idle and hit the brakes. The wheels locked but the Demon showed absolutely no tendency to slow down. The Taxi Director ducked as he disappeared under the left wing. With the edge of the flight deck approaching at an alarming rate and my heart in my throat, I released and reapplied the brakes but the skid continued unabated. My mind started debating whether it was better to eject before, during, or after I went over the side. I elected to wait until the nose wheel dropped into the catwalk, in hopes it might keep me from going over the side. I skidded over thirty feet before the airplane stopped, fortunately still on the flight deck, but just barely.

The Taxi Director reappeared and started signaling me to start easing forward. I was determined not to move another inch until they attached a tow bar and tractor to move the airplane. I kept shaking my head from side to side,

Who's the boss here?

which only made the Taxi Director even more persistent with his "come ahead" signal. I radioed Pri-Fly, "Fairfield, Bandwagon One Oh One, I don't think its safe to taxi, I want to be towed, Over." Pri-Fly's curt reply was direct and to the point, "Follow the Taxi Director Bandwagon, and get the hell out of the way." I followed the Director but at about half the speed he wanted me to go.

The Demon's nose wheel is located directly beneath the pilot. Consequently, when you taxi near the edge of the flight deck, from the cockpit it looks like you are actually hanging out over the water. This is especially disconcerting at night when the deck lights disappear behind you and you have no

Pilot's view of taxiing too close to the edge

idea where you are relative to the edge. You have no choice but to trust the Taxi Director completely. My insistence in not following his directions at the rate he wanted, resulted in his insistence that I was going to be taxied as close to the edge as he could get me. He parked me on the port bow by taxiing me at a forty-five degree angle to the edge and requiring a near minimum radius right turn, such that the nose wheel must have come within inches of the edge. He knew I was not happy about the nose hanging over the side while holding full right brake and using lots of power to complete the turn on the damp fuel-soaked deck. It was his way of letting me know who was the "boss" on the flight deck, and clearly it wasn't me.

Don't Dunk the sailors

One of the least favorite in-port requirements of the Junior Aviation Officers was standing boat duty. The draft of the Aircraft Carrier was too deep for most of the ports we visited. If a suitable docking facility was not available, we dropped anchor outside the port a mile or so off the beach and used Liberty Boats to transfer personnel between the ship and shore. A Liberty Boat is no small device, it can carry up to ninety people. The catch was that every boat required a Commissioned Officer onboard when carrying passengers. Of course none of us, except possibly the Naval Academy graduates, had any formal seamanship training. Fortunately the boat came equipped with a highly qualified enlisted Boatswain's Mate who did all the boat handling and made most of the decisions. The poor Boat Officer was along to help with disciplinary problems and to be held responsible in the event something went wrong.

We always hoped to get the day or early evening duty, because the ability of the sailors to negotiate the loading and unloading of the boat deteriorated rapidly as it got later and they became more inebriated. It was not unusual for

The Liberty Boat on a good day

waves to create five to ten feet of vertical motion between the Liberty Boat and the boarding platform at the ship. The vertical motion was exacerbated by the simultaneous, but not necessarily synchronized, lateral motion that created huge gaps between the platform and the boat. It was easy to slip and fall into the water, or worse, get crushed between the boat and the platform. It was at best a difficult task when stone sober, nearly impossible when drunk, and impossible when inebriated friends tried to help their barely functional shipmates off the Liberty Boat. It was always a relief when they showed up on the platform when it came back into view.

Part of our Navy issue clothing was a long heavy woolen coat. Mine received a lot of usage while standing boat duty during those freezing winter nights in the Mediterranean. By the time my second cruise was over, the gold braid on the sleeves was more green than gold. I felt lucky to have survived those periods of "Command at Sea."

Boat Officer's view of USS Saratoga inbound to port

Shore Patrol Duty

In addition to standing boat duty while in port, most of us had to stand at least one day and night of Shore Patrol duty. We always vied to have this "pleasure" on the first night in port. The idea was mostly to find out where all the "good" places to go were, so we could visit them the next night before they were declared "off limits." Shore Patrol duty was never fun. It is amazing, well maybe not, how much trouble twenty-five hundred sailors can get into in one night in a country where a seemingly insignificant incident could easily become an "International Incident," and bring discredit on the U. S. Navy and the United States. My approach to Shore Patrol duty was the same as for Boat Officer duty. Let the senior enlisted members do their job and back them up as required. It was a successful strategy.

Saratoga, Where Are You?

The Mediterranean basked under the kind of sun you see in the travel brochures for the French Riviera. I kept the canopy open as long as possible, enjoying the warmth. After launch, I made a left clearing turn, descended to 50 feet, punched the clock and enjoyed skimming along the azure surface for the next eighteen minutes. As was becoming the norm, the Saratoga was operating under Emergency Communication (EMCOM) conditions and I was assigned to provide intercept practice for a Destroyer-based Radar Controller on the perimeter of the task force. The mission went fine. I chased a couple of unsuspecting airliners and felt I had properly defended my sector of the air defense perimeter.

Demon clears left off Cat 4

When it came time to return to the Aircraft Carrier, things took a different turn. The controller gave me a vector for the Saratoga. To my dismay, when I arrived over the designated spot, the ocean was devoid of ships in any direction. I suspect he vectored me to the location where he had picked me up on his radarscope, which was a long way from where I had launched from the ship. We discussed the dilemma for a while and I was getting somewhat agitated, "Don't you know where you are relative to the Carrier, can't you vector me to that position?" The reply was an immediate but not very reassuring, "Standby." After a suitable pause, "Bandwagon One One Zero, new vector is one six zero degrees, Over."

"Now we're getting somewhere." I took the vector, flew on for about ten minutes, spotted the Carrier, thanked the controller, retarded the throttle to idle, and started to descent.

Lower now; I realized I had been vectored to "An" Aircraft Carrier but not "The" Aircraft Carrier. This one had a slightly curved bow rather than the sharp trapezoidal bow of the Saratoga. It was the French Aircraft Carrier, Clemenceau. As precious fuel pumped through the engine, I climbed back to altitude and reported my deepening dilemma to the Destroyer. Fuel, while not yet critical, was becoming a concern. I got another "Standby." This time a different and much more authoritative voice stated, "Bandwagon One One Zero, vector two four zero degrees for home plate, Over."

"Roger two four zero degrees, thanks." Precious minutes, measured in even more precious gallons per hour, ticked by. Bingo, Saratoga dead ahead, no sweat. The next guy up the ladder on that Destroyer really knows his stuff; I may even make my "Charlie" time. Down I go, fuel marginal but OK. As I got lower and more aligned with the Aircraft Carrier, I was surprised and dismayed to find that someone had painted large white circles along the flight deck. That wasn't

Which way is home?

the Saratoga, it was a Helicopter Troop Carrier and not about to accommodate an F3B, even one with low fuel.

With my fuel state now critical, I did the only thing I could think of on the spur of the moment. I announced on Guard Channel in a loud voice, "Fairfield, this is Bandwagon One One Zero, my fuel state is thirty-four hundred pounds, I don't know where you are, and if you don't turn on the TACAN so that I can get home, I'm going to eject, right now!" There was no verbal reply, but the TACAN needle swung smartly to my left and the DME clicked in solidly at forty-eight miles for several seconds. I called the ball with twenty-nine hundred pounds. No one mentioned the episode once I was safely aboard the ship.

Backward Sparrow III

Toward the end of the Med. Cruise, the ship decided to dispose of its outdated Sparrow missiles. We were quick to suggest we'd be happy to shoot them for practice. To our surprise they agreed. We apportioned the missiles. I lucked out and got to fire one, a rare treat. LTJG Hal Seaman was my wing man for the firing. I would reciprocate when it was his turn. LT Max Gore was the tow plane pilot. We cleared the target area and started a head-on intercept of the red Styrofoam Delmar target streamed almost four miles behind Max's Demon. Two well-spaced radar blips marched rhythmically down the center of the scope. I confirmed target and tow plane separation, called "Judy," locked on the target and set up the armament panel: Armament Master Switch-OFF, Weapons Selector Switch-SPW III, and APA 127 Power Switch-ON.

"Cleared to Fire."

Master Arm Switch-ON. I waited until the target was in the center of the in-range circle and pressed the trigger. "Fox Away." The missile launched off the rail in a brilliant burst of red flame and white smoke. Unfortunately it didn't have the foggiest idea where it was supposed to go. The guidance system had apparently failed. The missile arched gracefully upward to the left and then dove straight into the blue Mediterranean Sea. "Damn, I'm sure glad that wasn't for real." I was disappointed.

Hal made his run on the target and had even worse luck than I did. His missile wouldn't even fire. We checked with the ship to see if they wanted it back. The answer was, "No, jettison it." I moved back and to the left of Hal's Demon for a better view of the missile as it jettisoned from the wing pylon. For some reason, at the last minute, I decided to step up just a little since the missile would be ejected downward and I didn't want to hit it. Hal counted down from three and hit the jettison button. The missile started down as it should have and forward as it should not have. It then pitched up abruptly, careened over the top of Hal's wing, missing it by

Almost two Demons with one Sparrow III

less than a foot, and headed directly for my airplane. It went underneath my wing missing it by inches. We almost lost two F3Bs to one non-functioning Sparrow III missile flying backwards. That would have made a grand accident report. It was a good thing no one was shooting back.

Mother and Daughter Satisfactory

When we departed Mayport for the Mediterranean, Linda was due to deliver our first child in September or October. It was now October and her letters indicated birth was imminent. On the Saratoga it was business as usual. I was on the early afternoon Combat Air Patrol mission, had manned my aircraft and was standing by to start. Abruptly the Plane Captain disappeared beneath the wing. Puzzled, I figured he must have discovered a hydraulic leak, a loose panel or something I had missed on the pre-flight. Shortly, he reappeared on the steps beneath the canopy, and with a big toothy smile, handed me a yellow telegram. "LTJG Gene Hall, USS Saratoga, from NAS Jacksonville Hospital, stop, Daughter born 1032, 6 October, stop, Mother and daughter satisfactory, stop. "Ya-hoo! I'm a father, a baby girl and what's more on my birthday. What a fantastic birthday present! Ya-hoo! I'm a father. But wait, what does it mean, "Mother and daughter satisfactory?" When I think of someone in the hospital in satisfactory condition, I think of them as

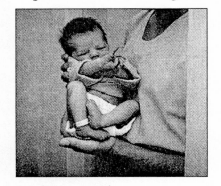

Pamela Lyn, age: 1 hour

being pretty sick. "Is everything OK?" I wondered. I flew the mission but was totally preoccupied as I vacillated between the elation of being a father and the agony of not knowing what was meant by, "Mother and daughter satisfactory."

Of course, I had been prepared for weeks with the duty cigars for everyone and enjoyed all the congratulations. I expressed my concern regarding the wording of the telegram to Commander Pierozzi. He suggested I talk with the Flight Surgeon. The Flight Surgeon went with me to the ship's Communication Center where we sent a telegram to NAS Jacksonville Hospital for more information. Several long hours later we learned everything had gone just fine. Both mother and daughter were in fact doing great. Trudy, our next-door neighbor, had taken Linda to the hospital the night before with false labor pains that turned into real ones the next morning. Linda sent me a Polaroid photograph that Trudy had taken of Pam within hours of her arrival. It was an awful picture but I loved it and couldn't wait to see her in person.

Pleasure Cruise

The Navy has always called their Aircraft Carrier deployments to the Mediterranean, "Med. Cruises." With the possible exception of visiting the numerous ports-of-call throughout the Mediterranean, a Carrier deployment bears little resemblance to your typical pleasure cruise. Days at sea entail long arduous hours of work in an environment that is intolerant of inattention or error. Twelve hour shifts are the norm and it is not unusual to conduct flight operations around the clock. When flight operations cease, there are a

A rare day of rest at sea

multitude of exercises and drills that are vital to the combat readiness of the Carrier.

During a particularly strenuous at sea period, the Captain decided we deserved a day off. We just happened to be in the southern portion of the Ionian Sea in the vicinity of the Greek Islands, so we toured the Islands from afar. We took advantage of the opportunity to mimic a pleasure cruise. We lounged about the flight deck and soaked up some rays. For me it was a once in a Navy tour event and an enjoyable one.

Cancel the Launch

Late in the cruise we were heavily involved in a conventional ordnance exercise off the coast of Sardinia. To maximize the training, we pushed the flight and flight deck crews to the limit of their capabilities. The autumn night came early. It was pitch dark as I made my way to my Demon spotted at the very stern of the ship. This was not unusual, as the F3Bs were almost always the last ones launched and the first ones recovered due to their limited fuel. The flight deck was especially crowded as red-shirted ordnance men worked feverishly to complete the required ordnance loadings. Bomb and rocket carts were everywhere. It was becoming increasingly obvious that this particular launch was going to be delayed. I patiently waited with the engine running and, as always, contemplating the oppressive blackness of the high-overcast night. It wouldn't be long before the airborne aircraft would be out of fuel before they could get us launched. As if reading my mind, Pri-Fly responded, "Cancel the launch, spot all airplanes forward and clear the deck for landing."

As is the case in most accidents, an inexorable chain of events was being forged that would end in tragedy. My Plane Captain removed the chains and placed them around his neck. Following the commands of the Taxi Director, I inched slowly forward and stopped. Two Skyhawks made approaches and were waved off by the Air Boss in Pri-Fly. My Demon was unchained a second time and I taxied several more feet forward and slightly to the right of the center line but still in the landing area. In an instant and without any warning, my world turned into a holocaust as the third airplane to approach the ship landed straight ahead and right through my aircraft. The sick deadening thud of the impact didn't seem especially violent, but the fireball that erupted was beyond belief. Pieces of both airplanes tumbled wildly about in the blazing yellow and orange mass of flaming fuel. Black, recognizable silhouettes of ailerons and rudders appeared, disappeared, and reappeared in the irregular flame as they flailed about in the inferno. Fortunately, my

Plane Captain was standing in front of the aircraft and was only bowled over and not seriously hurt.

The force of impact propelled my twisted, broken and blazing aircraft across the deck as if it was made of paper. Fortunately the push was to starboard rather than to port, which would have been over the side. The still intact nose section of my mortally wounded Demon crashed into and wedged itself against the tail of an F8 Crusader. The stop seemed more abrupt than the start. My brain shifted into low gear as I carried on this ridiculous conversation with myself: "Well, Warren, don't you think you ought to get out of here? Yeah, that's probably a good idea." I calmly actuated the electrical canopy open switch and the canopy started a slow migration aft. The intense heat from the conflagration, which, by this time, had engulfed the entire aft end of the Aircraft Carrier, sped up my thought processes considerably. I jerked the emergency release handle to disconnect the parachute and survival kit from the ejection seat and pushed upward. Even with an elevated and increasing level of adrenaline, I could barely lift the weight of the parachute, seat cushion, and survival kit. Hastily, I undid the quick release fittings for the parachute and dove headfirst over the canopy bow onto the nose of the profusely burning and rapidly disappearing Demon. I half slid and half fell onto the aft fuselage of the Crusader and tumbled down onto its elevator, landing with a thud. A sharp pain pierced my neck and I could no longer move my head. Somehow my helmet was attached to the F8. The microphone cord had apparently dropped into one of the small blow-in doors located near the vertical tail. I reached up, grabbed the cord, and with one yank, broke all four electrical wires. My strength was improving. By this time, the ship had gone to "General Quarters." Men were running in all directions in only semi-organized chaos.

Someone, still unknown to me, grabbed me and stuffed me bodily into the catwalk that surrounds the perimeter of the flight deck. It seemed to take an eternity to make my way to the Ready Room. I was convinced that whoever was in whatever had hit me, could not possibly have survived and was as relieved as everyone else to find that Ken Cornell was not even scratched. His hook had miraculously caught a wire and stopped his Demon on the deck. Most of the nose and right side was missing.

My Demon was burning so profusely the Crash Crew pushed it over the side. One pilot broke his wrist when, sans ladder, he made the giant leap from the cockpit of his A4C onto the flight deck. Four deck crewmen were killed and several more were badly burned. In all, nine airplanes

LCDR Cornell's F3B the next day; ugly

were destroyed. Airborne airplanes reported the fireball was visible upwards of seventy-five miles from the ship. August 15, 1963 was a tragic night for the USS Saratoga.

The sequence of events that forged the accident, had somehow allowed all runway lights and the Fresnel visual landing system to be turned on; an A4C Skyhawk to be positioned with its exhaust directly over the LSO's platform preventing him from giving a wave-off signal; and no one in Pri-Fly either observed LCDR Cornell's Demon approaching the deck, or if they did, they failed to call him or wave him off because of a fouled deck. The result was a major tragedy.

A Taxi Director, Jack Sherrill, Jr., AMS3, was posthumously awarded the Navy-Marine Corps medal for heroism that night. Realizing that the approaching aircraft was headed for a flight deck crash, he raced into the flight path of the incoming aircraft waving his flashlight director wands in an effort to wave-off the approaching Demon. The aircraft struck and killed Sherrill as it crashed on the flight deck.

Another deck crewman, Larry D. Sowers, AN, was also awarded the Navy-Marine Corps medal for his selfless and alert action in aiding injured flight deck personnel. He disregarded his own personal safety in pulling several men from the flames that engulfed much of the Saratoga's flight deck.

As with every accident, a full investigation was conducted. The Air Boss bore the brunt of the responsibility and was relieved of his job. One comic relief aside was a report that followed me around for about six weeks, noting in less than complimentary language, that I had lost a set of classified authentication codes. The security people would not accept the fact that those knee board size pieces of paper were securely deposited two hundred fathoms beneath the sea in the carcass of one severely damaged F3B. I honestly think they wanted me to dive down and retrieve them.

Surviving the Cruise

As the end of the cruise approached, it was natural to start counting the days until we transited the Straits of Gibraltar westbound for the good old USA, our loved ones, and for me, a daughter I had yet to meet. Now that I more clearly understood the risks involved in this extremely dangerous business, I began to contemplate, first the number of night landings I needed to survive, then how many more flights I would fly and, in general, developed a growing concern for completing the cruise. It wasn't a major preoccupation, mostly an awareness I had not entertained during most of the cruise. The nearness of the end seemed to amplify the risk. I guess I was ready to go home, seven months was a long

Launch the aircraft

time. The other squadron pilots likely had similar thoughts but it was not a subject we discussed. I don't believe it interfered with my flying, nor improved it either, it was simply there in the back of my mind. I was clearly more experienced now, certainly highly proficient, still anxious to fly, and more competitive than ever. I do know my pre-catapult prayer, "If this should be the end Lord, may I please come to live with you?" Was rendered a little more earnestly.

Rota Spain

Our relief Carrier was the USS Shangri-la with VF-13 aboard. VF-13 was the last Demon Squadron on the East Coast. Since we were scheduled to transition to the Phantom II, our Demons were to be retired to Litchfield Park, Arizona. F3B parts were already in short supply, thus it was prudent to station a couple of spare Demons at the Navy Base at Rota, Spain, in the event VF-13 required aircraft or parts replacement. Unfortunately the Saratoga was operating off the west coast of Italy, which meant the F3B had neither the range nor navigation capability to fly to Rota. The solution was a simple one. A VAH-9, A3D tanker could provide both the navigation requirements and, with its in-flight refueling capability, the additional fuel. Hal Seaman and I were afforded the opportunity to deliver the two airplanes. The flight required two

A3D Tanker provides navigation and fuel

in-flight refuelings and was the longest single flight I ever made in the Demon. We had two delightful days in sunny southern Spain before returning to the Saratoga by COD.

Approaching the A3D for fuel

The Landing Record

There is no place where the competitiveness we learned in Pre-Flight training is more evident than in the Carrier landing. A pilot's landing performance has always been an important indicator of his overall airmanship. It is vital to be at, or near, the top of that competition. Not only were we debriefed by the LSO after every landing; his comments were posted on a chart in the Ready Room for all interested parties to see. Three grades are used to describe a landing:

VF-31 Demon too low over the ramp

the best is an "OK" pass, the next is a "fair" and the worst is a "cut." The latter indicating you did something dangerous. The ideal is a no comment, "OK three wire." Each Squadron has its own convention for displaying the information. In VF-31 we used a cat's paw for an "OK" pass, with or without comment; descriptive symbols for a "fair" and a skull and crossbones for a "cut pass." Night landings were posted in red. The landing summary chart accomplished several things other than foster competition, which was fierce. It allowed the pilots and the LSO to look for trends. It allowed the Squadron Commander to compare performance within his Squadron and the CAG (Carrier Air Group Commander) to look at the pilots collectively across Squadrons. As we entered the closing week of the cruise, I was leading the Squadron for the most "OK" passes. The Squadron LSO, LT Jim Wood, was a close second. In the final outcome he beat me by one "OK" pass. I felt quite good about my landing record, especially for a first cruise aviator. I easily qualified as an F3B and a USS Saratoga centurion (100 Carrier landings), logging my 100th Saratoga landing on the night of August 18, 1963.

Plane in the Water

One of saddest events of the cruise occurred on the very last day of flying in the Mediterranean. Four Crusaders were practicing air-to-ground gunnery against a sled being towed behind the Carrier. It was fun to be up in vulture's row and grade the shooting prowess of the pilots as they dove on and raked the target with their twenty-millimeter cannons. LCDR Harvey apparently got target fixation or simply waited too long to start the pullout from his dive. His Crusader pancaked into the sea, exploding on impact. The splash and fireball lasted only a second or two and were swallowed up by the sea. None of the wreckage or the pilot was recovered. Another sad trip to the forecastle to memorialize a fellow aviator who had given his all, with another rendering of: *"Lord guard and guide the men who fly through the great spaces in the sky..."* Perhaps my concern for making it through the latter part of the cruise was warranted after all.

USS Shangri-la relieves the USS Saratoga, October 19, 1963

We were relieved by the USS Shangri-la and exited the Mediterranean on October 19, 1963, westbound for home.

Launch the Alert Aircraft

The U.S.Navy and the Soviet Air Force played a "Cat and Mouse" game anytime our Aircraft Carriers transited the sea-lanes between the mainland and the Mediterranean in either direction. It is easy enough to determine when one of our Carriers was scheduled to deploy from the states or even from the Mediterranean for that matter. The information is unclassified, and stateside, it is widely publicized in local newspapers.

The object of the game for the Soviet Air Force was to over fly the Carrier Task Force in International Waters and gather as much photographic and electronic information as possible. The object for the Aircraft Carrier was to remain undetected if possible and, if unable, to intercept the Soviet aircraft as far from the Task Force as possible. We fighter pilots liked the latter best of all. It did, however, entail many hours of standing alert duty during the crossings, with the possibility of a mid-ocean launch and recovery without benefit of a divert field. The Navy later coined the term "Blue Water Operations" for these open sea operations.

The normal readiness posture during these crossings was two Crusaders spotted on the bow catapults and two Demons on the waist Cats. If VFR weather conditions existed, the Crusaders were manned for a five minute alert during the day, and the Demons during the day if the weather was IFR and on a fifteen minute Ready Room alert at night. We stood two hour watches. We had not experienced any over-flight activity on the eastward transit.

About three days out of the Mediterranean on the way home, in what we pilots call "Dog Shit" weather, I was sitting my two hour alert in the Demon on the Number Three Catapult. From the cockpit, the ragged ceiling looked as if the top of the Carrier's mast was propping it up. Rain alternated between moderate and heavy, creating hundreds of rivulets along the canopy. As the Carrier rolled and pitched, sheets of foamy white salt-spray exploded backward over the bow. I was glad to be on Cat Three and not on one of the bow catapults. As I sat there contemplating the weather, I envied the Crusader pilots who probably didn't even bother to pre-flight their aircraft this morning.

I punched the sweep second hand on the clock to see if it was still running. It was, with forty minutes to go. I wonder what's for lunch? I craned my neck to look behind me. The flight deck is deserted. It's sure going to be nice to be home. I hope Linda is as excited as I am. I can't wait to see our new daughter. Thirty-seven minutes to go. No self respecting Russian pilot would dare venture out in this crummy weather. I know I don't want to. I'm surprised they're even keeping us on alert. I can't believe they would launch us in this mess; at least I hope not. Thirty-four minutes to go. Let's see, Jim Wood is my relief, I hope he's early. My butt's sore.

In concert with the flight deck bull horn blaring, "Launch the alert aircraft," an army of men poured out of Flight Deck Control into the pouring rain. I couldn't believe my ears. Surely they're not going to launch us into this weather, not in the middle of the ocean. Unfortunately, it looked increasingly like they were. I'd better stop day dreaming and start thinking seriously about some serious IFR flying.

A yellow shirt appeared to my left waving a plastic card and thrusting it toward the cockpit. I hated to open up in this rain. As he climbed the extended steps on the side of the aircraft, I cracked the canopy just far enough to retrieve the card. As I read the card, the air starter roared to life behind me. Vector 340 degrees, angels three zero zero, radiate at 1545 Zulu and contact Fairfield on 257.9. Expected Fox Corpen three two four degrees. Lost Com recovery at 1645Z. As soon as the huffer stopped sputtering, the Plane Captain gave me the two finger turnup signal. The Demon groaned as it began to suck the rain-laden air through its narrow intakes. I briefly wondered if the engine would start with all that water going through it. The J-71 didn't seem to notice the rain as the engine gages sprang to life and registered a normal start. No sooner had I given the signal to disconnect the starter unit than a drenched Taxi Director started inching me forward to take-up the slack in the catapult holdback. It was all happening so fast, too fast, there was no time to reflect on the atrocious weather. The excitement of intercepting a Russian aircraft transcended the negative feelings regarding the risks associated with a mid-ocean launch in a torrential rainstorm.

The ship was still slightly heeled to the left from its right turn, as the Catapult Officer signaled for full power. The ship rolled out of its turn with the bow several degrees above the horizon and starting down. I checked the instruments and saluted. As I pushed my head back against the headrest and focused my attention forward, white spray swept over the bow as it fell heavily into the sea. The bow was still considerably below the horizon when the Catapult Officer gave the signal to fire the catapult. All I could see was dark, frothy, greenish-gray ocean. Thank goodness he knew exactly what he was doing. The deck was nearly level as the wheels rolled off the end of the angle deck and the "all weather" Demon strived to earn its reputation. The wheels were barely in the wells when the outside world disappeared and I found myself inside the darkest, rainiest, gray cloud I had ever seen. Instinctively I reached for the cockpit lights and turned them up full bright. Glued to the instruments, I came out of burner, raised the flaps and turned to a heading of three four zero degrees. The time was 1532 Zulu. From day dreaming to flying in less than three minutes, not too shabby.

Rain pelted the aircraft as I continued the climb in basic engine. I kept reminding myself that the flight manual was emphatic that areas of heavy precipitation were to be avoided. With engine anti-ice selected, the old Demon literally ran out of steam at 22,000 feet. The clouds above me were only slightly brighter. It was going to require afterburner to get to 30,000 feet. Another caution from the flight manual flashed through my mind. "Flight tests have shown that sufficiently heavy precipitation while in afterburner can result in considerable rpm reduction and possibly cause the afterburner to blow out, even with an operative de-ice system." Besides I sure hated to give up the fuel. I wanted every drop I could squander for the landing. Typical of a well trained Demon driver, barely airborne and already worrying about the landing fuel. Reluctantly I selected afterburner and continued the climb. At 30,000 feet I was still in the clouds but it was much brighter. At 32,000 feet, I broke out into a brilliant blue above and a blinding white below and quickly lowered my visor. I've always felt that this is what it must be like to enter Heaven. The world is so dazzling white, so clean, so beautiful, and so serene. Skimming along the rounded cloud tops created an exhilarating sensation of speed even in a pokey F3B. The predominant sound is the rhythmic swish of pure oxygen as it alternately flows and stops with every breath. Thoughts of the gray wind-swept ocean being filled by streaks of torrential rain are lost in the beauty and tranquility of the moment.

The cockpit clock reads 1545Z. "Fairfield, this is Bandwagon One One Zero, on top at angels three two zero, heading three four zero, Over."

"Roger, Bandwagon One One Zero, continue heading three four zero degrees, go max conserve, Over."

Over the radio, "Roger, go max conserve."

To myself, "What on earth does that mean?" I pulled the throttle back and slowed to 180 knots, engaged the auto-pilot and peered intently into the rubber boot surrounding the radar screen. I flicked through several range scales and rotated the tilt angle up-and-down. The radar was working fine but it didn't show any targets.

Shortly thereafter, Bandwagon One Zero Six checked in at angels three four zero. It was Kenny Mase. The Saratoga also gave him the command to go max conserve and added, "Bandwagon One One Zero bears three five five degrees, twenty miles, Over." Kenny acknowledged and said he had radar contact. I started a left turn to facilitate the join-up. It was nice to have company way out here in the middle of a stormy wet nowhere.

Kenny joined on me, took the lead and reported, "Bandwagons One Zero Six and One One Zero, holding hands." We looked at each other and gave the both hands palms up Navy salute. Kenny continued the three four zero degree heading and I moved out a bit so I could also scan the radar. We flew along in silent formation wondering what was going on.

"Bandwagon flight, come left heading one seven five, do you read Fairfield's TACAN? Over" Kenny looked at me and I gave him a thumbs up. We were on the three four four degree radial at one hundred twenty-seven miles. Still no explanation. "Bandwagon flight, your signal is Charlie, we'll bring you down individually, Over." It was abundantly clear no Russian aircraft existed. We had been launched in the

Two Demons, "holding hands"

midst of a major winter storm in the middle of the Atlantic
Ocean on a false radar target. All of a sudden I didn't
appreciate the lack of regard for my personal safety by the
"Powers that Be" in the Combat Information Center (CIC). I
didn't have much time to dwell on that subject as I had the
more pressing problem of penetrating 30,000 feet of angry
rain-filled clouds and getting aboard a rolling, pitching deck
beneath a ceiling that was at or below landing minimums.

They broke Kenny off first. Over my left shoulder, I
watched his Demon disappear into the tops of the clouds
still in a left turn. I continued another five miles and they
gave me a turn reversal with a descent to fifteen hundred
feet. Thirty-two thousand to fifteen hundred feet, why not?
We were surely the only two airplanes out here in the middle
of the ocean. I called "Platform" at 5,000 feet, leveled off at
1,500 feet and configured for landing. The CCA controller
provided guidance in a professional voice that instilled confidence. As I got lower, the rain pounded the windscreen with

less ferocity. Occasionally I would catch a quick glimpse of white caps below.

"Bandwagon One One Zero, you're approaching the glide path from below, commence your descent, Over."

"One One Zero, Roger."

"Your heading is three two seven degrees, you're on center line, you're slightly below glide path and coming up, no need to acknowledge further transmissions, you're on glide path."

I was in and out of the clouds as I descended through 500 feet but still didn't hold the Carrier sufficiently well to continue on my own. The rain, however, was much lighter now. At 300 feet, I had the ball in the middle and was on center line. The ball alternately went high, then low, as the ship pitched in the heavy seas. "Please ship, be in the right phase when I get there," I said out loud to the meatball. I don't think I've ever concentrated so hard before. "Meatball, lineup, angle of attack." I started to over-control the pitching ball and had to caution myself to average it out, average it out slightly high I mean. Oh what a lovely feeling when the trusty hook grabbed the Number Four Wire as the Demon slammed onto the slippery rain-soaked deck. Home on the first try. "Thank you Lord," I said, eyeing the ragged gray clouds so close above. As I taxied out of the landing area, I wondered what was for lunch?

After Kenny and I had changed flight suits and were debriefed by the LSO, "High, fast, too much power in close, Number Four Wire." We went to lunch. Over lunch we decided we deserved some explanation as to what happened. Lunch was English curry, not my favorite. We made our way to the CIC office and talked with Commander Barker. He carefully explained they had had two strong radar contacts. One image was so sharp they were convinced they could make out the return from each of the four counter-rotating pro- pellers of the Russian Bear aircraft. Unfor-

What's for lunch?

tunately, the contacts faded sometime between the time we launched and when we came up on the radio at 1545 Zulu. He apologized but noted that it had been an excellent training exercise for everyone. Ken and I listened attentively and independently concluded the Commander had a vivid imagination, probably a prerequisite for the job.

Rank Has Its Privileges

One instance where the adage, "Rank has its privileges" is most respected is the day the flight crews fly the airplanes off the ship as it approaches the States on its return to home port, in our case, Mayport, Florida. Unfortunately, I was not yet of sufficient rank to rate that privilege.

I probably had several reasons for climbing the ladder (stairway) to "vulture's row" to watch the Squadron air- planes depart, not the least of which was envy, but with the rationalization that as the Aircraft Division Officer I wanted to see that they all got off. It would be fun to see that many Demons airborne. It would also be the last time VF-31 would deploy in the Demon. During the last week of the cruise we had proudly flown ten Demons on the same launch and

Ten Demons fly by USS Saratoga, 1964

had the Photo Squadron take our picture to prove it could be done. We started the cruise with twelve airplanes, lost two in the landing accident and Hal and I had flown two airplanes to Rota, Spain, as spares for VF-13 on the Shangri-la. All eight remaining airplanes were up and ready for the homecoming fly-off. Max Gore in Bandwagon One Zero Seven would be the last Demon off the ship. I was standing almost directly over his airplane when Max gave

F3B 107 makes the fly-off with the landing gear pinned down

the Plane Captain the signal to pull the landing gear pins. As soon as the left gear pin was pulled, the landing gear started to retract slowly into the wheel well. The Plane Captain stepped back in frustrated helplessness and watched the Demon lay down on its side like a tired old horse. Max shut down the engine but to no avail. The left wing tip rested squarely on the deck. Not to be denied, a jack was rolled out, the wing jacked up, the tip checked for damage, and the landing gear pins inserted and safety-wired in place. Bandwagon One Zero Seven made the next launch. Max flew to Cecil Field with the gear down and pinned. A little late but, nevertheless, all eight airplanes made the fly-off. I would be home tomorrow.

Welcome Home

A huge crowd awaited the docking of the USS Saratoga at the Mayport pier. As far as I was concerned it couldn't be soon enough. I was pleased to be a part of the "New Dad" brigade and exit the ship first. What a thrill to hold my daughter for the first time! Indescribable.

"Welcome Home, USS Saratoga"

Gray Hair

The Demon was almost my undoing. I had completed my first Med. Cruise about three months earlier and was eagerly awaiting the transition to the F4B, Phantom II. The Saratoga was operating out of Mayport with a group of VIP's on board. VF-31 was tasked with providing an aircraft for static display. In my youthful quest for more Carrier landings, I volunteered to fly one of our Demons out to the ship. It would be fun. Carrier Air Group Three was sending an F3B, an F8D, an A3D and an A4C. We were to fly out at 0830 and return around 1700. I was afforded a period of Field Carrier Landing Practice and felt comfortable about it. Three of us flew in formation from Cecil Field. The A3D came from NAS Sanford. It felt good to land on the SARA again. I even got an "OK three wire.""

As the day continued, the weather got progressively worse. Our launch time came and went. Finally about 1930, we manned our aircraft and prepared to return to Cecil Field. The weather was down to a 600 foot overcast with light rain and, of course, it was pitch black. I had not had a catapult launch for three months and a night one for longer than that. My Demon was positioned behind the Number Three Catapult, the inboard one on the angled deck. Engine start, checkout, and spotting onto the port catapult went fine, anxiety level moderate. Throttle to 100%, gages checked, afterburner selected, gages rechecked, navigation lights on, and head against the headrest. LAUNCH. At the instant I lifted off, a brilliant flash of blue-white light blazed momentarily across the windscreen totally blinding me. Flying only by instinct, with the good grace of God, and fortunate enough to have a lightly loaded aircraft, I was simply along for the ride. Unbeknownst to me, once airborne I made a climbing right turn (you always clear left off the port catapults) over the ship and into the overcast, gear and flaps down and still in full afterburner. I could hear the ship calling me on the radio but I was in no position to attempt one more task. I reached up, put my left hand on the ejection seat handle, started to pull, and made what was probably a dumb decision, saying to myself, "No, Warren, you're not wet yet," and did not complete the pull. Still not yet in control of the aircraft, I slowly began to make out some of the instruments at least enough to realize I was descending rapidly. I managed to level off at less than 400 feet above the cold dark of Davy Jones' Ocean. I finally acknowledged the ship, got out of afterburner and raised the gear and flaps.

Scared and shaking, I climbed back into the clouds (without clearance), leveled off at 2,500 feet, and flew direct to NAS Cecil Field. I used the TACAN and radar altimeter to make an illegal letdown to beneath the clouds somewhere south of the airfield. It took me two tries to land on the 10,000 strip at Cecil. I am convinced this episode was responsible for the early conversion of my then dark-brown hair to endearing gray.

It was later determined that the gun sight had shorted out during the catapult shot and caused the brilliant flash of light. Since none of our guns were operational, we summarily disconnected all the gun sights to preclude another occurrence. Had the airplane crashed into the sea, with or without me, the accident would most likely have been attributed to pilot vertigo, i.e., pilot error.

The Phantom II

When the F3B Demons were phased out of VF-31, only six Squadron pilots transitioned to the F4B "Phantom II." It was a thrill to go from the "lead slug" to the hottest airplane in the fleet. No longer would we have to take back seat to the Crusader drivers.

It was back to Key West, NAS Boca Chica and VF-101 for the transition. We ex-Demon drivers would get fifty hours of training for qualification. Several interesting interactions occurred between the "old" VF-31 pilots and the "new" VF-31 pilots. The six of us naturally considered ourselves to be VF-31, as all other pilots came from some place else. As it turned out, several of the new pilots were training command "plow-backs," who had more total flight time than we did, and had experienced the exalted role of instructor, or "God," to the fledgling student pilots. Furthermore, the new pilots received double the number of flight hours in the Phantom, were already at VF-101 and well into their qualification

The Phantom II, a pilot's dream

program when we ex-Demon drivers arrived. The stage was set for a healthy competition. Fortunately, many of our back-seaters or Radar Intercept Officers (RIO's) were nearly through the training program; consequently, we would fly with many of the people at VF-101 that we would when VF-31 reformed.

My first flight in the Phantom was as a back-seat passenger. Yes, passenger is the correct term, for there are no flight controls in the rear cockpit of a Navy F4B. It was the VF-101 instructor's opportunity to show me what the Phantom could do. The Phantom II was a pilot's dream come true. It literally had power to burn. Its climb schedule exceeded the normal level flight capability of a heavily loaded Demon. After takeoff you accelerate to and maintain 300 knots until reaching Mach 0.9, which you then hold until reaching cruise or intercept altitude. Unlike the Demon, supersonic flight was no longer a dive in full afterburner to reach a mere Mach 1.3. The Phantom could fly at twice the speed of sound in level flight. As a matter of fact, it was difficult to keep from exceeding Mach 1.0 in a climb. I was glad when my back-seat ride was over for I was itching to get my hands on the stick. This occurred the next day.

While Key West often harbors thunderstorms and low clouds that glide eastward from the Gulf of Mexico into the Atlantic, today was a sparkling blue, see-forever day, a fantastic day to pilot my first Phantom. This time the VF-101 instructor pilot was in the back seat and it was my turn to show him what a VF-31 fighter pilot could do with a Phantom.

Wow! What an incredible difference from the Demon, I could hardly hold the Phantom with full brakes much above 80 percent power on both engines. Responding to the tremendous power from the two afterburners, the F4B accelerated down the runway like a scared rabbit with its tail on fire. The takeoff technique in the F4B is unusual. On the takeoff

Supersonic over Key West in a steep climb

roll you hold the stick full aft and move it forward at liftoff to stop the rotation. On takeoff I promptly over rotated, but the airplane didn't seem to notice. It climbed like a homesick angel. I overshot my planned level off altitude and as I came out of afterburner created a slight pitch oscillation. So far I had definitely not impressed the instructor. He was pretty calm about it. He'd probably seen it all before. Our climb out took us over the center of Key West. My attempt at capturing Mach 0.9 for the climb resulted in my first supersonic flight, unintentional of course, and right over Key West. I couldn't believe I was so far behind the airplane. Things never happened this fast in the Demon. In spite of my less than sterling performance, it was an amazingly wonderful flight. We didn't bother to look at the radar. This was a pilot-pilot flight. The real reason for the existence of this missile-only airplane could wait until a radar operator occupied the rear seat.

At this time the F4B did not have any inclose weapons, i.e. no guns, so the primary goal was to get into a missile firing position. Also the F4B was not the world's greatest turning airplane so we were taught to use its excess power to engage another airplane in the vertical plane rather than trying to turn with it horizontally.

The Phantom was especially impressive in the landing pattern. It was highly stable and, compared to the Demon, its engine response seemed instantaneous. In addition, the engine pumped bleed air over the wings through a boundary layer control system, providing a form of direct lift control. Landing the Phantom was a delight.

The F4B was easy to land

The Guy in the Back Seat

I readily admit to NOT looking forward to having another person aboard "my" fighter. I felt I had done a great job in the single seat Demon and, after all, fighters were supposed to be single seaters; "Weren't they?" The idea of having to baby sit some guy in the back seat didn't sit very well. The last thing I needed was a back-seat driver. After all, I knew how to run the radar and how to make intercepts. The radar operator was going to be a royal pain in the backside. In reality, I guess I didn't like the idea of somebody looking over my shoulder all the time. I had had enough of that in the Training Command. The second guy was only going to complicate my life. I liked the freedom of being alone, the master of my own success or failure so to speak.

The Guy in the Back; a great invention

There wasn't one of those guys I wouldn't trade for an extra thousand pounds of gas. Who needed him?

It took two, or possibly three, flights to figure out that the guy in the back seat was the greatest thing that ever happened to an all-weather fighter. I found more uses for him than ever imagined. He tuned all radios and navigation aids. He was the secretary. He copied and checked clearances. He read checklists. He did a much better job of operating the radar, especially under less than ideal conditions. He conducted outstanding intercepts and for those that weren't good, there was someone with whom to share the blame. He cross-checked approaches. He called altitudes and courses. He provided another set of eyeballs during simulated dogfights. Most of all, he became an indispensable member of a highly integrated team. Where had he been all my life? It was a great arrangement. Every fighter should come equipped with one.

Ensign George Patton was a rusty-haired, freckled-faced country-boy from "down-on-the-farm" in southern Georgia and spoke with the most southern of southern drawls. My first impression of George was, "Are you for real?" It took just one flight with him to realize that this Aeronautical Engineer from Georgia Tech was a cut above the other RIO's I had flown with. We hit it off immediately. We made a great team.

In the airplane, George and I competed fiercely to see who would locate the target on the radar screen first. We perfected our intercept techniques through constant challenge and critique. We ultimately got to that enviable position of knowing what the other really meant to say when he stated the exact opposite. George almost always had the answer for me before I even got to ask the question. I enjoyed flying with George and always felt less comfortable when flying with someone else.

Mach 2

The only time we got to go Mach 2 was when we had a clean bird, i.e., no external fuel tanks or missile racks. This luxury only occurred when we were specifically scheduled for a high speed or high altitude flight or when we got the opportunity to fly a maintenance check flight following a major inspection.

Flying Mach 2 in the Phantom was an event that was fun but one that didn't last very long. It was also an event you planned in advance. You carefully figured out how long it would take to accelerate to Mach 2 and how long you could hold it, which is mostly a function of how much fuel you would need for descent and landing. You then convert time into distance, fly out that distance and start your Mach 2 run in the direction of home plate. The best acceleration altitude for the F4B was typically between thirty-six and thirty-eight thousand feet. My first Mach 2 flight was in the training syllabus at VF-101. I was really excited about it. I had done the fuel planning and knew exactly where to start the run and where it should end. I couldn't wait to make the world zoom by so fast. After all, the theory of relativity said, as speed increased time would slow down, allowing me to add a microsecond to my life span. I was convinced the world would be a blur.

I flew out 256 miles west, turned back toward Key West and shoved both after burners to full power. The Phantom responded appropriately. Mach 1.0 raced by, as did 1.2, and 1.3. Approaching Mach 1.5, the rate of acceleration slowed noticeably which took me by surprise. The world didn't seem to be going by any faster at Mach 1.5 than it did at Mach 1.0, as a matter-of-fact, it seemed to be slowing down. At Mach 1.55, out of the corner of my eye, I saw the engine inlet ramps start to open and the acceleration picked up but nowhere near what it had been at the lower supersonic Mach numbers. The outside world still wasn't going by any

Mach 2 plus, not bad

faster. The only thing that seemed to be happening fast was the rate at which the fuel quantity gages were going down, and that was alarming. The Phantom continued to accelerate slowly but steadily. By now my attention was almost totally focused on the rapidity with which my fuel supply was being depleted. I suddenly lost confidence in my fuel calculations.

We finally reached Mach 2 and let it slop over to slightly above Mach 2. I confirmed it with George, held it for a few more seconds and deselected afterburner. I was not at all prepared for what happened next. It felt like we hit a brick wall. The shoulder straps cut deeply into our shoulders as the airplane decelerated at an incredible and sustained rate. Surely the deceleration wasn't as great as an arrested landing but the sustained deceleration made it feel like it was more. If only we had the power to accelerate like that. It didn't take long before we were subsonic. There were only two differences between flying at Mach 1 and flying at Mach 2; one was the indication on the Mach meter and the other was the prodigious rate at which the fuel was being consumed. Of course, this would be a totally different story had it occurred close to the ground or over a cloud deck. It was mildly disappointing. However, I was proud to boast of having flown twice the speed of sound and nearly 1,500 miles per hour. Once on the ground, I didn't dare let on it had been a disappointment.

My fuel calculations had actually been pretty accurate but there was a time there when I wasn't so sure. We headed for Key West, landed straight in, not really low on fuel but lower than a Demon trained pilot likes to be. The entire flight had taken exactly thirty-seven minutes. George and I received our McDonnell Aircraft Company Mach 2 pins that afternoon.

Our training program in the F4B was ending much too soon. In much less than the allotted fifty hours, I found the Phantom, for all its ugliness, easy to love, pleasant to fly, and its weapons system, with its built-in weapons operator, outstanding.

Carrier Qualifications in the Phantom

As with all Navy flight training programs, the last requirement was the Carrier Qualification phase. Checking out in the Phantom was no exception. We accomplished our carrier qualifications on the familiar turf of the USS Saratoga. Again the requirement was for ten day and six night landings. The day landings in the Phantom were a breeze. The rapid engine response, the excess power and boundary layer control system made

F4B launches from Cat 1

F4B at instant of cable snatch

it much easier and infinitely more forgiving than the Demon. We didn't even use afterburner for the lightweight catapult shots.

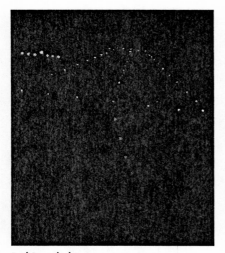

Red Drop-lights are great

The night landings went fine. A simple addition to the stern of the aircraft carrier had greatly improved the ability to attain and hold the lineup for night landings. The runway center line lights had been extended down the stern of the aircraft carrier as a string of red lights. When lined up, the white lights and the red drop-lights formed a straight line. When off to the left, the red lights angle to the left and vice versa if to the right. Anything that provided improved information for the night landing was a welcome addition.

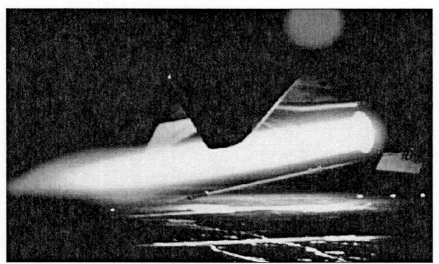

FB4 night afterburner launch

My first night mission was the highest weight aircraft I had ever flown. I had no reason to believe it would be any different from the day catapults and landings. Boy! Was I in for a surprise. As we taxied onto the catapult, "I kept thinking, it sure helps to have a good friend to share the blackness with." It was a lot less intimidating. The lighted weight board registered the high launch weight. Nose wheel extended, engines checked in full afterburner, "Are you ready George?"

"Does a bear shit in the woods?" Came the reply.

Navigation lights on. Stick full back. Head back. The catapult fired and the acceleration felt normal. As we ended the Cat shot, I over rotated by at least ten degrees nose up, although it felt more like sixty. I pushed the nose forward and felt like it was now sixty degrees nose down. The red and yellow glow of the afterburners reflected off the wet blackness below. I pulled the nose sharply upward. I followed this pattern for at least three more cycles, fortunately with decreasing amplitude. It scared the hell out of me. It was several minutes before I began to settle down. What had happened to that nice docile airplane we had flown during the carrier qualifications?

"George, that launch scared the shit out of me. I'm not sure I can get this thing back aboard tonight," I said.

"Sure you can," he replied, not as convincingly as I would have liked. We discussed my lack of confidence, off and on, for the next hour. I was serious about going to Cecil Field for the night. George became more convincing as the flight progressed and I agreed to make at least one attempt. I've often wondered how confident George really was. We got aboard just fine, but I never forgot how quickly the Phantom could change its disposition.

Factory Fresh Phantoms

When VF-31 completed its training at Key West and reformed at NAS Cecil Field in March 1964, we did not yet have all of our airplanes. Six of us flew commercially to St. Louis to pick up three brand spanking new F4Bs from the McDonnell plant. In the early 1960s, McDonnell Aircraft was making money hand over fist with its huge production run of Phantom IIs.

Only two of the airplanes were ready for pickup when we arrived. The third wouldn't be ready until two days later. McDonnell apologized for the delay and invited us six Navy types and four Air Force test pilots out for dinner. I had been around Navy test pilots at the Naval Air Test Center but hadn't socialized with them. We were escorted to the ritziest and most expensive restaurant I had ever seen, much less been in, with instructions to order whatever we wanted.

One of the Air Force test pilots was an exhibitionist from the word go. When the wine steward brought the wine, this test pilot elected himself to be the wine taster. The wine steward uncorked the bottle, handed the cork to the pilot and stood by in a detached, respectful manner with a folded white towel draped ceremoniously over his arm. The pilot studied the cork for a few moments and then passed it horizontally under his nose in both directions. He twisted it a half turn and repeated the sniff test. Finally he held it beneath his nose, damp end up, assumed an eyes closed, satiated look with a slight smile and took yet another deep whiff of the cork. Everyone at the table was looking at him but not a word was spoken.

Finally he laid the cork on the table and looked up expectantly at the wine steward. The steward carefully poured a quarter glass of wine and with a forced smile handed it to the pilot. The pilot raised the glass without any movement of the wine and held it up to the light. All eyes at our table stared at the glass. The patrons at several surrounding tables did the same. The wine steward shifted uncomfortably on his feet. After a complete visual study of the stationary liquid, the test pilot lowered the glass to nose level and took several deep inhalations. He carefully rotated the glass until the wine spun slowly within its enclosure. Again he raised the glass to the light and continued his in-depth visual study of the slowly rotating wine. He continued to swirl the wine as he lowered the glass for yet another eyes closed inhalation of its aroma. Of course it was necessary to visually study and sniff the wine in left and right hand swirls. A hush had fallen over the surrounding tables and the wine steward was becoming increasingly impatient. Without taking a taste, the pilot gently placed the glass on the table and continued to stare at the glass, as we all did, until the circulating wine came to a complete stop. The wine steward looked from the glass to the pilot and back again, not quite sure what was expected of him. The pilot paused long enough for everyone to feel expectantly impatient, but not long enough to lose his audience. He lifted the glass gently to his lips, closed his eyes and took a sip of the wine. He held the wine in his mouth for a few seconds and swallowed it. He paused for a moment, his eyes popped open, he placed the glass on the table, grabbed his throat with both hands, tumbled from his chair and crumpled in a motionless heap on the floor. A combined gasp emanated from the surrounding tables as all eyes riveted their attention on the limp body lying on the floor. The wine steward took two steps backward in shock and stared at the pilot in horrified disbelief. No one moved or said a word.

The young pilot looked up, lifted himself from the floor, smiled at the still immobile wine steward and said, "It's fine, we'll take it." His appreciative audience broke into spontaneous applause. It was a great performance. Test pilots were all right, obviously very thorough and definitely highly exhibitionist. The meal was outstanding. The next day we were given the VIP tour of the McDonnell plant. It was exciting to walk down the clattering production line and watch an airplane materialize from a million parts and pieces into a full operational machine with the capability of the Phantom.

Factory fresh Phantoms

Close-up of a new Phantom

The three Phantoms looked new, smelled new, were new, like brand new cars. Too bad there wasn't an odometer in the cockpit. I've always imagined it would have read some tiny number like 1.4 miles. On the flight home, we admired each other's airplanes as we flew along. No oil or hydraulic stains spoiled the clean undersides of the airplanes. All three planes carried three external fuel tanks, not because we needed the fuel, but as a means of delivering the tanks to the Squadron. Half the Squadron was waiting as we taxied into the chocks. As we climbed down from the cockpit, it was obvious no one was interested in us, only in the new Phantoms. They *WERE* beautiful. I never understood how an airplane as contorted as the F4B, with its wing tips bent up, it's horizontal tail bent down, a droopy nose, and huge flat plate boundary layer fences at the front of each engine inlet, could look so ugly on the ground, yet be so beautiful in the air.

George and I didn't have a single discrepancy on our airplane, although I suspect it did after our maintenance folks completed their acceptance inspection.

Where did he go?

The contest between the old Demon drivers and the newly assigned pilots continued after the Squadron reformed. Our most difficult, and the most practiced intercept maneuver, was the low altitude head-on intercept. We typically flew at 400 knots at 300 feet starting head-on with a nose-to-nose separation of 40 to 50 miles. One Phantom

Where'd he go?

acted as the target and the other as the interceptor. Of course the target airplane, assuming his radar was working, had the same information as the interceptor. We delighted in waiting until the interceptor was within a second or two of firing his simulated missile or calling "Fox away," before hauling back on the stick and zooming straight up. Unless the other crew just happened to be staring at the steering dot at that instant, they wouldn't see it jump smartly off the top of their radar screens. They would believe they had simply lost lock at a most inopportune time and would figure they were too close to reacquire a radar lock for the head-on attack and would reverse course for a re-attack or tail aspect shot. It was easy to join on them unobserved during the turn. Both crewmen would be so absorbed looking for us on their radar that we could fly formation, sometimes quite closely, for several seconds before they realized we were there. Obviously we only got away with this maneuver once and then the word was out!

Straight up

The F4B was an impressive airplane. When down to about 4,000 pounds of fuel, the thrust-to-weight ratio was very nearly one-to-one. It was fun to skim low over the Okefenokee Swamp, a few miles north of Jacksonville, at 400 knots, engage the double afterburners and haul back on the stick until the nose was pointing straight up. The non-tumbling attitude indicator had two black and white concentric circles at the top of the rotating sphere

Straight up, impressive!

that look like a small bow and arrow target. You could center the top of the attitude indicator and climb straight up for 15,000 feet and lose less than 10 knots. It was an exhilarating experience.

None of the other airplanes I had flown could fly straight up for any sustained period of time. A sixty degree climb angle was about all you could attain and even then not for very long. To maintain positive "g" in the recovery, we almost always rolled inverted and pulled back on the stick to lower the nose to regain the airspeed. Of course if you are going straight up, rolling the airplane has absolutely no effect on your relationship to the horizon. It had become so natural to roll prior to pulling the nose through to the horizon, that it was nearly impossible not to do it from vertical flight in the Phantom. It was a fantastic ego trip to command so much power. Of course, at the low fuel state you headed for Cecil Field shortly thereafter.

Night In-flight Refueling

My first opportunity to conduct night in-flight refueling with the Phantom occurred during an early evening sortie out of Cecil Field. Arrangements were made to rendezvous with one of Attack Squadron Thirty Six's (VA-36) A4D tankers. The tanker was on time and we quickly joined on his left wing. As he extended the hose, we confirmed the proper sequence of lights and that the basket was stable. There was no difficulty lining up the probe with the tanker's drogue because the F4B's refueling probe is located very near the same relative position to the cockpit as on the Demon. As I approached the basket it was obvious the Phantom was sensitive in pitch and had a tendency toward a mild pilot

Air refueling; it's easy in the daytime

induced oscillation. In the Demon, once you had the probe lined up, you pushed the throttle forward several inches and the probe coasted into and locked in the basket. I tried a similar technique with the Phantom. As I advanced the throttles, the airplane leapt forward like a sprinter coming out of the chocks in an Olympic one hundred meter dash. The probe crashed into the center of the refueling basket. The take-up reel on the tanker didn't stand a chance of taking up the slack I had created in the hose. The hose formed a quick "S" in the down direction, followed immediately by half an "S" in the up direction, and promptly severed at the connec-

tion to the refueling basket, which was now firmly attached to my refueling probe. Fuel gushed out of the free flying hose indignantly spraying the Phantom and its accurate, but overly zealous pilot. We

Closing on the tanker for fuel

were lucky we didn't ingest enough fuel to cause a fire. Needless to say, the tanker pilot was not pleased that I had so ingloriously captured his refueling drogue.

What a predicament! There was no way to hide this unusual and quite obvious addition to my Phantom. While not the least bit funny, George and I couldn't help but laugh at my latest faux pas. I desperately wanted to wait until it was real dark, sneak back into Cecil Field and have the ground crew quickly and quietly extract the basket from the probe, while I slinked stealthily into the Ready Room. No such luck!

A small but curious crowd awaited my arrival in the chocks. Everyone had a good laugh as we joked about how ridiculous the slightly cocked refueling basket looked as it clung limply to the Phantom's extended refueling probe.

The refueling basket was returned to VA-36 with full military honors. I bought the tanker pilot a quart of Chivas Regal.

Out of airspeed but not out of ideas

The deep blue skies and brilliant yellow sun featured in Florida travel brochures are not wholly representative of Jacksonville weather. Moisture laden weather systems bring their share of low dense fog, deep dark rain clouds, not to mention the occasional destructive hurricane gnawing its way out of the Caribbean and, last but not least, the ubiquitous Florida thunderstorms that delight in menacing airports. Most of us enjoyed the challenge of bad weather flying but freely admit the anxiety level is inversely proportional to the height of the cloud ceiling at the destination airport.

More than one way to fly

I have touted the Navy's strong reliance on angle of attack as the primary instrument for attitude/airspeed control in the carrier approach. Angle of attack also allows you to optimize climb and cruise profiles and, in at least one instance, to fly a full instrument approach and landing without an operable airspeed indicator. During one of those dark, turbulent, heavy rain fronts that had settled over Cecil Field, my RIO, Phil Anselmo, and I were leading a flight of two returning from an air intercept training mission. We entered the clouds around 20,000 feet and were cleared into a holding pattern south of the field. Shortly after breaking up the flight for individual instrument approaches, and while on descent, I noticed my airspeed was lower than I wanted and eased the nose down to speed up. In spite of my efforts, the airspeed continued to decrease. My intuition started telling me something was wrong but it wasn't immediately obvious. The airspeed was decreasing but my rate of descent was increasing. The speed decay was insidious and took several nose down corrections before I figured out I had an airspeed indicator problem. The real clue was that the angle of attack was also decreasing. Two out of three indications confirmed I had an airspeed problem. I eased the nose up to reduce the rate of descent and achieve a more normal angle of attack. The airspeed continued to decay to zero. "Pitot heat" was on the descent checklist and I reconfirmed that it was turned "on" and double-checked that the circuit breaker was "in." Once the problem was diagnosed, I simply flew the rest of the approach on angle of attack and felt quite comfortable doing so.

Alert Duty

Following the Cuban missile crisis, it was decided to station a fighter detachment at NAS Boca Chica and keep it on twenty-four hour alert. This particular duty was rotated between the Navy and Marine Fighter squadrons along the East Coast. Almost as soon as we completed the transition to the F4B, VF-31 received orders to man the alert commitment at Key West.

Standing alert duty is not my most favorite activity. It is hours of boredom cooped up in a one-room metal trailer next to the tarmac and alert aircraft. Typically two airplanes and two crews stood ready alert with two backup airplanes. We rotated flight crews back to Cecil Field about every three weeks. It was slightly less than 400 miles from Jacksonville to Key West which meant, when we ferried airplanes to Key West, we always had an excess of fuel when we arrived. We typically went feet wet (go from land to water) a few miles west of Tampa. One of the requirements when flying in the FAA's Area of Positive Control (at that time above 24,000 feet) was to notify the ground controller whenever you increased

"Miami Center...increasing air speed to 1,000 knots"

your airspeed more than ten knots. Normally we flew in the mid thirty thousands of feet and filed for a true airspeed of 550 knots. As soon as we hit the coast outbound to Key West, we delighted in advising; "Miami Center, Bandwagon flight increasing air speed to 1,000 knots, Over." It had a lovely ring to it and captured the envy of every non-F4B fighter pilot, real or imagined, on the frequency. Personally, I just loved to go fast.

During the time we stood alert duty, the Cuban, or we suspect, Russian pilots started flying the MIG-21, Russia's newest and highest performance export fighter. With a mere eighty miles separating Florida from Cuba, they could easily cover that distance in a very few minutes. Most of

the time they flew up and down the island and seldom ventured out over the water and even less often toward the United States.

The elusive MIG-21 Fishbed

On rare occasion they would test our defenses by heading toward Key West long enough to make us launch the alert airplanes. As soon as their radar detected airplanes headed south or southeast out of Key West, the MIGs turned tail toward their island sanctuary. We patrolled outside their twelve mile territorial limit, often on parallel flight paths with the MIGs. I never got close enough to get a positive identification of what type of airplanes we were mirroring flight paths with, but close enough to know they were at our altitude over the island.

I always wanted to sneak north out of Key West, never getting above fifty feet like we did off the carrier, and circle around to the south to see if we couldn't pop up between the MIGs and their coastline when they were challenging us. It was probably a good idea but not a practical one to implement. We never did see them fly at night.

Booming the Keys

Early in the sixties there had been enough complaints and damage done by airplanes flying supersonic over land that we were no longer allowed to do so. The single exception was when we were on an actual intercept mission whether we suspected it to be a friendly airplane or not.

Since the majority of air traffic in our area of responsibility was inbound to Miami, most intercept missions were flown toward the northeast, which meant we flew straight up the Florida Keys as fast as we could go, which at low level was about Mach 1.2. I'm sure the locals and all the wildlife in the keys hated it, but we absolutely loved the legalized flat hatting.

Flying Target for the Army

In addition to the alert aircraft, the Army stationed several Hawk anti-aircraft missile batteries along the Keys. We provided training for their missile crews. When we first flew against the missile installations, we enjoyed buzzing the launchers at low altitude and high speed. Apparently there was a rotational limit for the launchers that was exceeded when we did this. It was over-driving the launchers and creating maintenance problems. We were requested to please keep a little more separation from the sites, so as not to wreck their systems. How were we supposed to know? I never felt totally comfortable watching a battery of missiles faithfully tracing my pathway through the sky.

Intercepting the Friendlies

During a real intercept mission, for our own protection we always launched as a flight of two. One aircraft covered the other as the first one made the identification check. We often flew closer to airliners than was really necessary, but after all, it was they who had triggered the intercept and we were "just doing our job." Once the ID check was complete, we usually flew formation with them long enough for the pilot to think he was in serious trouble for not having reported the proper ADIZ entry point or squawking the correct IFF (Identification Friend or Foe) code. The natural reaction of any airline pilot when he sees an F4B with its wing tilted up as it rendezvoused with him is to turn away from the interceptor. We cleverly placed the second fighter on the opposite side

A Phantom on your left and a Phantom on your right

so that as the airliner banked he was immediately presented with a mirror image of another F4B on the other side. The result was predictable. He rolled wings level and stared out the cockpit window wondering what he was supposed to do now and how much trouble he was in.

Our job was essentially done once we had made the identification but we enjoyed the role of fighter escort, at least until we were sure any passengers on board had the opportunity to get a good look at our new Phantoms. It was a nice touch to include an aileron roll in our breakaway maneuver as we headed for Key West, another successful air intercept mission accomplished. Time to go home.

Hollywood Beware

Standing alert duty, especially against the Cuban Air Force, can be excruciatingly boring, so boring that we decided to produce a movie to capture the excitement. It was easy to capture the boredom. Simply make a boring movie. Capturing

Cinema of the Century

the excitement was not so easy but most of the fun. Technical problems abounded, not the least of which was that none of us knew what we were doing and the handheld camera only operated about three minutes before it ran out of film and had to be reloaded. Right in the middle of a big scene the photographer would yell, "STOP!" and everyone was supposed to hold their last position until the camera was reloaded. We were not very good mimes and therefore only marginally successful. Lastly, we were ad libbing the whole process with a group of egotists, each of whom wanted to hog the limelight. We quickly discovered that the dimly lit trailer was not a very good stage, not to mention that when all the flight crews were present (which was

Felix - The Director

not the case for a normal alert condition), we barely had enough room to move about, much less don the required flight gear. However, we weren't about to let little details like that deter the production of Naval Aviation's "Cinema of the Century."

The plot was simple. The "Cuban Bad Guys" were coming and the world's greatest fighter pilots were to ensure that they never reached the U.S. mainland. It was especially important to capture the "drama" that went along with defending our country from the dangerous threat of the Cuban Air Force to the south. A pivotal character was the enlisted orderly who manned the phones over which the Air Defense Radar Sites announced suspicious contacts and initiated the launch of the intrepid defenders.

Waiting... Boring

The movie opens with an idyllic scene of flight suit clad pilots and RIOs reading intellectual books like "Playboy," playing Acey Duecy, simply resting, or faking doing paper work and all looking terribly bored. Keep in mind that this is a silent film so we made judicious use of the chalkboard in the back of the trailer for subtitles. The phone rings and we are put on five minute alert status. To demonstrate that this was a military operation, the entire Chain of Command had to be individually alerted in order of seniority. Every officer had his own telephone and ended up with the poor orderly being nearly strangled by the numerous phone lines wrapped around his neck.

After a full confirmation of the change in alert status, we calmly put on our flight gear in anticipation of a launch. It wasn't long before the five minute alert was canceled. We doffed our flight gear and the boredom resumed.

The Cubans are coming!

The next phone call was the real thing and chaos abounded as we scrambled to don our flight gear and race off to man our aircraft. The scene cuts to the outside of the trailer where a sailor with a tray of food is approaching the double trailer doors. At the instant he reaches the door, twenty-six energized flight crew burst through on the way to their aircraft. A yellow van waits at the end of the ramp to collect the dedicated and determined airmen. Unfortunately the van won't start and needs a push. Since most aircraft systems are redundant, it follows that the alert air-

Lunch arriving...

Gang Way!

Redundant transportation

craft transportation system should also be redundant. When the van is finally pushed away, the flight crews are already sitting on an operable flatbed conveyance. "Wait! Where is the Executive Officer?" Here he comes with the Squadron Mascot, a brown and white stray dog, close behind.

Wait again! Where is the Commanding Officer?

The double doors open and a roll of brown packing paper starts down the ramp but hangs up on the left railing about a third of the way down.

Cut!

Take two.

The double doors open and a roll of brown packing paper starts down the ramp but this time hangs up on the right railing about a third of the way down.

Cut!

Take three.

The double doors open and a roll of brown packing paper descends majestically down the center of the ramp and stops at a chair adorned with a garbage can umbrella attached to two side railings manned by four burly

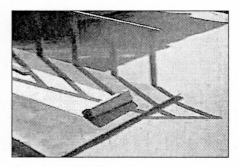

The paper makes the grade

CO transportation

enlisted "throne bearers" naked from the waist up.

The Commanding Officer strolls purposefully down the ramp, coffee cup in hand with two Junior Officer escorts brandishing mop swabs over his head to ensure "Le Majesty" does not suffer from the excessive heat of the Key West sun. Safely on his "throne," the bearers carry him off to his alert aircraft with the "swab bearers" dutifully doing their duty. At the airplane, a forklift manned by a stern looking Marine elevates the CO's chair to the level of the cockpit. With a "Shazam" motion of his hand, the canopy slowly rises upward followed closely by his helmet ready for donning.

Shazam!

Meanwhile, some of the other air crews had devised alternate modes of transportation to their aircraft. The most innovative was a diesel-powered steamroller. Confusion abounded as at least eight people attempted to man

Not fast, but sturdy!

the first aircraft. There were airplanes without pilots and airplanes without RIOs. One RIO, whose airplane did not have a pilot, knew that the pilot started the engines simply by holding up two fingers and rotating his hand. The RIO simply climbed from the rear seat to the front, held up two fingers, rotated his hand and, as expected, the engine started. Returning to the rear cockpit, he saluted the Plane Captain and the airplane started to taxi sans pilot.

Who needs a pilot?

Right engine won't start

One crew couldn't get their right engine started. The Crew Chief crawled into the engine intake and emerged from the afterburner section with the dog in his arms.

Hey, wait for me!

The quickest way to the cockpit?

Another aircraft taxied out without the RIO who was running along behind at full trot. The pilot stopped the aircraft on the runway and the RIO climbed into the engine intake and appeared backward in the rear seat.

Ready for takeoff!

All aircraft eventually make it to the runway for takeoff. The Cuban Air Force never challenged our efforts, so we declared ourselves successful. We decided, however, we'd better not quit our day jobs, as we were much better alert crews than movie makers but we enjoyed our brief sojourn into Hollywood.

Unidentified Flying Object

It was another typical, long and boring night in the alert trailer. Time crawled by snail's pace slow. Most often the only fun we would have was a practice launch near the end of our alert period, that is, if enough airplanes were available to continue the alert. Tonight proved different.

The scramble alarm sounded with a loud urgency of its own. Normally we were given advanced warning by telephone any time there was air activity over Cuba, but not tonight. We quickly shook off the surprise, donned our torso harnesses, dashed out the trailer's double doors and raced toward the waiting Phantoms. The ground crew was already in action and the huffer (air starter) was belching red flames straight up into the moist night air, reminiscent of a recalcitrant afterburner. George and I clamored up the steps and into the cockpit. As the crewman helped us strap in, the Telephone Watch arrived with a slip of paper containing the initial intercept heading and altitude. Too busy at the moment to look at it, I slid the paper under the clip at the top of my knee board. The right engine was commanding my attention as the air starter spun the turbines up to starting rpm. A quick glance at the ever important EGT (Exhaust Gas Temperature) and oil pressure gages indicated the start was progressing normally. Even though the engine was not fully up to idle speed, I diverted the starter air to the left engine. To the left, my wing man was in sync. When it came to doing one of these things for real, we weren't doing half bad.

A short radio check between the two airplanes was followed immediately with takeoff clearance from the tower without our having requested it. I took a quick peek at the small white slip of paper not very neatly attached to my knee board. Surely this heading must be wrong. It wanted us to turn west after takeoff and climb to 10,000 feet. The last time I looked at a map, Cuba was south and most of the airspace to the west was either restricted airspace or warning areas. I relayed the heading and altitude to George as the four afterburners lit up the night sky and the two Phantoms raced down the runway.

George had had the presence of mind to punch his watch when the alarm sounded and noted that we were airborne in three minutes and twelve seconds from the time the clacker had sounded, not bad for a sleepy crew. It wasn't until I started my left turn toward the west that I became aware of how inky black it was. There were no stars and no horizon. Shortly the other Phantom tucked in comfortably close on my right wing. As we checked in with the GCI (Ground Control Intercept) Controller he confirmed our initial westerly vector and the 10,000 foot altitude. He had a single bogy bearing two seven eight degrees for one hundred eight miles, smack dab in the middle of warning area W-174B. The red glow of the airplane's clock showed it to be 0127 local. Who on Earth would be in that part of the Gulf of Mexico at this time of night? We charged madly toward the lone target which, at this time, was only a voice command from the GCI Controller.

George picked up a small radar target at fifty-seven miles and acquired a lock-on at forty-three miles. The radar indications were unusual. Whatever it was, it was not moving very fast. George directed a slight turn to the right to set up a collision course and minimize the time to intercept. We were doing 490 knots at 10,000 feet. I instructed the wing man to drop back and take a little more distance behind to cover us during the intercept. He disappeared out of sight as he eased back and to my right.

George and I were perplexed by the bogie's location and excited by the realness of it all. Since we needed to make a positive ID and would end up in Sidewinder range first, I set up the fire control system to launch a Sidewinder missile. The night sky was as black as those I remembered from the Aircraft Carrier, no moon, no stars, and, out this far in the Gulf, no shrimp boat lights. Our closure rate was only 560 knots, which also seemed strange.

Suddenly, a brilliant white light blossomed about fifteen miles directly in front of us. I called the sighting to the other Phantom and reported it to the GCI Controller. I descended slightly and flew directly at the suspended white light. It never wavered. When we were almost directly underneath, it moved rapidly off to our left and stopped in midair. My eyes must have widened tenfold, as I had no idea what it was. I didn't know of any man made machine that could maneuver that quickly, much less hover in midair. I reported to my wing man that whatever it was, it was doing a lot less than 400 knots. His "Roger" was followed shortly by a not very professional, "Holy Shit, did you see that?" I knew exactly what he was thinking. I started a wide left turn keeping the motionless light in sight, slowed to 250 knots, and turned directly toward the tantalizing brilliance. As I approached the light for the second time, once again it moved smartly off to our right and stopped. What on Earth could it be? Or maybe it wasn't.

Simultaneously George and I came to the same conclusion: we were dueling with a UFO that was quicker, more maneuverable than we were, and possessed the uncanny ability to hover in midair. Any minute now I expected a tractor beam to dart from the eerie suspended brilliance and whisk the two of us inside the celestial intruder. Our wing man's lights were visible across the circle as we continued our Lufberry maneuver around the UFO. I could already envision the newspaper headlines and most assuredly the entire front page of the National Enquirer: "Two Navy fighters disappear while dueling with UFO over Gulf of Mexico." The subscript was even worse: "Fate of crews unknown."

Our wing man wasn't having any better success than we were and I wasn't quite sure what to do next. I did know that I wasn't going to be satisfied until I found out what it was. I had one more idea. Slowing down, I dropped the gear and flaps, turned on the landing lights and once again turned toward the motionless light. Staggering along at as high an angle of attack and as low an airspeed as I dared fly, I hoped the UFO would remain stationary long enough for me to capture it in the landing lights and get a good look at it.

As we approached, the UFO, in an obvious attempt to avoid my lights, started a slow drift to the left. I made a minor correction and stopped the drift. If only it would hover a few more seconds I would have it in my lights. So far so good. My imagination was running wild. I was certain it was going to be saucer shaped. George was convinced it would be cigar shaped. For good measure I relayed our progress to the GCI Controller. "Come on now, hang in there a couple of more seconds and I'll know what you are," I said out loud in a determined but pleading voice. George was uncharacteristically silent.

Again the light started to move slowly to our left. I banked a little more to the left. My lights were now shining only slightly behind the UFO. Hold it UFO, hold it. I was reluctant to bank any further but it was obvious I would never get my lights on it if I didn't. Keeping an eye on the angle of attack chevron, I increased the bank angle. The landing lights began to illuminate the intruder. George and I stared at the UFO in amazement. We couldn't believe our eyes. It was not saucer or cigar shaped, nor was it a brilliant, shining, metallic object, nor was it from outer space. It was a dark-blue, twin-engine, propeller-driven Navy S2F,

"Tracker" Anti-Submarine Warfare Aircraft putting along at 120 knots at 10,000 thousand feet. What a disappointment! We could barely keep from laughing as we reported the identification to the GCI Controller.

The pilot of the S2F had either forgotten to turn on his navigation lights or they were inoperative. The only light showing was a bright white light on the bottom of the fuselage. As we found out later, he had departed NAS New Orleans around 2330 local en route to Key West. Apparently the crew had not been able to establish over-water communications nor had NAS New Orleans passed his route and proposed arrival time to Key West. In either case, he should not have been blithely flying through warning areas without permission.

The lack of motion we perceived was due to his slow speed and total lack of any visual reference against which to measure it. The rapid movements left and right were primarily the result of our high closure rates and varying angles off as we flew at the solitary light, akin to watching the lights of a distant car coming directly at you. There is little perception of relative motion until the car is quite near at which time the lights blossom in size, blaze in brilliance, separate and storm rapidly by.

Had we not made a positive identification, or had the S2F turned out his light and dove for the deck, two fighter pilots, two radar operators and one GCI Controller would have provided an accurate and fully believable account of an encounter with a visitor from another planet. The UFO would have gone down in the record books as being able to do all the antics most often ascribed to those unearthly vehicles. As for me, I would have sworn on a stack of Bibles that it was all true. Ever since that encounter I admit to a mild skepticism when it comes to UFO sightings. I often wonder what the pilots of the S2F must have thought, as two fighters made repeated passes on their airplane in the middle of the night.

Welcome the Marines

At the completion of our first alert duty tour at Key West, VF-31 was relieved by a Marine Corps F8 Crusader Squadron, with undoubtedly the most arrogant bunch of pilots I ever encountered. Two VF-31 crews remained for a couple of days in an attempt to provide some degree of continuity during the transition. The Marines refused all but the most rudimentary help getting situated and assured us they didn't need any assistance with their flight operations.

Beware of Marines carrying missiles

George and I were standing outside the alert trailer to observe their first practice alert. Their time from alert to takeoff was impressive. It was on takeoff that the real fireworks began. The two Crusaders did not quite make a formation takeoff but there was barely a couple of seconds between their takeoff rolls.

As the second Crusader lifted off, George and I stared at the two planes for a moment and then looked at each other utterly dumbfounded. When the second airplane's landing gear started to retract, a live Sidewinder missile blasted off each side of its fuselage and whizzed past the leader's airplane. The missiles couldn't have missed the first F8 by more than twenty feet. The pilot of the second F8 either had a serious missile system malfunction or had taken off with the system armed and his finger on the trigger. When he raised the landing gear handle, both missiles fired. Fortunately the lead aircraft was close enough that the missiles did not have time to activate their guidance systems. The two missiles bracketed the leader's aircraft with telltale trails of white smoke and continued on a straight course arching gracefully into the Atlantic Ocean. We then understood why the Marines preferred a closer takeoff interval than we did.

Assuming the pilot of the lead aircraft saw the missiles, and I can't imagine he didn't, for they went right by his canopy, I'm sure he had a much browner flight suit seat than when he started out. I almost did and I was watching it from nearly two miles away. It would have been interesting to be a fly on the wall at the debriefing of that flight!

Not that the takeoff incident wasn't bad enough, they had another and more serious incident the next day. They loved to hot-rod around the traffic pattern and always requested a low altitude fan-break for landing. Those of us who had trained at Key West, knew how quickly the weather could change and almost always flew some type of instrument approach to landing. On day two, two Crusaders, who had

Crusader 1 lands normal

Crusader 2 lands long

also achieved a creditable scramble time and hadn't tried to shoot each other down on takeoff, were approaching for landing. Their high-speed fan-break looked neat; although it appeared that Number Two was a little close to Number One on final. It looked like a sloppy section landing just as the previous day's takeoff had looked like a sloppy formation takeoff.

The first F8 touched down normally and Number Two was barely a second or two behind him. Unfortunately Number Two landed longer or Number One either landed slower or decelerated faster than Number Two, for the second F8 ran into the rear of the first. The rudder of the first ended up with a perfect "V" cut out of its vertical tail that matched the silhouette of the radome of the second. The second airplane had the imprint of an afterburner nozzle in its intake duct. Needless to say, both airplanes were going to be down for a while until the beginning of one and the ending of the other were repaired. Knowing the Marines, they probably took the front of one and the back of the other and made them into one flyable airplane. George and I were happy to lift off in our Phantom for Cecil Field. I hoped the Marines survived their alert tour at Key West. I'm sure the Naval Air Station was never quite the same. I concluded that if you were going to be that arrogant, you had better be good enough to warrant it. What's more, be able to prove it to your peers.

Space Suit

Unlike the Demon that struggled to get to 35,000 feet, the Phantom easily exceeded 50,000 feet. Flying over 50,000 feet required encasement of the flight crew in a full pressure suit. At great expense to the government, we were individually fitted for pressure suits. For me it was deja vu, a throw back to my college days at the Naval Air Test Center. We did the standard high altitude chamber runs, including rapid decompressions. Our last training exercise was primarily a confidence builder. We donned a full pressure suit, not our own, weighted ourselves, submerged in the swimming pool and walked around under the water. It seemed the antithesis of a space suit

High flyers reach 73,000 feet

and more like a deep-sea diving suit. The principles are the same. I actually flew two flights up to 55,000 feet and another flight where we had the opportunity to fly the Phantom as high as we could coax it to go. With Jon Steele as my RIO, we were lucky to draw a "slick" (no armament racks or external fuel tanks) Phantom for our high altitude attempt. The operational procedure was to accelerate in full afterburner to Mach 1.5 at or about 38,000 feet, make a "2 g" pull up to 45 degrees nose up and fly over the top at a maximum of 9 units angle of attack. Jon and I took off and headed out over the Atlantic into Warning Area W-158. To preclude an inadvertent pressurization of the suit, we always flew the climb out with the wrist attachment of one glove disconnected. At 35,000 feet we reconnected the gloves and depressurized the cockpit to inflate the suit to check for proper operation and leaks. Trust me, it is a lot harder to fly with the suit inflated when your arms are lifted up and forward and are as stiff as a board. The helmet does its utmost to lift and separate your head from your body. It is also difficult to feel the controls through the inflated gloves. It was a relief to repressurize the cockpit.

As we approached the eastern boundary of the Warning Area, I turned back to the west, went to full afterburner and accelerated rapidly to Mach 1.6. I increased the "g" to two as smoothly as I could, trying to capture as much energy as possible. At 45 degrees nose up the altitude indicator spun upward in a blur. At 66,000 thousand feet, both afterburners blew out simultaneously. I deselected the non-functioning afterburners and concentrated on keeping the engine exhaust gas temperatures from over temping. Shades of the budding seventeen year old test pilots in their Ercoupe. Knowing that a normal landing

Mach 1.6, nose up 45 degrees, altimeter a blur

was made at 19 units angle of attack, and that the stall warning was set to activate at 23.3, I had already planned on going over the top at 21 units angle of attack. I eased the throttles back but did not need to shutdown either engine. The throttles were nearing the idle stop position as we passed through 70,000 feet, which had kind of become the Squadron's high altitude benchmark. We were still climbing. I let the angle of attack increase as the rate of climb decreased, being especially careful not to disturb the aircraft laterally or to exceed 21 units of angle of attack for fear of spinning out at the higher angle of attack. We topped out at 73,000 feet. At that point we were mostly at the whims of gravity with little influence from aerodynamics. Thankfully, the cabin pressure did not decrease to the point where the protection of the suit was required, i.e. the suit did not inflate. The sky is in fact darker at the higher altitudes but we had precious little time to enjoy the view. The nose fell through slowly and the airspeed increased rapidly. This flight was likely as close as I will ever get to being an astronaut.

Dead in the Water

The USS Saratoga had undergone extensive overhaul in the Portsmouth Naval Shipyard between the Demon cruise in 1963 and the Phantom cruise in 1964. While the Saratoga was a Forrestal class aircraft carrier, internally

USS Saratoga undergoes major overhaul in 1963

it had one major difference. The Saratoga had a 1200 psi steam system rather than the standard 600 psi system of the Forrestal. The high-pressure steam system was harder to maintain and more susceptible to leaks. Although there had been several upgrades to the ship during its overhaul, it did not seem to be in as good a shape as it was in 1963. While we aviators had nothing to do with the operation of the ship, it was not unusual for the ship to be steaming happily along, launching and recovering aircraft one minute and dead in the water the next. Obviously this did not exactly instill a lot of confidence in the flight crews. We did several training operations off the Florida coast in preparation for the upcoming deployment.

Southeast Air Defense Command

In the early 1960s, the Russians had developed some fairly sophisticated air-to-surface missiles providing them with a significant stand off bombing capability. One such missile was carried beneath the fuselage of their Bear and Bison bombers and had a supersonic speed capability. They were especially well suited for attacking the fleet. We simulated these missile attacks by flying two Phantoms together between thirty and forty thousand feet in to a distance of about a 150 miles from the fleet. At a predetermined point, one F4B would simulate the profile of the missile by making a diving supersonic run on the carrier.

On this particular day we were operating from the Saratoga about 75 miles off the Georgia coast in preparation for

USS Saratoga cruises off the Georgia coast

our upcoming deployment to the Mediterranean. LTJG Ferg Norton and I made a low-level departure from the ship to the north. At 200 miles we climbed to 35,000 feet and turned toward the ship. I was the simulated bomber and Ferg the simulated missile. At a 150 miles we activated our radars and Ferg started his dive toward the carrier. As I watched him disappear below and in front of me, a single glint of sunlight slightly below, behind, and to my right caught my attention. I called the target to George and we craned our necks to see who or what it was. I wrapped the airplane into a sixty degree banked turn to the right long enough to identify two Air Force delta winged F-102s in the final stage of an intercept on us. Someone had obviously forgotten to inform the East Coast Air Defense sector that we would be operating in the area. Since the two F-102s were already slightly sucked (behind) in their turn, I decided valor was the better part of discretion this time, and started my own supersonic dive toward the ship. I rolled inverted, unloaded the airplane (reduced the "g") and tapped the powerful double afterburners. The Phantom responded, as I knew it would. We accelerated downhill so fast it looked like the two F-102s had simply stopped in midair. By their relative positions I suspect they were already in full afterburner. They had little choice but to watch their two targets disappear right before their eyes.

When we recovered on the Saratoga, we reported the incident to the Combat Information Center and filled out an incident report in the event the pilot's in the F-102s filed a formal violation. We never heard anything further, so we assumed we had violated the ADIZ (Air Defense Identification Zone) and gotten away with it.

Caribbean Cruise

It was normal for the Aircraft Carrier with its Air Group aboard to undergo a short deployment to the Caribbean for its Operational Readiness Inspection (ORI) prior to deploying to the Mediterranean. The

Cruising the Caribbean

Saratoga's mechanical problems severely hampered a good ringing out of the ship's capabilities as most of the Caribbean deployment was devoted to getting the ship up to a deployable level.

New Airplanes

When we departed for the Mediterranean on December 14, 1964, VF-31 was not the only Squadron sporting new aircraft.

VF-31 F4B Phantom II

The Heavy Attack Squadron, VAH-9, now known as RVAH-9; had transitioned from the A3D to the North American RA5C, "Vigilante," a two-place, supersonic, reconnaissance aircraft capable of carrying nuclear weapons. It was a

RVAH-9 RA5C Vigilante

beautiful sleek airplane, but its heavyweight and high landing speed made it a challenge to land aboard the ship.

HU-2 UH-2 Seasprite

The Rescue helicopter detachment, HU-2, was now flying the Kaman UH-2A "Seasprite" Helicopter.

Avoid the Russians

The Russians continued to demonstrate their ability to find and overfly the U.S. Carriers. One of the requirements of this deployment was to transit the Atlantic undetected. To this end a decoy Cruiser followed the normal deployment route and the Saratoga took a more southernly route. The Cruiser broadcast recordings of full flight operations and the Carrier went to full EMCOM silence, i.e. no electronic emissions. As far as I know, neither ship was overflown. It didn't mean, however, that we didn't have to stand alert duty during the crossing.

Steam problems continued throughout the cruise creating numerous nuisance factors, like restricted water hours and "Navy" type showers. Unfortunately the tempo of flight operations did not always coincide with the ship's water schedule.

Phantom stands "lonely" Alert Duty

Our Russian shadow

The Russians were actively pursuing the development of their first Aircraft Carrier. To this end, it was not unusual for us to encounter Russian Naval vessels while on deployment. This deployment was no different. They were getting bolder and more persistent.

Partway through the deployment, our Russian shadow showed up. A Russian Cruiser joined the Task Force and attached itself to the Aircraft Carrier. For the most part he behaved nicely and interfered little with our operations.

During launch and recoveries, the Cruiser always stationed itself fairly close to the aft port side of the Carrier to observe our flight operations. Unfortunately for

A Russian Cruiser shadows the USS Saratoga

Fuel for the Russians

him, it positioned him right under our flight path slightly beyond the one eighty degree position. When we knew he was going to be there, we saved a little extra fuel in our outboard wing tanks and dumped it on the cruiser as we flew low overhead. That had to be the dirtiest, greasiest, and slipperiest ship in the entire Russian Navy.

Poopy Suits

When the water temperature was fifty-nine degrees or below, or the outside air temperature was thirty-two degrees or below, or the combined air/water temperature was one hundred twenty degrees or below, we were required to wear exposure suits, affectionately known as "Poopy Suits." These suits were skintight rubber suits that covered you from the neck to the bottoms of your feet. The poopy suit only kept you dry, so we wore thermal underwear beneath it. Once you were encapsulated inside the suit it was too late to decide that you needed to take care of nature's call. I always said that the last item on the pilot's checklist was to make one last head call. It also meant you were going to sweat it out until you had flown your sortie. Donning the suit worked a lot better when you had someone to help you put it on. Getting your head through the neck hole while not quite fully in the torso of the suit was not easy. Of course none of us ever expected to go into the water, but had we done so, we would not have survived without it. Your flight suit and boots went over the poopy suit, followed by the "g" suit that looked a lot like cowboy chaps. The "g" suit attached to an air connector on the left console in the cockpit and used pressurized air to inflate it under high "g" conditions. The inflated "g" suit restricts the blood flow in the abdomen, thighs and calves, allowing us to pull higher "g" levels without blacking out. Next came the survival vest containing lots of useful equipment should you find yourself in a survival situation. After that we strapped on our thirty-eight caliber pistol loaded mostly with tracer bullets since we were not in a wartime situation. A tracer looks a lot like a neon light in the blackness of the sea. We were cautioned never to aim the pistol at the rescue helicopter if we wanted to get picked up. At this time in the dressing process, you are literally sweating and can't wait to "Man your aircraft," and cool down. While this may sound like a lot of trouble, you get used to it in a short period of time. After all, your life may very well depend on this equipment.

The Disappearing RIO

It was one of those dazzling blue days when the brilliant sunlight shimmered off the Mediterranean Sea like millions of diamonds. George and I were about a mile astern of the ship heading into the break for landing with our hook already extended. The quiet of the beautiful morning was interrupted abruptly as the radio exclaimed, "Plane in the water port side, Plane in the water port side!" As we passed

Now you see him, now you don't

over the ship, we craned our necks to see what had happened.

Without warning, there was a tremendous BOOM! And a horrendous blast of air as George ejected from our Phantom. For a moment I was stunned. In the rear view mirror all I could see was a big hole where George should have been. My first thought was, "Why the hell didn't he tell me we had a problem?" Without hesitation, figuring George obviously knew something I didn't know, I reached up and placed both hands on the ejection seat handles located above my head. I was making one last check of the instruments before I yanked the ejection handle (fortunately none of the dials wavered), when a wee tiny, and very high-pitched voice exclaimed, "No! Don't! I'm still here!"

For some unexplained reason, the aft canopy had separated from the airplane! Simultaneously, George had ducked down into the cockpit. Consequently, when I looked in the mirror all I saw was open space. I really was going to pull the ejection handles. George gave the LSO the finger through the open cockpit as we landed. A broken cam on the closing mechanism was identified as the cause of the canopy separation.

Lonely Christmas 1964

I spent my first Christmas ever away from home in port at Naples, Italy. The Saratoga hosted a Christmas party for local Italian orphans but it didn't fill the void of not having one's family near on Christmas.

A Christmas party for Naples' orphans

Cat Shot Serenade

Ever since we transitioned to the Phantom, Jim Carnes had been itching to take a flight from the Aircraft Carrier. One day we were scheduled to do something we seldom got to do, other than during Carrier Qualifications and that was "run-the-deck" or get several Cat shots and landings on the same flight. We finally convinced the Skipper to let me take Jim for a ride. George showed Jim how to operate the necessary systems and set up the switches in the backseat. It was a beautiful summer day and the calm Mediterranean Sea reflected the puffy white cumulus clouds floating overhead in the gentle breeze. Jim had flown with me at Cecil Field but he had never flown off the ship. The inter phone betrayed his

"Are you OK Jim?"

nervousness and amplified his anxiety. As we taxied onto
the catapult Jim's breathing rate doubled.

"Are you OK Jim?"

"Yeah, yeah I'm fine."

"Make sure you put your head firmly against the headrest when we launch."

"OK."

When the catapult fired, every ounce of air expelled from
Jim's lungs as a most God awful O-O-O-Omph echoed in my
headset the entire length of the run. I probably should have
been concerned for his safety but it was so funny I was on
the verge of laughter.

"Jim are you sure you're OK?"

His now hyperventilating, "I'm fine, that was great,"
was more than I could handle, I burst out laughing. On
downwind, Jim's breathing increased to at least three times
its normal rate. As we turned toward final he followed me
through the before landing checklist confirming each item.

"Confirm your shoulder harness is locked," I cautioned.

"It's locked and I'm ready for landing," came the reply.

I focused my attention on flying the approach. On arrestment, I was serenaded by yet another, but much shorter, "O-Omph" and an excited, "Wow!"

"I agree, Jim, an arrested landing is difficult to describe and hard to appreciate until you've actually been there," I added.

As we taxied toward the catapult, I couldn't resist, "Jim, don't scare me like you did last time, make sure your head is pressed tightly against the headrest."

"I won't, I know what to expect now."

I'm sure he tried, but his "O-O-O-Omph" this time, and the next, was equally as loud. I told him those were the loudest catapult shots I had ever taken. He enjoyed the flight, as did I, but there was no way I could resist telling the rest of the Squadron about Jim's "Cat Shot Serenades." We relived the flight many times. He was a great roommate.

Taking care of the Boss

Jim and I worked in maintenance, which meant we had a lot of interaction with the enlisted men. Whenever the ship conducted an at sea replenishment, our Aircraft Division provided the extra manpower the ship's company required. Jim was highly regarded and especially well liked by his men and they took good care of him. On this cruise, we were more senior, had a larger stateroom and the luxury of all shipboard luxuries, a refrigerator. The goodies that appeared in our refrigerator after every replenishment, compliments of our enlisted friends, were impressive. My favorite was #12 cans of strawberries. We lived "high on the hog" for several days following each supply operation.

Airborne Replenishment

Ship-to-ship is not the only way the Carrier can be replenished while underway. Most Cargo ships have a helicopter platform located at the stern that allows provisions to be airlifted by helicopter. It was impressive how efficient the operation was. A single Sikorsky

Fancy flying H-34

H-34 helicopter typically carried three cargo nets on a hook beneath the aircraft. The helicopter looked like a honeybee flitting between a flower (the Cargo ship) and the honeycomb (the Carrier). It would pick up three loads and deposit them on the forward flight deck of the Carrier. By the time it returned to the Cargo ship, another load was ready for pickup. When it returned to the Saratoga, the previous load had been moved and the three empty nets were ready for return to the Cargo ship. The transfer was kept up for several hours and required some very precise flying by the helicopter crew.

Another "Routine" Hydraulic Failure

George and I launched one afternoon for a routine Combat Air Patrol mission and had been airborne less than five minutes when we experienced yet another utility

Low and fast to use up the gas

hydraulic failure. We called the Air Boss and reported our problem. For several minutes we discussed whether we should land during the present recovery or wait until our normal landing time. It didn't matter to us. We had had five previous hydraulic failures and felt comfortable staying in the air. The Air Boss decided we should land on the current recovery, which meant we had to get down to landing weight quickly. The choices were: dump fuel, burn fuel or both. We elected the second alternative.

What fun to have all this gas and so little time in which to use it! Of course, the quickest way to expend the fuel was to plug in those big double afterburners and charge around at low altitude and high airspeed. We had a grand time. We were quickly down to landing weight and joined the landing pattern near the end of the recovery.

It was George who first noticed the TACAN bearing becoming erratic. In rapid succession, we began to have radio and inter phone problems. As we turned down wind for landing, George reported several unusual circuit breakers had popped. Something was definitely wrong with the electrical system. On final, George called over the intermittent inter phone that he was getting faint smoke in the aft cockpit. Without explanation I told the LSO we had a problem and intended to shut down both engines as soon as we stopped. His only reply was, "Roger." It turned out to be a good decision.

The half-flap landing was uneventful, even good. Of course we had had several practices during previous hydraulic failures. As soon as we came to a halt, I stop cocked both engines. We were used to being towed out of the landing area by now.

When maintenance inspected the engine compartment, they discovered we had developed a small bleed-air leak in the main boundary layer cross tube in the center of the fuselage, probably during the catapult shot. The high-temperature air had melted several hydraulic lines, hence the hydraulic failure. No one, except possibly the Good Lord above, could explain why the hydraulic fluid did not ignite and cause an explosion or a major fire. The electrical anomalies resulted from several charred wire bundles located in the same area. The metal shielding along the right side of the fuel tank was badly burned. It was estimated that the metal was less than three minutes from being burned through. The rubber fuel bladder would have lasted only seconds and the entire right side of the airplane would have been engulfed in flames. It had been a lucky decision to recover the airplane on the current recovery and a good decision to shut down the engines on landing. It had been a stupid choice to charge around at low altitude in full afterburner rather than simply dumping the fuel, but then we would never had made it to the next recovery even at reduced power.

Within two weeks, LT Vince Knaus and LTJG Roger Brokaw experienced a similar but catastrophic failure and ejected midway through their catapult stroke. Both crewmen survived the ejection without injury.

NATO Exercise

The most exciting part of any NATO exercise was the opportunity to test our air-to-air skills against aircraft and pilots from other countries. Even though the F4B did not carry a gun, it was impossible to resist playing fighter pilot when the opportunity presented itself. During one such exercise, George and I were flying a low level Combat Air Patrol mission when we intercepted a flight of four, French, twin-engine, Vautour fighters. We passed the flight head-on at about 250 feet. They immediately broke up into two flights of two. One pair started a hard level turn to the left and the

A French Vautour fighter

other pair climbed up and right. I pulled back hard, lit the afterburners and climbed straight up affixing my attention on the two climbing fighters. High above them I rolled left until inverted, yanked the throttle to idle, pulled the nose through to keep the pair in sight and started down. The two Vautours, with their noses still pointed upward, rolled left as I passed them canopy to canopy on the way down. I eased my descent and started a hard left turn. The pair ran out of airspeed and continued their left turn as they nosed down

Phantoms fight vertical

to regain speed. I lost track of the two lower fighters. I continued my hard left turn and pulled the nose upward again to achieve additional vertical and horizontal separation from the descending pair. The wing man was doing an excellent job of staying with his leader. The leader either lost sight of me, or didn't have enough energy to decrease his turn radius any further, or get his nose up to stop his decent, for he continued the same descending left turn toward the water. Again I lit the afterburner and hung at altitude just long enough to maintain the separation and started down. It was too easy. I put the speed brakes out and practically rendezvoused on the descending fighters. Unfortunately, I closed faster than expected and went under the leader at less than 500 feet over the water. I lit the burner and pulled up steeply to insure we were seen. We must have taken the wing man by surprise for he broke hard right and ended up nose down and almost inverted less than 300 feet above the water. We were sure there was no way he could possibly recover before he hit the water. I banked hard right anticipating the inevitable splash. To our amazement he somehow managed to roll wings level and pull out at less than a 100 feet, leaving a distinct wake in the water. It was a masterful piece of flying but I'm sure he was one frightened French fighter pilot, for he sure scared me.

George was the first to catch a glimpse of the other two Vautours still in a steep left turn at our eight o'clock position and closing. I reversed my turn, tapped the afterburner and started to climb. The two Vautours didn't stand a chance of catching us. As I rolled

Where are the other two fighters?

out of the turn, two small delta wing airplanes appeared high above us and to our right. It was obvious that they were intent on helping their beleaguered friends. The arrival of the two French Mirage III fighters would have presented a real challenge because it was a great fighter and easily climbed with and out turned the F4B. None of us looked forward to meeting them one-on-one. A quick check of the fuel gages indicated we had no choice but to head for home. The low altitude maneuvering and excess afterburner use had taken its toll. There would be no more fighter pilot heroics this morning. We dove for the deck and raced toward the Saratoga. Too bad, it would have been a challenge and fun.

Orange, France

During one of these NATO exercises, LTJG George Shirley and I were invited to Orange Military Airfield as observers and guests of the French Air Force. We arrived at the Air Base by COD (Carrier Onboard Delivery aircraft) in the late afternoon. Three young, English speaking, French Air Force pilots were assigned to "take care of our every need."

After we checked into our quarters, we were met and given the royal tour of Orange. I have never eaten so many things I didn't recognize, all delicious, in my life. The evening passed quickly and the early morning even quicker. It was fun but we were not used to such rich food, late hours, and so little sleep.

George didn't look any better than I felt as we reported to the Officer's Club for lunch the next day as guests of the Base Commander, Colonel Charles. I handled the amenities gracefully but lunch was not as easy. The first course consisted of a whole fish entombed in a clear jelly-like substance. I took one look at that fish and it looked me right back. It wasn't any happier about my eating him than I was about eating it.

I quietly excused myself, made my way to the men's room, and not so quietly lost the remnants of the previous evening's dining. I washed my face with cold water, took several deep breaths, and returned to the table. I cautiously scraped off the jelly and gingerly dabbed at the gray carcass. I was relieved when the steward arrived to take away the fish delicacy. I'm sure Colonel Charles felt we didn't enjoy his luncheon because we ate so little.

At Orange, we observed a couple of Navy A4s fly over the base but agreed we would rather have been participating in the war games than sitting on the sidelines. It was while we were at Orange that Vince Knaus and Roger Brokaw ejected during a catapult launch.

Air Show

On occasion we hosted foreign dignitaries, particularly those of our NATO allies. We would put on an air show to demonstrate the capability of the Aircraft Carrier. The Attack Squadrons, especially the A1H, Skyraiders, were impressive with their fire power demonstrations. They dropped real bombs and rockets about a quarter-mile off the port side of the ship. It was amazing how much water was destroyed during these demonstrations. It made a believer out of me. I never wanted to be the recipient of any of those weapons. The RA5C Vigilante broke the sound barrier close enough along the side of the ship that you could actually feel the shock wave. The Willy Fudd and the Kaman helicopter flew

Daisy chain refueling

in formation with the helicopter breaking left abeam the ship and making a three sixty degree turn to a hover. Two A4D Skyhawks and a Phantom refueled in a daisy chain with one A4D taking fuel from the first, while the Phantom tanked from the second. It looked like the lead tanker was towing the other two aircraft through the sky.

The F8U-1P, Photo Reconnaissance Crusader used explosive magnesium flares to provide illumination for night reconnaissance. The "flash bulbs" were fired upward from the fuselage aft of the cockpit. The Crusader performed a low altitude loop with a three sixty degree roll at the top, popping flares all the way around. If there was little wind, the puffs of smoke from the flares made a near perfect heart in the sky.

The finale of the show was an en masse formation flyby of at least four aircraft from each Squadron. The real finale was the recovery of the aircraft aboard ship. It was an excellent demonstration of the enormous warfare capability of the Aircraft Carrier and its aircraft.

Goodbye Drone

Vince and I drew the long straws for the opportunity to fire Sidewinder missiles at a free flying drone. Since I was junior I would shoot second. The drone arrived right on schedule. As we entered one end of the restricted area, it entered the other. Both airplanes got good radar targets and Vince started his intercept. George had his trusty movie camera running as we hung loosely onto Vince's

Sidewinder splashes drone, Drat!

Sidewinder launch on film

wing. Following some rather abrupt maneuvering, George actually filmed the missile leaving the rail. The white smoke trail from the Sidewinder was a beautiful sight as it traced it's snake-like intercept of the drone. We were excited for Vince as we watched the missile guide to the target and relished the opportunity to get our chance to shoot. Our excitement was short lived. Vince's Sidewinder scored a direct hit on the drone. We watched our only chance to fire against a live drone spiral lazily into the blue sea below. Vince was ecstatic. I was very disappointed.

Pay Attention to Stay Dry

On yet another day, during a live Sidewinder firing against a towed low-altitude Delmar target, George and I almost ended up in the ocean ourselves. Flying low over a rough sea made the small Delmar target extremely difficult to pick up on radar. George finally got a return but not until we were quite close to the target. We did our best, but ended up too near the target to fire the missile. The lighted flares on the target burned brightly and I wanted to destroy it in

Too low, too slow, dangerous

the worst way. If only the F4B had a reverse gear. With idle power and full speed brakes, I slowed down faster and to a much slower speed than I intended. As the nose of the airplane started to slice left and right (an indication of an incipient stall), the chase plane called just as I was adding power. We were about to depart from controlled flight only 300 feet above the ocean, not a healthy thing to do. I swallowed my pride and pulled up beside the target. There would be no live firing on that pass. I learned a good lesson about flying that day. We were given a second chance and got our missile away. While the missile did not hit the target, it was judged a lethal miss.

In Port Too Often

During the cruise, the United States was becoming increasingly involved in the Vietnam War. Although the war was halfway around the world, it created a major resource problem for the Sixth Fleet in the Mediterranean. On the previous cruise, we were typically at sea for ten days to two weeks and in port three to five days. On this cruise these numbers were almost reversed. We spent considerably more time in port. The disturbing effect was a reduction in air crew proficiency, especially for night operations. Most of us would rather have been flying.

A Memorable Easter

We spent Easter of 1965 in Athens and held a very moving Sunrise Service on Mars Hill near the Acropolis, the place where Paul had preached to the assembled Greeks nearly 2,000 years ago. In the cold morning air, the Chaplain

A memorable Easter on Mars Hill

presented a suitable sermon, but most memorable was the beautiful singing of one of our Filipino Wardroom Stewards named Vibat. His voice matched the grandeur of the sun as it broke the horizon and flooded the calm hazy sky with a crimson red as deep as blood.

War Games

When Commander Wissler became the Squadron Commander, he was the first CO to show any interest in furthering the tactical education of his officers. During in-port periods, we developed and played complex War Games. A typical scenario pitted the Carrier Task Force against an aggressor country capable of defeating the Task Force. We were divided into three teams, the good guys, the bad guys, and the team that conducted and refereed the war game. One set of detailed maps showed the deployed Task Force and the other the Aggressor Force distributions. Typical intelligence reports were provided to the opposing teams. Offensive and defensive maneuvers were passed

F4B attacking Mt. Etna

to the processing team who evaluated their effectiveness and provided appropriate feedback based on the interaction of the opposing proposals. Typical of the flight crew ego, competition was intense and much ire was vented, mostly at the processing team. No matter which team we were on, we all learned a lot.

At the end of the game, the processing team provided a complete debriefing. Commander Wissler, with his Air Warfare College background, provided outstanding feedback. Discussions often continued for days after the exercise regarding better tactics, or more often, as to how the processing team had screwed up the interpretation of the intended maneuvers. I believe we were all enriched by the experience. If nothing else, the War Games gave the junior officers a better understanding and appreciation of the difficulty and potential outcome of decisions made with sketchy and incomplete information.

Dedication

The angriest George ever got with me was on a flight the day before we were to put into the port of Palma de Majorca. Shortly after takeoff we experienced a problem with our right engine and shut it down. We discussed our problem with the Air Boss and he suggested we proceed to Palma and land. I honestly felt the best place for the airplane was on the Sara-

Will it be the ship or the shore?

toga where we had engines and maintenance people to work on it. I argued with the Air Boss, while George did his best to make me see the Air Boss's position. To George's dismay, I ended up convincing the Air Boss to let us land aboard. In retrospect, George was right. We wasted a full night in Palma without 5,000 sailors around and the maintenance people would have loved to work on the airplane on terra firma. Besides, no one seemed concerned but me. I should have gone to Palma as originally proposed but I had no idea what we would have done for two days in our smelly orange flight suits. George always maintained he would have gladly bought us enough clothes to solve that problem.

A Trip to the Captain's Office

For three days we flew nearly continuous fighter cover for the Skyhawks, Skyraiders and Vigilantes supporting a practice Marine amphibious assault landing on the Island of Sardinia. It was relatively boring because all we did was fly high overhead while the attack types had all the fun. On the fourth day, the air war was over and we knew the Marines had landed successfully. LT Mike Fleming, LTJG Gary Ferguson and I were scheduled for a practice intercept mission. I'm not quite sure whose idea it was, but we decided it would improve the morale of the Grunts slugging it out on the Island, if we gave them an air show. Besides, for three days now, we'd been itching to fly down in the dirt like attack pilots. We were spectacular. Mike led the flight through a series of low-level high "g" turns and a few vertical maneuvers for good measure. We were sure the spectators below had enjoyed our show as much as we had performing for them.

The low level flying and the afterburner maneuvers had used up most of our fuel so we headed back to the Saratoga for "practice" aerial refueling with the duty tanker. I'm sure the tanker pilot didn't really buy our story about all three Phantoms needing a wet transfer to check out their air refueling systems. Anyway, he obligingly gave each of us 500 pounds of fuel so we wouldn't be too embarrassed when we called the ball with low fuel states.

We even improvised the approach and break over the ship. Rather than our normal right echelon formation, Gary flew Mike's left wing and I was on his right. The formation was especially tight. We felt great. Gary broke left on Mike's kiss off, then Mike. I took my interval and turned down wind in trail. I even got an OK, three wire. The six of us were in great spirits as we strode into the Ready Room.

Three F4s in the break, Three pilots to the Captain's Office

The elation was short lived. As we entered the Ready Room, the Skipper met us at the door. It seemed the Captain wanted to see the three "Phantom" pilots in his office right away. We knew we had put on an impressive aerial display, but we really didn't believe it warranted a commendation from the Captain.

We waited anxiously in the Captain's outer office, not quite sure what to expect. I was sure glad it was Mike who had led the flight and not me. The Yeoman at the desk, without speaking, motioned that we should enter. We filed in, Mike, me, then Gary. Standing at attention and in unison, "Reporting as ordered, Sir." It was painfully obvious from the Captain's expression that we were not about to receive a commendation for superior airmanship.

"Do you gentlemen know how close you came to getting yourselves killed this morning?" The side glances between the three of us varied only by our relative locations. We wondered, "What does that mean?" The Captain continued, "Admiral Townsend is angry as hell. Your antics this morning caused him to shut down a large scale and very important live artillery exercise for the Marines. I have directed your CO to take appropriate action. You gentlemen are dismissed." Without a word, we turned toward the door, the Captain cleared his throat and with a slight twinkle in his eye, added a post script, "I understand it was a pretty good show, just don't let it happen again."

Commander Creaseman was not as generous as the Captain. He restricted the six of us to the ship for the entire in-port period in Marseilles, France. Fortunately it was only a five day visit. I felt especially sorry for Mike, for when the LSO debriefed us on our landings, he had gotten a low, slow, taxi to the number one wire, "cut" pass. It was not his day.

"Look Maw, No Nose Wheels"

The landing approach and wire engagement appeared perfectly normal, even good, that is until the nose wheels hit the deck and the nose fell through much further than usual and I found myself starring down at the deck. The front axle had cracked on touchdown. One wheel bounded off the left side of the angle deck and splashed harmlessly into the sea. The other careened to the right and crashed through the extended flap of one of VA-35's Skyraiders, leaving a jagged rectangular hole. We were lucky no one was hit by the errant wheels. I shut down the engines. George and I remained in the cockpit as a four-wheeled dolly was placed under the broken nose strut and the Phantom was towed out of the landing area. The whole process took less than five minutes. The ground crew painted the outline of a Skyraider beneath the canopy rail of my aircraft to commemorate the "kill."

Wake up Time

Night Combat Air Patrol missions from the ship were not always the most exciting. Most of the time was spent in orbit and the rest doing radar intercepts on another Phantom. It was more fun when there was enough

Two Phantoms airborne at dusk

moon (night flying was always better when there was even the slightest hint of a moon) to allow positive identification of the intercepted aircraft. It was especially fun when you knew you had intercepted another military airplane. It was an irresistible urge to let them know the U.S. Navy was awake and doing their job. I can only imagine the surprise many a sleepy C-130 flight crew experienced as we accelerated underneath them in full afterburner and timed our pull up so as to flash vertically in their windshield as we climbed past them. If they didn't see the afterburner lights, I'm sure they felt the turbulence. It's too bad those legalized flat-hatting days are gone.

Allemande Left

Normally when we conducted exercises against the other Aircraft Carrier in the Mediterranean, we flew with all our electronic navigation aids turned off in what we called EMCOM conditions. Someone cleverly decided that for one exercise we would leave the Saratoga's TACAN station (Navigation aid) on the air with one minor change. The TACAN bearing information was rotated ninety degrees either left or right. We briefed our crews that in order to track into the Carrier, it was necessary to place the TACAN bearing needle on either the left or right wing as appropriate. It worked for a while as the "Bad Guys" flew in circles around the ship thinking they were tracking into the Saratoga (and how dumb we were to leave our TACAN station on the air). Except for a couple of our pilots who either didn't listen closely during the briefing or didn't understand it and circled the ship themselves, we Saratogan's had the last laugh.

Bombs Away?

As George and I assumed our Combat Air Patrol position eighty miles northeast of the Saratoga at a hundred feet, the bright milky gray sky reflected off the glassy smooth Medi-

Low altitude Combat Air Patrol

terranean. We had relaxed and were scanning the radarscope for possible bogies when, without any warning, a fusillade of practice bombs splashed into the water slightly forward and to the left of the airplane. Their telltale columns of white smoke ascended straight up and hung for several seconds in the calm morning air.

My first thought was, "What a dumb shit thing to do, you could hurt someone." My second, and more logical, thought was to find out who did it. I pointed it out to George and started a steep climbing left turn hoping we would pick up whomever it was on our radar. We made a second 360 degree turn at 1,000 feet and didn't have a single radar return. Perplexed, we descended back to 100 feet and headed back to our designated position. Less than a mile from the CAP point, yet another volley of practice bombs crashed into the water. Whoever it was had to be right in front of us. I pulled up again hoping to get a visual contact but the gray haze was too opaque, and still no radar return. I decided it was prudent to move our CAP location to the east. Following a foolish afterthought, I decided to fly over our assigned position en route to the new one. As we crossed the original position, we were treated to yet another practice bomb display. This time, however, it was obvious the smoke plumes were not being generated from above the water but from below. We had flown over a pod of eight whales making their way through the glassy Mediterranean Sea. What a sight, and what a relief!

Ramp Strike

One of the toughest decisions a commander has to make is what to do about a pilot who demonstrates marginal performance around the ship where the risks are high and lives are at stake, especially at night when the margins for error are even lower. I often wondered how the RIOs must have felt who entrusted their lives to the skills of a marginal pilot. LT Bill McMurry was one such pilot: not bad enough to warrant the decision to take him out of Carrier Aviation, yet not good enough that there was a great deal of confidence in his ability, especially at night.

On March 1, 1965, the night Bill hit the ramp, I happened to be the Duty Officer. We could usually ignore the PLATT system (the television screen that shows the airplanes approaching for landing) when other Squadrons were landing but were drawn to it when our own aircraft were approaching. We had two Phantoms on the recovery and the first one was safely aboard. As Bandwagon One Zero Four called the ball, I glanced at the scheduling board and mentally noted Bill and George Shirley were in the airplane. When I shifted my attention back to the PLATT, I agreed with the LSO's call, "Bandwagon One Zero Four, you're low

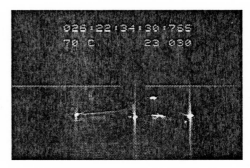

The PLATT confirms "Low"

bring it up." The white specks of light on the TV screen sank even lower and completely disappeared off the bottom of the screen. I came up out of my seat as the LSO frantically screamed, "Power, POWER" and then "WAVE-OFF, WAVE-OFF, YOU'RE LOW!" Three widely spaced lights streaked upward from off the bottom of the screen. For just a second a ball of white light with sparks radiating in all directions blossomed in the lower center of the screen and the screen went black.

The silence was deafening. You could cut the tension with a knife. The few of us in the Ready Room looked at each other; not yet willing to accept what we knew was the inevitable. Someone summed up the event in a single word, "Damn!" Two lives taken in a single heart beat. This was definitely a dangerous business we were in.

Finally the Air Boss's voice broke the silence. "Bandwagon One Zero Four do you read, Over?" Why in the world was Pri-Fly calling Bandwagon One Zero Four? Again, "Bandwagon One Zero Four, do you copy, Over?" A shaky, but very much alive voice, replied, "Bandwagon One Zero Four, I've got a problem, Over." Again we looked from one to the other for conformation that someone else had also heard the transmission. Pri-Fly responded, "Roger, Bandwagon One Zero Four, your signal is Bingo, Son San Juan (Palma de Mallorca) bears zero three two, five four miles, we'll have the tanker join on you, go Channel Four and state your problem, Over."

"Roger, Bandwagon One Zero Four going Channel Four."

We'd have to wait until later to find out what really happened. What we did know was Bill and George had joined the lucky few who had hit the ramp and lived to tell about it.

The morning revealed Bandwagon One Zero Four had indeed hit the ramp. The imprint of its hook was measured fourteen feet below the round down. The tips of the inverted "Vee" of the horizontal tail had carved two graceful red arcs along the flight deck as they reassumed their more normal shape from the wrenching stress they had endured. Bill and George were lucky. The F4B was cocked up and climbing when it crossed the round down. The main landing gear had barely cleared the ramp. While the hook had destroyed a major portion of the tail section, the "all-flying" stabilator worked well enough to keep the airplane flying. It was Bill's last flight from the Aircraft Carrier. He left the squadron in Naples.

How Good We Had It

When the Aircraft Carrier USS Roosevelt (CVA 42) relieved us, VF-14 was short one Phantom and we were tasked to give them one of ours. George and I drew the long straw to get to deliver the aircraft. I was especially looking forward to it because I had never landed the F4B on any ship other than the USS Saratoga. It would be imperative that we fly an "OK three wire" landing.

How easily spoiled we get! When we broke left over the USS Roosevelt, it appeared to be about half the size of the USS Saratoga. I achieved my "OK" pass but when we snagged the arresting cable it reminded me of my first Carrier landing in the T2J Buckeye. I swore I had never before stopped in such a short distance. We were literally thrown forward in the straps but only for an instance. When I looked to my right, I was practically eye level with the Captain's Bridge. It took me totally by surprise. The landing distance on the Roosevelt was slightly less than two thirds of the Saratoga. It is hard on the human and even harder on the airplanes. VF-14 was pleased to have the airplane. After the required paper work was signed, they treated us to lunch and we caught the next COD back to the luxurious Saratoga. We didn't have it half bad.

End of the Cruise

The Officers and men of Fighter Squadron Thirty One completed a highly successful Mediterranean deployment on July 12, 1965 with the loss of one aircraft and no personnel. Numerous problems were solved with a relatively new aircraft and weapons system. Over all, I achieved 312 Carrier landings including 68 night landings becoming a Saratoga bi-centurion (200 Carrier landing) on October 30, 1964. It had been a most exciting time for me.

VF-31 Officers, 1965: 1ˢᵗ Row:, L to R: Hall, LT; Fleming, LT; Groat, LT; Garret, LCDR; Wissler, CDR; CAG 3, CDR; Kraus, LCDR; Cornell, LCDR; Lusk LCDR; Knaus, LCDR; 2ⁿᵈ Row:, L to R: Norton, LT; Turner, LTJG; Patton, LTJG; Lines, LTJG; Shirley, LTJG; Brown, LT; Leach, LTJG; Anselmo, LTJG; Ferguson, LTJG; Seaman, LT; Rogers, LTJG; Diedrich, LTJG; Davies, LTJG; Brokaw, LTJG; Steele, LTJG; Creed, LTJG; Morrow LT

"Charlie Tuna"

Before it was fashionable for all Naval Aviators to have a nickname that became their call sign, some nicknames were inevitable. LCDR Charles Lusk predictably became "Charlie Tuna, Chicken of the Sea." Nearing the end of

Launch "Charlie Tuna"

the cruise, Charlie became the Maintenance Officer. I have previously talked about the importance of the Air Group fly-off as we neared the U.S. Coastline on the way to home port. Depending on our rank in the Squadron, we had our names stenciled beneath the canopy rail of the appropriately numbered aircraft. The night before the fly-off, some of the JOs decided to re-stencil Charlie's airplane to read "Charlie Tuna." Charlie discovered the re-stenciling early on the morning of the fly-off and was furious. He quickly issued a direct order that his name be changed back to LCDR Charles Lusk. After all, he was the Maintenance Officer. The ground crew complied with the direct order but just happened to stencil out the "Charlie Tuna" with the outline of a pink fish and stenciled LCDR Charles Lusk in the center of the fish. It was too late to do anything about it when "Charlie Tuna" manned his aircraft for the flight to the beach. He was still furious. The main-tenance crew had fol-lowed the letter but not the intent of the direct order.

Beware of departed drag chutes

"OOPS"

We looked great, and smoky, as three flights of four Phantoms each streaked into the break at NAS Cecil Field. The home folks had to be impressed and proud. Some of the "impres-siveness" was destroyed when the still packed drag chutes of two of the first four Phantoms simply plopped onto the runway when their drogue chutes were deployed. The rest of the flight had to go around while the still packaged drag chutes were removed from the runway. To preclude further foreign objects on the runway, the rest of us landed sans drag chutes. Not a problem on a 10,000 foot runway.

Home at Last

It was great to see Linda and Pam. They looked like Goddesses. Unfortunately, Pam was not so sure she was glad to see me. After all, who was this stranger hugging and kissing her mother? I took Pam in my arms but she turned away to Linda in tears. It would take a little time for us to get reacquainted. With her typical foresight, Linda had rented a small apartment for our remaining month in the Navy. She was thoughtful to allow Pam and me time alone to rediscover each other. It only took a couple of hours before Pam decided I was okay and that she would adopt me as her Dad. After all, she had spent more time with my father than she had with me and carried a real fondness for her Grandfather. It was nice to be home.

My Thirteenth Hydraulic Failure

George and I continued our string of hydraulic failures once we returned to Cecil Field. One morning as we taxied onto the runway, the old Phantom seemed a bit more sluggish than usual but I didn't think too much about it. We experienced a slight swerve early in the takeoff roll but that wasn't unusual either, especially if the nose wheel steering was slightly misaligned. Otherwise the takeoff seemed normal.

Except for a slight gray haze, it was a beautiful day for charging low level around the flat Florida countryside at 450 knots. George had just assured me we were right on track, when we scared the hell out of some unsuspecting light

A great day for flying

plane pilot by streaking underneath his Cessna as he was on final approach to a small private airstrip somewhere in northern Florida. I say somewhere, because our maps didn't show any usable airstrips anywhere along our planned low level route. If the Cessna pilot saw us, I'm sure he was as surprised as we were.

Shortly after we buzzed the airfield, the yellow master caution light blinked twice and came on steady, directing attention to the illuminated "check hydraulic gages" light on the warning light panel. The utility hydraulic pressure gage on the panel between the rudder pedals was slowly rotating counter clockwise toward zero. It seemed all too familiar. We had been there before. This was our thirteenth Utility Hydraulic System failure in the short two years we flew the Phantom.

The pieces of the puzzle began to fit together. The sluggishness during the taxi onto the runway and the swerve on takeoff could mean only one thing. We had suffered a flat tire on takeoff and the hydraulic failure likely resulted from remnants of the tire scraping against the hydraulic lines in the wheel well as it spun down. My first concern was that the wheel itself might be jammed in the wheel well and the air pressure in the accumulator for the emergency landing gear extension system might not be sufficient to blow the gear down. It was entirely possible the blown tire had also cut the air lines. We broke off the low level and headed for Cecil Field. It would be best to know the answer to all those questions while there was lots of fuel remaining. Besides, it would take some time to get the arresting gear rigged and an LSO out to the runway.

We radioed the Squadron and explained our problem. They said they would take care of getting an LSO. I called the tower, declared an emergency, and notified them of our requirement to make an arrested landing. As luck would have it, the arresting gear on the main runway was down for repair, but the one on the off duty runway could be made ready in about fifteen minutes. We didn't really have any choice. It did mean we would have to make our landing toward the east with the wind from the north. I would have preferred that it be in the other direction.

Prior to pulling the gear handle outward to activate the emergency landing gear extension, I slowed to our minimum half flap speed to give the one shot of compressed air the best possible chance to work. Although it seemed to take forever, the air bottle functioned properly, the landing gear extended, showed three green lights and the air pressure indicated a comfortable 3,000 PSI. No sweat, we had been there before.

Emergency landing gear extension

In accordance with the published emergency procedure, I touched down at the end of the runway, retarded the throttles to idle and pulled the drag chute handle. We got a good chute and the airplane decelerated nicely. The intent was to engage the midfield arresting gear before the rudder lost its aerodynamic effectiveness. As we approached the arresting cable, we were getting pretty slow, requiring nearly full left rudder to keep the Phantom straight but it looked like we would snag the wire only slightly right of center line. Again, no sweat. I felt the nose wheel bump over the arresting cable. Immediately thereafter we got a rapid deceleration and a large swerve to the right as the right landing gear grabbed the wire and dragged it several feet down the runway. I felt the wire release from the wheel and waited for the hook to engage it. The anticipated deceleration never occurred. Immediately the LSO exclaimed, "Hook skip, hook skip!" But provided no additional information.

It was another of those times when time slowed to a crawl. We were at a dangerously slow speed, power at idle, drag chute deployed, the nose cocked off toward the right side of the runway and full left rudder barely holding the Phantom straight. Even at the slow speed, the last half of the runway was disappearing beneath us at an alarming rate. My first thought was at least a constructive one. I decided I had better do something and do it fast. My first option was to try to get the airplane straightened out enough to continue down the runway and engage the overrun barrier at the end. The tower helped me rule out the barrier option as a possibility when it came up on the radio excitedly and exclaimed, "Bandwagon One Zero Four, raise your hook, raise your hook, the barrier is not rigged for engagement." Raising the hook seemed like a good idea, but if I could raise the hook, I wouldn't be in this predicament in the first place, for it requires utility hydraulic pressure to raise the hook. Besides, at this point, it wasn't a sure thing I was going to be able to keep the airplane on the runway long enough to even reach the barrier, rigged or not.

I decided I had best get airborne and real soon. I started talking to myself. "You should probably release the drag chute? Now that's a good idea." I lowered the drag chute handle located on the left side of the seat. The chute departed the airplane but with no noticeable change in deceleration. We were so slow by this time the chute was no longer effective. I jammed both throttles full forward and felt the lightweight Phantom start to accelerate toward the unrigged barrier. The tower issued yet another warning, "Raise your hook, Bandwagon One Zero Four, Raise your hook!" God bless the rapid acceleration of those two beautiful General Electric J-79 engines, but this time it wasn't fast enough. We weren't going to make it over the barrier. "Damn!"

I pushed both throttles outboard and as far forward as my arm could possibly make them go. The Phantom leapt forward as both afterburners ignited. "That was more like it, but would it be good enough?" My directional control improved as the speed picked up but that wasn't my immediate problem. We still didn't have sufficient airspeed to fly. Thoughts of vertical afterburner climbs over the Okefenokee Swamp flashed through my mind along with the reminder that all those climbs had occurred at 400 knots.

I waited until what I thought was the last second and hauled full aft on the stick. The Phantom rotated nicely but stayed firmly on the runway. We were still too slow to fly. The unrigged barrier was looming larger and larger all the time. The airplane seemed to sense the dilemma for it lifted off. Unfortunately, with the extreme nose high attitude, the hook was still dragging along the runway. Not only were we going to engage the barrier, we were about to have an in-flight engagement. If the hook didn't tear out of the airplane or snap the cable, we were about to enter the Guiness book of records for the shortest, and possibly the hardest landing, in the history of the F4B. That is, of course, if it, and we, survived the aftermath of the arrestment. I waited for the crunch. The old Phantom finally remembered the afterburner climbs over the swamp and lived up to its reputation. The two J-79 engines, with their pointed sheets of diamond studded afterburner flame, lifted the hook over the menacing barrier with only inches to spare. It was sure nice to be airborne again.

The euphoria was short lived. The right landing gear indicator now showed the right wheel to be unsafe and the precious pneumatic pressure that had so nicely lowered the gear and shared the responsibility for keeping it down, was reading zero. We weren't exactly fat on fuel either.

We talked it over with the LSO and decided to make a low speed fly-by to see if he could confirm the position of the gear. Not that it made any difference, because we couldn't do any thing about it anyway. The piece of mind was worth the flyby and it might allow us to be a little better prepared should the gear collapse. We also decided to make a midfield arrestment rather than rolling half the runway length before engaging the arresting wire. The LSO added a nice Post Script: "Bandwagon One Oh Four, you were leaving a large sheet of sparks, flame, and smoke behind your right gear. It didn't look real good." Thanks a lot LSO. We needed that kind of encouragement right now.

As far as the LSO could tell from our fly-by, the right gear was down but there was only half the right wheel remaining. Again, thanks. On the next pass, we set up for a midfield arrestment. The LSO provided encouragement when we were on the proper glide slope and coached us up or down when we weren't. When the hook snatched the wire, it was a lovely feeling. We swerved dramatically to the right as the airplane decelerated and had a noticeable list to the right when it finally came to a stop.

Old habits die hard. We patiently waited until the ground crew indicated the landing gear pins were in place prior to shutting down the engines. Quite a crowd had gathered around the right landing gear as George and I climbed down from the cockpit.

We completed the age old aviator ritual as we walked from the left front of the airplane, lightly running our hands along the leading and trailing edges of the wing, around the tail, carefully inspecting the well worn tail hook still grasping the arresting wire, and made our way to the center of attention, the right main landing gear. The crowd parted as we approached to let us inspect the wheel or at least what was left of the wheel. What a mess! The wheel and brake assembly were little more than an inverted half moon seared totally black. The only recognizable pieces of the tire were two bands of black fuzzy rubber, which must have been the beads of the tire. The inside of the wheel well confirmed our suspicions. Two hydraulic lines had been chafed and one completely severed by the spinning flat tire. Closer inspection revealed the broken pneumatic line. The underside of the wing was also severely damaged. The honeycomb structure had thousands of pieces of broken steel wire embedded in it by the disintegrating radial tire as it raced along the runway. The wing looked like it had a three-day stubble that needed shaving.

A disquieting conversation developed around the possibility that the cost of replacing the underside of the wing might escalate a simple flat tire to the level of a reportable accident. I hoped the Cessna pilot had a less eventful landing.

Stay or Go?

After many discussions, lots of what ifs, and much agonizing, Linda and I decided to get out of the Navy. I had actually received my first choice for a second tour assignment, which was orders to the Naval Postgraduate School in Monterey, California. As my luck would have it, I would be on cruise until mid-July and would end my active duty tour in mid-August. All in all, I had been deployed twenty-five of the last thirty-six months I had been in the Navy and it did not look like the commitments were going to get any less, especially with the build-up for the war in Vietnam.

Using the college placement manual as my guide, I sent out a slew of resumes to a number of aircraft companies. On the positive side, engineers were in high demand and airlines were hiring pilots at a prodigious rate. I rejected the airline idea because I didn't like the "Union" approach to advancement and I wanted to use the Aeronautical Engineering degree I had worked so hard for at the University of Virginia. I had pretty well given up on the idea of employment including flying. At that time I didn't understand that flying opportunities, other than airlines, might even be a possibility. I knew I had enjoyed working with the wind tunnel and liked aerodynamics and had expressed interest in aerodynamics, wind tunnel operations, and flight testing in my resume. On the basis of the resume alone, I received firm offers from Boeing, McDonnell, and North American. I had also sent a resume to Cornell Aeronautical Laboratory because they operated one of the finest transonic wind tunnels in the country. I did not receive a job offer from Cornell Aeronautical Laboratory, but I did get a letter indicating that they were interested in my flying background as well as my aeronautical engineering education. I was cautiously elated. The catch was that they wanted to talk with me when I returned to the States. I made arrangements for an interview with them the last week of July. On the way to Buffalo, New York, Linda and I stopped off in New York City and enjoyed the World's Fair for a couple of days. Our Operations Officer, Rudy Kraus was from Buffalo and showed Linda around while I interviewed. It turned out that Cornell Aeronautical Laboratory was the research component of the old Curtis Wright plant that had been sold to Cornell University for the proverbial one dollar as a tax write-off. It was operated as a non-profit independent research laboratory. Their Flight Research Department primarily worked on aircraft handling qualities using in-flight simulators. They also used these in-flight simulators or variable stability airplanes to teach stability and control at the Air Force and Navy Test Pilot Schools. Needless to say, I was impressed but overwhelmed by the technical aspects of the job that seemed well beyond my capabilities. Fortunately for me, they were looking for an Aeronautical Engineer with a military jet background that they could train to do their very specialized type of work. I liked them and it must have been mutual because they offered me a job. When we finally got around to talking about salary, I mentioned the highest salary offer I already had from the three aircraft companies. Cornell Aeronautical Laboratory offered me fifteen hundred dollars more per year than my best offer plus the opportunity to continue to fly. The latter made putting up with the notoriously nasty Buffalo weather bearable. In fairness, it was Linda that had the bigger problem with the weather because I spent a fair amount of the winter flying out of Edwards Air Force Base, California or some other warm place. I was discharged from the Navy on August 13, 1965 and reported to Cornell Aeronautical Laboratory the next week. As exciting as the Navy flying had been, the Love Affair with flying did not wane with my departure from the Navy. Quite to the contrary, it blossomed. I flew exciting flight programs at Cornell including the unique X-22A VTOL aircraft and then joined NASA as a Test Pilot in 1977. But these are stories yet to be written.

1 Track of the Tomcatters, A History of VF-31 Part One: Fighting Six-The Shooting Stars, 1935-42, by Thomas F. Gates, (<u>The HOOK, Fall 1984</u>)

2 Track of the Tomcatters, A History of VF-31, Part two: Fighting Six at Guadalcanal, by Thomas F. Gates, (<u>The HOOK Winter 1984</u>)

3 Track of the Tomcatters, Part Three: VF-3, Finishing the job, 1943-45, by Thomas F. Gates, (<u>The HOOK, Spring 1985</u>)

4 Track of the Tomcatters, A history of VF-31, Part Four: New Planes, New Missions, by Thomas F. Gates, (<u>The HOOK, Summer 1985</u>)

5 <u>Naval Aviation News August 1973</u>

— *G. Warren Hall* —

Photography Credits

1. The yellow Navy Trainer – Daniel C. Dugan
2. White wooden roller coaster – G. Warren Hall
3. Aeronca 7AC Champion – G. Warren Hall
4. Bobby Brown, 1955 – Virginia Aviation Museum
5. Air sickness epidemic – Unknown
6. F-86 Sabres at Langley Air Force Base, circa 1951 – G. Warren Hall
7. Northfield Airport, circa 1951 – Virginia Aviation Museum
8. Northfield Operations Building – Virginia Aviation Museum
9. Northfield lounge and snack bar – Virginia Aviation Museum
10. Northfield entrance – Virginia Aviation Museum
11. Mr. Bailey and Bobby – Virginia Aviation Museum
12. Runway roller – G. Warren Hall
13. Aeronca 7AC Champion – G. Warren Hall
14. Aeronca instrument panel – G. Warren Hall
15. You always remember your first solo – G. Warren Hall
16. Piper Cub shows the way – G. Warren Hall
17. That looks like Bugg's Island Lake – G. Warren Hall
18. Refueling Northfield Aeronca Champion – Virginia Aviation Museum
19. Linda (2) – G. Warren Hall
20. Budding test pilots – G. Warren Hall
21. Not as it's supposed to be!!! – G. Warren Hall

22. My first passenger; my Mom – Virginia Aviation Museum
23. Captain Don Henderson, USAF – USAF Photograph
24. Smile for the camera – NATC – U.S. Navy Photograph
25. First jet ride with LCDR Austin– U.S. Navy Photograph
26. Temco TT-1 Pinto Trainer – U.S. Navy Photograph
27. NATC T2J Trainer – U.S. Navy Photograph
28. NATC Grumman F11F Tiger – U.S. Navy Photograph
29. Beware of "Ground Effect," or the lack thereof – U.S. Navy Photograph
30. Swearing in by CDR Rolston – U.S. Navy Photograph
31. NAS Pensacola Main Gate, 1960 – U.S. Navy Photograph
32. Marine Gunnery Sergeant Hustler – U.S. Navy Photograph
33. AOC Hall official photo – U.S. Navy Photograph
34. Harder, Hottle, Kelly – U.S. Navy Photographs
35. The "Infamous" Grinder – G. Warren Hall
36. AOC Class 30-60, November 1960 – U.S. Navy Photograph
37. Marching to church – G. Warren Hall
38. The obstacle course... It goes on forever – G. Warren Hall
39. My Nemesis – G. Warren Hall
40. Aviation Cadet Recreation Center – G. Warren Hall
41. NAVCAD Haven – G. Warren Hall
42. Swimming requirements, mandatory and tough – U.S. Navy Photograph

43. Dilbert Dunker halfway... – U.S. Navy Photograph;
    ...Crash with a splash, sink up side down – U.S. Navy
    Photograph
44. Survival Training Center – G. Warren Hall
45. Graduation day parade and graduation – Linda D.
    Hall
46. Ensign Hall – U.S. Navy Photograph
47. Saufley Field entrance marker – U.S. Navy Photograph
48. Anxious to fly – Stanley Primmer
49. A new T-34B Trainer at NAAS Saufley Field – U.S.
    Navy Photograph
50. T-34B Procedural Trainers – U.S. Navy Photograph
51. "Fly Navy" – Navy Museum – U.S. Navy Photograph
52. "Sorry Sir, I don't remember our parking spot" –
    G. Warren Hall
53. Getting serious about flying – Stanley Primmer
54. T-34B Trainer on final approach – Navy Museum –
    U.S. Navy Photograph
55. Soloing the T-34B –Navy Museum – U.S. Navy
    Photograph
56. Something's wrong here! – G. Warren Hall
57. Spins are fun? – Navy Museum – U.S. Navy
    Photograph
58. Primary complete, jets next – Stanley Primmer
59. Ensign and Mrs. Hall – N. N. Fleming III
60. Naval Auxiliary Air Station Kingsville entrance
    marker – G. Warren Hall
61. VT-7 T2J Kingsville, Texas – U.S. Navy Photograph
62. Overhead view of the T2J – G. Warren Hall
63. Out climbing Texas thunderstorms? – Navy Museum
    – U.S. Navy Photograph

64. Solo flight at NAAS Meridian – U.S. Navy Photograph
65. Hurricane evacuation from Pensacola to NAAS Meridian (4) – G. Warren Hall
66. Early student formation flying – Navy Museum – U.S. Navy Photograph
67. Wow! I look like that! – LTJG Michael Hazelrig
68. Instructors fly formation – U.S. Navy Photograph
69. The hard part, joining up – U.S. Navy Photograph
70. First graduates from NAAS Meridian – <u>Naval Aviation News</u>, August 1973
71. VT-4 T2J flight line, Forrest Sherman Field, NAS Pensacola – G. Warren Hall
72. T2J with a gun pod under each wing – G. Warren Hall
73. A flight of four for gunnery practice – LTJG Michael Hazelrig
74. T2Js in right echelon formation – Navy Museum – U.S. Navy Photograph
75. The mirror landing system – G. Warren Hall
76. T2J in FCLP pattern – Navy Museum – U.S. Navy Photograph
77. USS Antietam departs for Carrier Qualifications, November 1961 – G. Warren Hall
78. USS Antietam with a deck full of T2Js – U.S. Navy Photograph
79. "Meatball," Lineup, Angle of Attack – G. Warren Hall
80. Ball centered, lineup good – G. Warren Hall
81. First time with the hook down – U.S. Navy Photograph
82. T2J snags a number 3 wire – Navy Museum – U.S. Navy Photograph
83. An impatient Taxi Director – U.S. Navy Photograph

104. Reluctant to land – G. Warren Hall
105. Demon with 4 Sparrow III Missiles – U.S. Navy Photograph
106. F3B cockpit, large and roomy – U.S. Navy Photograph
107. VF-101 "Grim Reapers" F3B – G. Warren Hall
108. A typical Key West thunderstorm – G. Warren Hall
109. VF-101 F3B in the FCLP pattern – G. Warren Hall
110. Demon over the ramp – G. Warren Hall
111. Demon Main Instrument Panel (Flight Manual) – U.S. Navy Photograph
112. Hot-refueling at the base of the island – G. Warren Hall
113. A4D in Carrier Landing configuration – U.S. Navy Photograph
114. Night launch of a Demon in full afterburner, 1964 – G. Warren Hall
115. Felix the Cat Insignia on Boeing F4B-4 – U.S. Navy Photograph
116. Felix the Cat patch – U.S. Navy Photograph
117. VF-31 Demon lives up to the Squadron Motto, "We Get Ours at Night" – U.S. Navy Photograph
118. CDRs Creaseman & Pierozzi – U.S. Navy Photograph
119. USS Lexington cruising south of Cuba, 1962 – U.S. Navy Photograph
120. Contrail in the sky; join the fray – G. Warren Hall
121. A Demon at a Crusader's six o'clock – G. Warren Hall
122. VF-31 F3B in preservation at Litchfield Park, Arizona – U.S. Navy Photograph
123. Reserve crews, casual but good – U.S. Navy Photograph
124. One cold wife - G. Warren Hall

146. USS Saratoga transits the Straits of Gibralta – U.S. Navy Photograph
147. VF-31 Officers 1963 – U.S. Navy Photograph
148. Spanish World War II Hienkle 111s -Unknown
149. A3D gets a "Pinky Landing" -G. Warren Hall
150. Sometimes you just don't get it right the first time – U.S. Navy Photograph
151. Me, Jim Carnes & Pat Rogers – Vince Knaus
152. Emcee Hal Seaman explains the procedure – G. Warren Hall
153. Dr. Von Carnes, "The moment of delivery" – G. Warren Hall
154. Dr. Denio Padrick and Baby Felix – G. Warren Hall
155. Amber back home – George Patton
156. Who's the boss here? – G. Warren Hall
157. Pilot's view of taxiing too close to the edge – G. Warren Hall
158. The Liberty Boat on a good day – G. Warren Hall
159. Boat Officer's view of USS Saratoga inbound to port – G. Warren Hall
160. Demon clears left off Cat 4 – G. Warren Hall
161. Which way is home? – U.S. Navy Photograph
162. Almost two Demons with one Sparrow III – U.S. Navy Photograph
163. Pamela Lyn, Age: 1 hr – Trudy Ritchotte
164. A rare day of rest at sea – James Carnes
165. LCDR Cornell's F3B the next day; ugly -The HOOK, Summer 1985
166. Launch the aircraft – G. Warren Hall
167. A3D Tanker provides navigation and fuel – U.S. Navy Photograph

192. "Miami Center… Increasing airspeed to 1,000 knots" – George Shirley
193. The elusive MIG 21 Fishbed – G. Warren Hall
194. A Phantom on your left and a Phantom on your right – U.S. Navy Photograph
195. Cinema of the Century – G. Warren Hall
196. Felix – The Director – G. Warren Hall
197. Waiting… Boring – G. Warren Hall
198. The Cubans are coming! – G. Warren Hall
299. Lunch arriving… -G. Warren Hall
200. Gang Way! – G. Warren Hall
201. Redundant transportation – G. Warren Hall
202. The paper makes the grade – G. Warren Hall
203. CO transportation – G. Warren Hall
204. Shazam! – G. Warren Hall
205. Not fast, but sturdy! – G. Warren Hall
206. Who needs a pilot? – G. Warren Hall
207. Right engine won't start – G. Warren Hall
208. Hey, wait for me – G. Warren Hall
209. The quickest way to the cockpit – G. Warren Hall
210. Ready for takeoff! – G. Warren Hall
211. Beware of Marines carrying missiles – U.S. Navy Photograph
212. Crusader 1 lands normal – G. Warren Hall
213. Crusader 2 lands long – G. Warren Hall
214. High flyers reach 73,000 feet – James Carnes
215. Mach 1.6, nose up 45 degrees, altimeter a blur – George Patton
216. USS Saratoga undergoes major overhaul in 1963 – U.S. Navy Photograph

242. Low altitude Combat Air Patrol – George Shirley
243. The PLATT confirms "low" – G. Warren Hall
244. VF-31 Officers, 1965 – U.S. Navy Photograph
245. Launch "Charlie Tuna" – G. Warren Hall
246. Beware of departed drag chutes – U.S. Navy Photographs
247. A great day for flying – U.S. Navy Photograph
248. Emergency landing gear extension – George Shirley

Mr. G. Warren Hall learned to fly while working as a "line boy" at Northfield Airport in Richmond, Virginia. He earned his private pilot's license at age 18. After graduation from the University of Virginia in 1960, with a degree in Aeronautical Engineering, he became a Naval Aviator logging more than 300 carrier landings in the F3B Demon and F4B Phantom II aircraft.

Mr. Hall began his flight test career in 1965 as an Engineering Test Pilot with Cornell Aeronautical Laboratory of Cornell University where he logged over 100 hours in the Bell X-22A V/STOL aircraft. Mr. Hall joined NASA Ames Research Center in 1977 as a Research Test Pilot where he is now the Assistant Director for Aviation. He has flown over 65 different types of aircraft including the X-14B, XV-15 and the unique Rotor Systems Research Aircraft.

Mr. Hall completed 28 years of military service before retiring as the Commander of the California Air National Guard's 129th Rescue and Recovery Group at Moffett Field, California with the rank of Colonel.

In 1992, Mr. Hall was recognized by his peers for his excellent engineering and piloting contributions as a NASA Test Pilot and awarded the coveted rank of Fellow in the Society of Experimental Test pilots.

Mr. Hall has authored 73 Technical Reports including three international awards for technical excellence.

Printed in the United States
32261LVS00005B/40-111

9 781414 017051